TORRID ZONES

PARALLAX ⬛ RE-VISIONS OF CULTURE AND SOCIETY
Stephen G. Nichols, Gerald Prince, and Wendy Steiner, *Series Editors*

TORRID ZONES

Maternity, Sexuality, and Empire
in Eighteenth-Century English Narratives

Felicity A. Nussbaum

THE JOHNS HOPKINS UNIVERSITY PRESS
Baltimore and London

© 1995 The Johns Hopkins University Press
Published 1995
Printed in the United States of America
on acid-free paper
04 03 02 01 00 99 98 97 96 95   5 4 3 2 1

The Johns Hopkins University Press
2715 North Charles Street
Baltimore, Maryland 21218-4319
The Johns Hopkins Press Ltd., London

Library of Congress Cataloging-in-Publication Data
will be found at the end of this book.
A catalog record for this book is available from the
British Library.

ISBN 0-8018-5074-6
ISBN 0-8018-5075-4 (pbk.)

Contents

ACKNOWLEDGMENTS

I have been very lucky while writing this book in various venues to have been surrounded by good friends and colleagues. My debts are deep, but none so great as to Jean E. Howard, with whom I have shared ideas and female friendship for almost two decades. Carol Barash, Toni Bowers, Laura Brown, Terry Castle, Margaret Doody, Roxann Eberle, Margo Hendricks, Cora Kaplan, Pat Parker, Ruth Perry, James Turner, and Bill Warner each contributed to the manuscript in ways they have probably forgotten but for which I am very grateful. Dympna Callaghan and Harriet Guest read several chapters and spurred me on with spirited critique, and John Bender offered generous and sage counsel.

The Stanford Humanities Center provided a lively intellectual community as I drafted the bulk of the book, and the community of fellows contributed to making it a most memorable year, especially Kathleen Canning, Sandra Greene, Kate Hayles, and Ana Zentella. Herbie Lindenberger, Charles Junkerman, and the skilled staff at the Center encouraged my work at every turn. The John Simon Guggenheim Memorial Foundation also granted a fellowship for the completion of the book. Audiences too numerous to name have improved this work with their penetrating questions and interest, including especially the David Nichol Smith Seminar in Melbourne, Australia, the Bay Area Eighteenth-Century Group, and the University of Pennsylvania Early Modern Culture Seminar. The students in my graduate seminars, as well as Sara Gadeken, Michelle Jensen, David Weed, and Roxann Wheeler, contributed to the ideas in embryo.

I want to thank especially the staffs of the rare books collections at Stanford University libraries, the Cornell University Libraries, The British Library, and the Syracuse University Library. Carolyn Moser's editorial expertise greatly improved the manuscript. A version of Chapter 2 appeared in *Cultural Critique* 20 (Winter 1991–92) and was reprinted in *Eighteenth-Century Life* 16, n.s. 1 (February 1992); and a version of Chapter 3 was published in *Women, "Race," and Writing in the Early Modern Period,* ed. Margo Hendricks and Patricia Parker (New York: Routledge 1993). *Australian Women's Book Review* (Fall 1993) published a short section of Chapter 1.

Annika and Peter Ekman and their family have provided good

conversation and delicious meals to distract me happily while I conducted research in London. Alexandria Currin, Michelle Galvin, Bob Littlehale, Valerie Sheffield, and Carrie Stock offered much-appreciated child care. Beverly Allen, Sari Biklen, Kokkie Buur, Paula Freedman, Donna Guy, and Lleni Pach have regularly buoyed my spirits. Margaret Cooley and Luther Nussbaum and their families have offered steady, loving support.

This book would not have been written without the inspiration of my children, and it is my abiding hope that it will speak to my daughter, Nicole Wilett, whose courage and commitments I admire as she forges her original own path; and to my son, Marc Wilett, who constantly shares his optimistic spirit and beatific smile.

This book is dedicated to my parents, Leo Lester Nussbaum and Janet Gladfelter Nussbaum, who have always acted globally, and who continue to make manifest their zest for life and learning.

TORRID ZONES

England's Other Women

I

This book analyzes the connections between eighteenth-century women in England and women in the emergent British empire. The invention of the "other" woman of empire enabled the consolidation of the cult of domesticity in England and, at the same time, the association of the sexualized woman at home with the exotic, or "savage," non-European woman. I argue here that a particular kind of national imperative to control women's sexuality and fecundity emerged when the increasing demands of trade and colonization required a large, able-bodied citizenry, and that women's reproductive labor was harnessed to that task. The English nation came to represent its eighteenth-century woman as happier than women of the past, happier than the "savage," and happiest as a mother. In the chapters that follow I consider the representations of women at home and abroad during the expansion of commercial and imperial authority in order to analyze the interrelations that evolved among sexual, racial, and class hierarchies. My departure is to read reproductive and sexual issues, usually imagined as confined to the private sphere, within larger social structures and even global manifestations of the family, of production, and of desire. Throughout the book I explore the interpenetration between the domestic and the exotic, the civil and the savage, the political and the sexual.

Centering on literary representations, this book considers novels ranging, for example, from Daniel Defoe's *Roxana* (1724), Charlotte Lennox's *The Female Quixote* (1752), and Phebe Gibbes's *Hartly House, Calcutta* (1789), to the more broadly defined texts of culture—travel narratives, medical documents, visual artifacts, and legal records—as sites of struggle over cultural meanings. My analysis extends beyond representations to focus on specific material practices, including infanticide, prostitution, polygamy, the seraglio, and homoerotic activities. All these practices embody attitudes toward sexuality and maternity that emerge as loci for defining differences between Englishwomen and "savage" women, as well as women of the Middle East, the Caribbean, India, and Africa. I seek to avoid a simple binary opposition between the Englishwoman and her Others, in part by considering women in a variety of geographical locations, in part by tracing the alignment between lower-class women in England and other women, in part by acknowledging and analyzing the different power relations among the women of the eighteenth-century world even as feminism emerges to assert the identity of "Woman."

Most critical studies of the "noble savage" in the period have focused primarily on exotic male subjects and the similarities among them, replicating a view common to many in the eighteenth century. As Samuel Johnson expressed it in his contempt for South Sea voyages, "One set of Savages is like another."[1] This book centers instead on the diverse *women* of empire to document their representation as homogeneous but also to counter, for example, stereotypes of Eastern women as veiled figures of seduction or victims of self-immolation, or African women as naked, polygamous, and barbaric (see Figs. 1–3). At the same time I argue that as various as the asymmetrical relations of domination might be, the differing positions of women at home and abroad should not blind us to the affinities among them. While Englishwomen and the women of empire came into literal contiguity only rarely, their geographical separation is bridged by their common interests as women. In fact, I mean to imply that the term "women of empire" encompasses European women in their complicity in the formation of empire *and* in their being scapegoated as the focus of luxury and commercial excess. The term unites women around the world in the eighteenth century in Europe and the colonies, because they share the threat of unregulated sexuality and the promise of maternity; what unites them in feminist theory is their mutual oppression.

The domestic virtue demanded of Englishwomen ensured the legitimacy of family and property, of course, but regulating sexuality in the eighteenth century (as now) also was often an attempt to define and legislate racial purity through such policies as natal alienation and antimiscegenation laws. These policies systematically interrupted family life and skewed sexual and maternal behavior. "Sexual control was more than a convenient metaphor for colonial domination," remarks Ann Stoler; "it was . . . a fundamental class and racial marker implicated in a wider set of relations of power."[2] The power relations between nations also involved power relations between the sexes and "races." These "mutually exclusive categories of experience and analysis," as Kimberle Crenshaw has pointed out, are nevertheless heavily coded in their intersectionality.[3] For example, while colonizing men usually imagined European women to be domestic and maternal figures rather than sexual objects for themselves—perhaps a projection of their racist conditioning to assume greater sexuality in the woman of color than in the European woman—European women are curiously considered to need protection from the sexually passionate indigenous men of the empire.

Some rather questionable claims have been made that the impulse for empire is a masculine sexual impulse that can be quelled only by the conquest of territory and peoples. Nupur Chaudhuri and Margaret Strobel comment that "theories about colonialism have stressed its 'masculine' nature, highlighting the essential components of domination, control, and structures of unequal power."[4] Correlated with this view is often a feminization of the colonized, so that the territory inhabited and penetrated by the colonist is figured as woman.[5] British explorers in their travel accounts often made something coherent, consistent, and feminized of the foreign peoples they encountered in the interests of consolidating the nation's imperial energies and shaping a national identity. Others have argued that the culture heightened Englishwomen's sexual desires to encourage satisfying those desires through the consumption of foreign goods.[6] In the logic of empire these formulations imply that for men to satisfy women sexually, they must participate in raiding foreign countries to prove their manliness. The Other, whether man or woman, is gendered as something that the man must pass through in order to satisfy the Englishwoman. Yet Englishwomen also participated at some level in imperial activities, sometimes as the beneficiary of empire's spoils rather than its violated object, to consolidate the national cultural identity and to accumulate the capital necessary for the expanding empire in the nineteenth century. Western women of a certain status were both implicated in empire and victimized by it. The means by which race and sex function together in history is only beginning to be delineated, and this study, part of that larger feminist and postcolonial project, is distinguished by its attention to historical specificity during the formation of England's nascent empire.

I approach the task of defining the economic, political, and social relations between eighteenth-century Englishwomen and the Other women of empire with great caution because I speak within feminism while offering a critique of it, in part as a response to Hazel V. Carby's resounding challenge to white feminists that "instead of taking black women as the objects of their research, white feminist researchers should try to uncover the gender-specific mechanisms of racism amongst white women."[7] In addition, in discussing veiling, maternity, prostitution, and other aspects of sexuality among non-European women, one has to be very wary of simply replicating the very terms of hierarchy and domination. Chandra Mohanty points out that "images of the 'third world woman,' images such as the veiled woman, the powerful mother, the chaste virgin, the obedient wife, . . . exist in universal, ahistorical splendor, setting in motion a colonialist discourse which exercises a very specific power in defining, coding and maintaining existing first/third world connections."[8] The "Other" woman, like the popular shorthand "Third World," is justifiably a contested term. The potential to reproduce colonialism and its binaries is particularly acute if victim and agent are the sole categories available for women—one of the difficulties of speaking of the "Other."[9] Such stereotypes have considerable restrictive force. The point in including women from around the eighteenth-century world is to avoid their "assimilation within a sole western-european herstory" that Audre Lorde warned some time ago was unacceptable.[10] By objectifying the Other woman, Western women may ignore the way that women of all cultures share the effects of a historically and culturally contingent patriarchy.[11] In addition, questions of agency and victimization need to be deeply imbedded in history and in the material conditions of production and transmission in order to consider the political and economic use of women's erotic and maternal bodies. In the narratives I discuss, the concept of empire is often translated from the global geographical picture and written onto the local and domestic; it includes the metaphorical and the material. By "materialist" I mean to focus on the emerging global processes and structures of the political economy that produce the power relations of empire that can be calibrated for racial, class, and sexual variations within the logic of colonialism. By "material" I do not mean "things" so much as the materiality of ideology that connects the domestic to the exotic to construct the social real.

Seeking women's agency within the social real may also, however, silence the very agents who are least empowered. Exploring the conditions under which one *should* speak for others, Linda Alcoff attempts to distinguish between the times when the privileged speaking for the unprivileged increases or alleviates oppression, and she cautions that there is a necessity to reflect on one's own political, economic, and social position: "Anyone who speaks for others should only do so out of a concrete analysis of the particular power relations and discursive effects involved."[12] I agree with Alcoff's thoughtful argument that "such representations are in every case mediated and the product of interpretation" (9). Yet at any time that I speak for anyone, even for "myself," I am historically and culturally removed from eighteenth-century Englishwomen of all classes as well as from eighteenth-century African and Eastern women. Rather than speaking in the place of another, ideally one would speak "nearby or together with" rather than "speak for" or "about."[13] But any articulation of Other women is a hybridization of tradition and modernity, of the native informant and the displaced Westernized woman, and of the implication of First and Third World together.[14] To discuss women of empire here is an attempt to identify the ideological work of fixed images and "authentic" identities as they serve the interests of colonialism.

Another obvious difficulty inherent in my project is the historical problem of locating women's agency when women's public voices are only beginning to be heard in published writing, and there is no obvious equivalent movement of women into the literary marketplace in Africa, Asia, or the Caribbean. While the histories of Englishwomen such as William Alexander's *History of Women from the Earliest Antiquity* (1779) were beginning to be written in the eighteenth century, the histories of non-European women were scarcely visible, especially from the imperial domain. In what follows, I have located contests to that colonial erasure in the African or Middle Eastern woman who resists through the muted mockery of a song, through a gaze averted, in the refusal to put on European clothing, or in choosing not to speak or write in the master's tongue. The voices and acts of resistance recounted here are always mediated, but they nevertheless embody resistance—in the satiric song of the African women encountering Mungo Park, in Queen Clara's refusal to dress in the manner deemed appropriate by the Englishwoman Anna Falconbridge, in transforming the veil from religious dictate or fashion to political resistance, and in the homoerotic pleasure exercised within the seraglio. These traces qualify the model of the silent subaltern who must be spoken for. For example, in regard to the Hindu practice of *sati* (burning oneself on the funeral pyre of one's husband), we might take up this challenge by locating the hesitations, contradictions, and inconsistencies that call the idea of women's "voluntary" self-immolation into question and complicate the female subaltern's situation in the early nineteenth century to find agency in unlikely locations.[15]

Such a "countersentence" in locating the Other's voice is fraught with its own perils for the white feminist.[16] It may disrupt the terms of the current historical narrative, but it may, in turn, produce a new history of the colonized that assumes an authentic Other who possesses an essential truth. Chela Sandoval proposes an antidote to such identity politics as she interrogates the very paradigm by which Anglo-American feminism has constructed female identity: "It has remained inconceivable that U.S. third world feminism might represent a form of historical consciousness whose very structure lies outside the conditions of possibility which regulate the oppositional expressions of dominant feminism." Sandoval conceives of a new subjectivity formulated through U.S. Third World feminism as "a political revision that denies any one ideology as the final answer, while instead positing a *tactical subjectivity* with the capacity to recenter depending upon the kinds of oppression to be confronted."[17] The idea of a tactical subjectivity (similar to the strategic essentialism many have discussed) is very compelling, and it is a considerable advance over the concept of contradictions and heterogeneity voiced by many postmodern feminists. A simple pluralism, however, in which any one ideology is equivalent to any other, will undermine such a tactical strategy.

"Global" feminism, on the other hand, has been critiqued because of its tendency to operate from a Western feminist perspective. While this is a just critique, it need not be inherent in global feminism, and I hope here to revise the term to invest it with another valence. Inderpal Grewal and Carla Kaplan argue for a transnational practice that compares "multiple, overlapping, and discrete oppressions rather than [construction of] a theory of hegemonic oppression under a unified category of gender."[18] They usefully focus on the historical condition of postmodernity and its variations within various hegemonies. We can, however, work within the large category of gender without assuming an identity or equivalence among women while recognizing that women's situations are historically specific. The concept of the transnational is less applicable to the early colonial period I treat here, since that is the very moment in the post-Enlightenment period when nations begin to emerge and are implicated in postmodernism. Alternatively, I posit a postcolonial global feminist strategy that remains flexible in its response to varied oppressions yet cognizant of their

unity, since a worldwide feminist collectivity must develop a comprehensive logic of feminist material praxis in spite of differing historical and social locations. Such a strategy helps to distinguish between a
pluralist feminist community that places primacy on individual rights
and consciousness (and Western and Enlightenment notions of the
unified self) versus a feminist collectivity that is distinct from liberal
pluralism, coalition, or affinity, and thrives through opposition, resistance, and critique within its ranks.

In this formulation the heterogeneity and the hybridity of the
colonized and the colonizers may always be kept in view while we
steadfastly remain focused on the universality of certain kinds of oppression—patriarchy, capital, and colonialism. We can, for example,
differentiate productively between indigenous patriarchy and colonial
patriarchy, since the men who were subject to empire were positioned
differently from European white men within patriarchy.[19] This tactic
reveals the difference between making something fixed and essential
of the Other and recognizing the systemic global relations of labor and
production. Empire is unstable and contested, and the relations between metropole and periphery shift constantly. Further, British imperial policy was itself heterogeneous, and contests among competing
interests were involved in producing it. While I agree that the tensions
between colonizer and colonized are not fixed but "problematic, contested, and changing," the overarching realities of domination and
exploitation remain the crucial fact in analyzing metropole and colony
within a single analytic sphere.[20] It is the aim of this book to figure the
heterogeneity of empire into the equation of European women's complicity with empire without forfeiting the larger conceptualization of
patriarchy in its historical formation.

II

I take as a central metaphor for the consideration of maternity and
sexuality the concept of torrid zones, both the geographical torrid
zones of the territory between the Tropic of Cancer and the Tropic of
Capricorn, and the torrid zone mapped onto the human body, especially the female body. A premise of my study is that the contrasts
among the torrid, temperate, and frigid zones of the globe were for-
mative in imagining that a sexualized woman of empire was distinct
from domestic English womanhood. These distinctions among peoples based on climatic variation appeared in the natural histories that
began to be written in the eighteenth century. Oliver Goldsmith, for

example, voices conventional sentiments in claiming real differences between people of varying climates: "It is not, therefore, between contiguous nations we are to look for any strong marked varieties in the human species; it is by comparing the inhabitants of opposite climates, and distant countries; those who live within the polar circle with those beneath the equator; those that live on one side of the globe with those that occupy the other."[21] As is well known, popular Renaissance accounts gave gendered inflections to the theory of humors, so that men and women were divided into hot and cold, dry and wet. But by the eighteenth century, geography substitutes for these humors and writes the effects on the world map. The geography of sexual desire described in Adam Ferguson's *Essay on the History of Civil Society* (1767) claims that passion is strongest in the locations least known to Europeans.[22] In Ferguson's formulation (as with other natural histories of the period, especially of the Scottish Enlightenment), hot climates produce sexual desire, while more temperate climates require greater control and more elaborate ritual. Domesticity, believed to be antithetical to sexual heat, increases the farther one resides from the equator. Warmer climates naturally intensify the amount of sexual activity and consequently produce a larger population that freely indulges its libidinous energy. Ferguson elaborates on the connection between sun and sexuality in his chapter "Of the Influences of Climate and Situation":

> The burning ardours, and the torturing jealousies, of the seraglio and the haram, which have reigned so long in Asia and Africa, and which, in the Southern parts of Europe, have scarcely given way to the difference of religion and civil establishments, are found, however, with an abatement of heat in the climate, to be more easily changed, in one latitude, into a temporary passion which ingrosses the mind, without enfeebling it, and which excites to romantic achievements: by a farther progress to the North, it is changed into a spirit of gallantry, which employs the wit and the fancy more than the heart; which prefers intrigue to enjoyment; and substitutes affectation and vanity, where sentiment and desire have failed. As it departs from the sun, the same passion is further composed into a habit of domestic connection or frozen into a state of insensibility, under which the sexes at freedom scarcely chuse to unite their society. (115–16)

According to these formulations, the torrid zone exists in an eternal past, permeated with sexual passion. Traveling from hot places into northern regions fosters a move into history, industry, and politics: "The torrid zone, every where round the globe, however known to the geographer, has furnished few materials for history; and though in many places supplied with the arts of life in no contemptible degree, has no where matured the more important projects of political wisdom, nor inspired the virtues which are connected with freedom, and required in the conduct of civil affairs" (110). Ferguson continues: "The melting desires, or the fiery passions, which in one climate take place between the sexes, are in another changed into a sober consideration, or a patience of mutual disgust. This change is remarked in crossing the Mediterranean, in following the course of the Mississippi, in ascending the mountains of Caucasus, and in passing from the Alps and the Pyrenees to the shores of the Baltic" (115). As the geographical terrain shifts from hot to cool, so do human desires and social relations. In Ferguson's representation, sexual passion varies according to the world's topography and climate, yet its unrestricted expression is predictably linked to the torrid zone's failure to nurture civilization or political freedom. With Ferguson and other early natural historians, sexuality as it is connected to civilization is zoned on a world scale.

John Millar's *Origin of the Distinction of Ranks; or, An Inquiry into the Circumstances* similarly contends that tropical climates encourage indolence while temperate zones foster industry and vigor.[23] To judge from the footnotes in Millar's treatise, he closely studied contemporary travel narratives as documents from which to draw what he believes are systematic conclusions. Millar claims uncertainty as to whether an exact rendering that explains differences among all countries is possible, since sexuality varies so widely across history and geography. Although seeming to argue that warm climates heighten sexuality, Millar paradoxically contests environmental determinism to assert that the savage may be less interested in sexual subtleties because he dares not distract himself from grubbing out an existence, "has no time for cultivating a correspondence with the other sex," and has sexual desires that are "barely sufficient for the continuation of the species" (18). Also unlike Ferguson, Millar argues that marriage among the inhabitants of warm climates, arranged rather than based on mutual attraction or individual desires, evolved naturally as an expedient way to care for children and leads to indifference. According to Millar, savages, both contemporaneous and historical, are caught in the contradiction of sexual desire without romantic passion or affection, on the one hand, and without restraint on the other: finding "nothing blameable in that instinct which nature has bestowed upon them, they are not ashamed of its ordinary gratifications; and they affect no disguise. . . . From the extreme insensibility, observable in the character of all savage nations, it is no wonder they should entertain very gross ideas concerning those female virtues which, in a polished nation, are supposed to constitute the honour and dignity of the sex" (35).

Montesquieu and David Hume also addressed the question of the relation between climate and sexual behavior, and they quarrelled over the extent to which both factors are connected to government. Montesquieu emphasized the relationship between temperature and passion in *De l'esprit des lois* (1748): "If we draw near the south, we fancy ourselves removed from all morality; the strongest passions multiply all manner of crimes, every one endeavouring to take what advantage he can over his neighbours, in order to encourage those passions" (14.2). Those who live in temperate climates are most responsive to liberty, while warm climates lend themselves to tyranny. For Montesquieu, climate influenced sexual behavior and political conditions by contracting or relaxing the nerve endings of bodily fibers; the climate's material effect on the body means that Hume, however, found Montesquieu's argument for climate's influence morally outrageous because the supposed harmonious relationship between humans and their environment encouraged *laisser faire au climat.*[24] Others, such as William Falconer in *Remarks on the Influence of Climate* (1781), countered that European travellers of the higher social classes would escape the debilitating effects of climate: class counteracts climate. Though Montesquieu, Hume, Millar, Ferguson, and others map the world somewhat variously, each connects climate and sexual desire to define a temperate, civilized Europe that possesses the sexual constraint necessary to engage in the work-discipline productive of political liberty and civic virtue, in marked contrast to the libidinous and indolent torrid zones.

The zones I deal with here fall under the general auspices of "hot climates." Yet equally important, because the women in both torrid and frigid regions possess bodily torrid zones, women of all regions threaten to inject sexuality into the most temperate geographical domains even as imperial discourse strains to confine it to certain areas. Androgynous, transgressive, "monstrous," lesbian, and working-class women—indigenous *and* colonizing women—are all linked metaphorically to bawdy women and are located on the fringes of respectability akin to brute savagery. The general category of "woman" muddles the binaries between mother and whore, Other and prostitute, center and periphery. These connections also make possible the forging of common interests on a global scale, even as they, contradictorily, enable nations to identify a category based on biology that is subjected to disciplining.

As natural histories of the entire eighteenth-century world began to explain past societies, primitive contemporary societies were put forward as evidence of earlier stages of gender relations. Enlightenment debates on women engaged the question, according to Sylvana Tomaselli, of whether woman's "slavery or enfranchisement . . . [was regarded] as the measure of the liberty prevalent in any one form of government."[25] In her pathbreaking article, Tomaselli demonstrates that in spite of the differences among Diderot, Montesquieu, Rousseau, Antoine-Léonard Thomas, John Millar, William Alexander, and others, Enlightenment thinkers generally believed that woman's status determined the level of civilization. The point for these European intellectuals, conceptualizing for the first time that women *have* a history, is, of course, to demonstrate to newly literate women that their situation is far superior to that of their counterparts in the past or to contemporaneous "primitive" societies. Among the privileges European women enjoy is increased leisure, which allows them to expect greater reciprocal love and affection from men. In addition, more leisure in a civilized society makes possible greater attention to the aesthetic instead of the brute desire of primitive societies. The histories of the female sex urge European women to appreciate their differences from women of the past and from women of less "civilized" countries, including their supposedly superior virtue. As Tomaselli puts it, "What [such histories] revealed and highlighted instead was the fact that, however bad conditions were for women in civilised nations, they had been a great deal worse in primitive societies" (110).[26]

I would like to suggest that construing the history of women to reflect Enlightenment progress also aims at convincing European women of their right to dominance over the other women of empire. In other words, the increase in commerce and the accumulation of capital in the West is interpreted as benefitting European women by distinguishing them from their less fortunate counterparts. Civilizing women is also an important aim for Mary Wollstonecraft in *A Vindication of the Rights of Woman* (1792).[27] She wishes that savage, or exotic, women might be incorporated into the revolution in manners to help all women escape their lack of education, their supposed physical weakness, and their emotional delicacy. Yet in all these accounts, civilization is also a curse, since it sometimes leads women to escape cloying domesticity through frippery and consumerism.

A civilized woman freed from the physical labor that her more primitive counterparts undertake finds the strictures of modern society liberating because she benefits from man's increased attention to her. In more advanced societies, "love" extricates women from simple obedience to men because the savage, unlike the civilized man, chooses his female partners without their consent.[28] Rousseau argued that women became empowered by the tensions of such desire, which allowed them to manipulate an empire of love: "Now, it is easy to see that the moral in love is a factitious feeling, born out of life in society, and celebrated by women with great cleverness and care in order to establish their empire, and make for the dominance of the sex which ought to obey."[29]

Enlightenment constructions of women write history as a movement away from man's tyranny toward greater self-determination. Tomaselli, for example, draws analogies between the political and the domestic in that absolutism breeds slavery for women while monarchy creates freedom. She cites Montesquieu's *De l'esprit des lois:* "Everything is closely related: the despotism of the prince is naturally conjoined to the servitude of women; just as the liberty of women is tied to the spirit of the monarch." Islamic regions such as Turkey and North Africa act as magnets for representations of tyrannical masculinity, yet they are envisioned by some as occupying a middle state between savagery and civilization. The concept of despotism, closely tied to climatic conditions because people made slothful from heat are too enervated to resist, may have been largely a construction of Europeans to vindicate their oppression of Asia.[30] Such arguments served colonialism in that they encouraged European women to assume that their alleged superiority was a privilege inherent in their nationality.

As we have seen, since property and the subsequent inequalities that arise from its possession were "the great source of distinction among individuals," the savage has no time for pleasure in the opposite sex. John Millar's famed four-stages theory of society posits a hunting and gathering period, next a pastoral age, then an agricultural era, and finally a commercial stage; and he incorporates arguments about sexual stages as well. Hunting and gathering societies from earlier times are conflated with contemporaneous savage nations that "entertain very gross ideas concerning those female virtues which, in a polished nation, are supposed to constitute the honour and dignity of the sex."[31] During the earliest stage women were bought and sold, subjected to toil and drudgery, and consistently subjugated to men. Just as the pastoral age carried new advantages for women, the agricultural stage contributed to still greater refinement of sentiment in spite of the fact that it also meant that sexual rivalries increased. The feudal knight became enslaved to his lady: "A woman who deviated so far from the established maxims of the age as to violate the laws of chastity, was indeed deserted by every body, and was universally contemned and insulted. But those who adhered to the strict rules of virtue, and maintained an unblemished reputation, were treated like beings of a superior order" (Millar, 95). What derived from this period and still exists in the eighteenth century is "great respect and veneration for the ladies, which prevailed in a former period, [and] has still a considerable influence upon our behaviour towards them" (104). Women's status improved, Millar argued, when men had greater difficulty gaining sexual access to them and when the leisure to conduct courtship increased.

The four-stages theory argues that commercial advancement creates still greater freedom between the sexes. Such freedom may at first increase friendship and companionship, but it ultimately diminishes women's dignity. At the same time, women in the highest form of civilization yet achieved by man paradoxically cultivate their domestic talents and take their greatest pleasure in the reclusive life of the family. Since the commercial society relies on the cult of domesticity, public display of sexual desire is perceived to be un-English and associated with primitive women of earlier stages of development. Their heightened sexuality and its public display encourage "the same free communication between the sexes as in the ages of rudeness and barbarism" (123).

Englishwomen, then, were seen to possess the ideals of reciprocal affection, refined sexuality, and private domesticity, which were equated to the highest levels of civilization. Yet William Alexander's history of women also contends that female virtue is on the decline in the eighteenth century, a belief he connects to consumption. He makes the argument by remarking on the disparity between European women and women of other parts of the world and between savage and civil life. He divides women into three categories, from the savage and uncultivated, to the middle degree between barbarity and civilization, and finally to civil society:

In savage countries, [women's proper behavior] consists mostly in performing the tasks of labour assigned them; in yielding the most abject submission to their husbands; and taking proper care of the children they have by them. In the East, it consists in resigning themselves with a seeming alacrity to confinement; being perfectly skilled in all the arts of pleasing, and avoiding, with the utmost circumspection, every cause of jealousy. In Europe it is more unlimited; it consists in good-nature, sensibility, delicacy, chastity, the domestic virtues, and a thousand other qualities; which, when joined to a competent share of beauty and female softness, are almost sufficient to soothe the most rugged nature, and change the cruelest temper into gentleness and humanity.[32]

Mutable, variable, and subject to shifting fashion, European women contrast to the other women of empire, who, figured as outside the consumer society, are represented as always and everywhere the same because they occupy the timeless geographical terrain of the torrid zones, which are supposedly impervious to the commercial changes of more advanced societies. Alexander worries, however, that recent trade with Europe has turned Asian and African women toward the European love of conspicuous consumption. When Alexander gazes around the world from a position of patriarchal confidence, he finds disturbing consistency, a lamentable sameness, among women: "We are, like the man, who from an eminence surveying the surface of a placid ocean, looks out in vain for variety or diversity" (128). The resolute conviction of Enlightenment debates was that savage tyranny and despotism over European women had ended and that liberty and progress had been irrevocably awarded to them. Yet women's identity, their imagined sameness, provided fertile ground for the birth of feminism at the same time that the natural historians furnished the philosophical basis for Englishwomen to profess their superiority to other women of the empire in formation.

III

Empire afforded a convenient metaphor for feminism in that it variously conceptualized domestic sovereignty and tyranny. "Empire," like "slavery," gained primacy in early feminist descriptions of women's exploitation, and there is considerable slippage among at least three definitions: the actual British empire, men's empire or dominion over women, and women's empire of love. Domesticating empire to make it seem to be only a metaphor (as did many early women writers) trivializes the material reality that emerged in the colonies of the Americas, and extended beyond to Africa, India, and the South Pacific.[33]

The "first" British empire involved a mercantilist policy, the immigration of British settlers toward North America and the West Indies, and the establishment of the slave trade. Until after the Seven Years' War the British empire consisted principally of the American colonies, and trade was controlled by the mandate that British-owned and -staffed ships must carry all goods. Debates ensued over economic policy between the mercantilists—who thought that the exchange of raw materials for the manufactured products of European countries, along with tariffs to protect the metropole, would ensure a favorable balance of trade—and others who supported Adam Smith's liberal ideal of a marketplace in which all nations would share the wealth. Mercantilists constructed a national policy of protectionism, argued in behalf of industrial Britain's establishing a monopoly over the marketplace, defended colonial expansion rather than allowing for free trade, and were actively hostile toward competing imperial powers.[34] Smith's policy of free trade and enlightened rationality contended that while the colonies provided a useful market for the metropolis, mercantilist militarism and aggressive expansion were not productive.

This book attends more particularly to the heterogeneous "second" British empire, which turned toward commercial exploitation of Africa and the East. The concept of empire carried increasing material force in the later part of the century, which was characterized by crises, revolts, and resistance to colonialism. In the history of empire, the period from 1763 to 1815 is regarded as a loosely defined interim period between the loss of the American colonies and the more closely regulated empire of the nineteenth century that turned to more profitable trade routes supported by increased naval power. England gained preeminence on the high seas over other European nations (especially Holland, Portugal, Spain, and finally France) in commanding trade routes and laying claim to territory, in spite of its loss of the American colonies. In addition, England's own notion of itself shifted geographically with the absorption of Scotland into the newly formed British nation in the 1707 Act of Union.[35] During the later eighteenth century England annexed new possessions, which contributed to commerce and naval traffic, rather than principally seeking new settlements. Among the very few new colonies actually established during this time were Sierra Leone—determined to be a place for West Indian slaves because of Lord Mansfield's judgment in the Sommersett case (1772) and because slavery no longer was legal in England—and New South Wales, which became a penal colony in 1788.[36] Gambia and the Cape of Good Hope were also added in 1795.

This period saw an evolution in colonial policies in which private company interests became intertwined with government policy. The Royal African Company had, of course, controlled the slave trade. Also during this period England shifted its noninterventionist policy in India to one of increasing domination of the subcontinent and of attacking India's wealth through trade.[37] The East India Company, founded in 1600, became in the later eighteenth century less a joint-stock trading company and evolved instead into an administrating body with governmental supervision. Winning Bengal in 1757 and the nearly complete conquest of India after 1764 gave England precedence in the contest with France over the possession of the country. As D.K. Fieldhouse has pointed out, "The British empire in the later eighteenth and early nineteenth centuries inherited not only the inherent liberalism of the first phase of British colonization, but also the principle that colonies must be under effective imperial control. In the first British colonies the principle of liberty had been predominant: in the modern empire it was coupled with authority."[38] Mustering that authority also involved engaging Englishwomen's tacit approval and complicity in the "masculine" mercantile activities and territorial acquisition of empire.

Turkey also figures importantly, though differently, in relation to Britain's empire because the Ottoman Empire, another kind of empire, persistently held considerable force in the collective imagination and came to represent men's incontestable dominion over women. But by the later eighteenth century, travel narratives mock the former power of the Ottomans:

> Ridiculous as it may appear, the Turks still indulge the foolish vanity in private, to think that they are a power superior to all others upon earth. Their national pride, therefore, has been cruelly mortified, as often as they beheld the British fleets triumphantly commanding the Mediterranean, and so numerous, that they had squadrons upon almost every ocean. They also envied the flourishing state of the British commerce; and whenever they drew comparisons between the great maritime force of England, and the despicable state of their own, the Ottoman pride broke forth in execrations against this formidable nation.[39]

By the end of the century the Turkish empire was near complete dissolution and its political leaders were characterized as slothful and sensual. Major John Taylor writes: "The enervation of the Sultans, from the period that they ceased to head their armies in person, and shut themselves up in the haram; the indolence, ignorance, and selfish sensualities of the great officers of state; the insubordination of the Pachas; the disaffection of the Provinces . . . announce . . . the subversion of the Ottoman throne, and that the Eastern empire is soon to become the grand theatre of contention among the predominant powers of Europe."[40] The East is represented as a failed power defeated by its sensuality and vulnerable to European penetration.[41]

Turkey and Persia, while not literally dominated by England, embodied male prerogative, manifested in polygamy, as the frightful antithesis to Christian monogamy and the liberty that eighteenth-century Britain proudly claimed for its women. Through Turkey the struggle for masculine authority, of the sovereign over his female subject, was displaced from Europe and simply relocated to other imperial climes. In Turkey, the empire of patriarchy, or male prerogative over women, was closely tied to political empire because the ruler of the kingdom also ruled the household. Turkey afforded an arena for playing out the crisis of absolutism in England (the decapitation of Charles I and the demise of the Stuarts) at a distance, since patriarchal authority was persistently troubled in its coexistence with the bourgeois family in the Restoration and the eighteenth century. Judith Drake in *An Essay in Defence of the Female Sex* (1696) drew early feminist affinities between Eastern women's oppression and slavery: "As the World grew more populous, and Mens Necessities whetted their inventions, so it increas'd their Jealousy, and sharpen'd their Tyranny over us, till by degrees, it came to that height of Severity, I may say Cruelty, it is now at in all the Eastern parts of the World, where the Women, like our Negroes in our Western Plantations, are born slaves, and live Prisoners all their Lives."[42] The passage elides the difference between confinement and slavery at the same time that it attends to the affinities among oppressions.

The final figure of empire I consider, women's empire of love, portrays the seductive power of female sexuality in the romantic heroine as well as the prostitute. Women's empire of love may also offer an arena for potential resistance to men's imperial dominance. The heroine may, as in the case of Lennox's Arabella in *Female Quixote* (1752), contest the romance conventions that confine her or, as in the case of

Amelia Opie's *Adeline Mowbray* (1804), refuse the restrictions of bourgeois marriage. At the same time, Englishwomen's feminist resistance
may rest upon the manipulation and exploitation of Other women.
The divisions within female labor in the eighteenth century and the
emerging patterns of international labor produced cultural practices
that pitted women against women. Examining the differences among
women in the eighteenth century in their historical configuration assists us in constructing a genealogy of feminism's reigning exclusions,
even though they may not match current differences. I hope by identifying those differences in their historical particulars to contextualize
the struggles, and thus to reimagine the future of feminism rather than
to celebrate the differences.

IV

These competing interests among women in the context of empire are
among some of the issues that I address in the chapters that follow.
The first chapter of the book engages conflicts between sexualized
mothers and chaste daughters at opposite ends of the century as they
are filtered through women of empire in Defoe's *Roxana* (1724), Opie's
Adeline Mowbray, and the Foundling Hospital petitions from destitute mothers. These texts struggle to reconcile women's sexuality to
bourgeois domesticity by displacing it onto Turkey, the prostitute, and
the working-class woman to pit the sex against itself. Roxana's highly
sexualized impersonation of the Other woman contends for dominance with her maternity and domesticity. This chapter, like the one
that follows, analyzes the connections between maternity as a central
trope for female difference and maternity as a figure for allegiance to
"mother" country.

Chapter 2 looks at mid-century narratives of maternity in Samuel
Johnson's *Life of Savage* (1744), representations of Queen Caroline,
and British travellers' visions of the indigenous mother, especially
William Snelgrave's account of Guinea, Robert Norris's of Dahomey,
and Mungo Park's of the African interior. *The Life of Savage* accuses
Savage's alleged mother of being unnatural in refusing to acknowledge
her son and akin to savage mothers capable of infanticide. I connect the male appropriation of the maternal procreative reproductive
power, the reproduction of life in text, and the writing of biography
with the threat imposed by the movement of women into the literary
marketplace.

Chapter 3, "Polygamy, *Pamela*, and the Prerogative of Empire," examines polygamy in the English setting when the domestic realm intersects with notions of multiple marriages occasioned by men's exploration of the larger empire. In Hume's essay on the subject as well as in Martin Madan's *Thelyphthora; or, A Treatise on Female Ruin* (1780) and the surrounding pamphlet controversy, polygamy becomes synonymous with barbarity and the debate aims at distinguishing a monogamous Christian English nation from its polygamous heathen empire. Much remarked upon in the travel narratives of Africa, polygamy was also an embarrassing problem for male colonizers who took a second "native" wife. The dilemma, interwoven throughout with issues of class, is particularly poignant in Mr. B's threat to become polygamous if Samuel Richardson's Pamela insists on breast-feeding their child rather than hiring a wet nurse. Women of different classes are set against each other within England, and Englishwomen themselves (such as Mary Wortley Montagu and Anna Falconbridge) exhibit feminist racism in their travel narratives as they make difference a justification for domination.

Another example of sacrificing one part of womanhood to preserve the other occurs in the practice of prostitution. Prostitution at home threatened to allow the torrid zones of empire to encroach on the nation so that the Other seemed troublingly near. Chapter 4 details the sexual division of labor in its relation to empire as Bernard Mandeville's *Modest Defence of Publick Stews* (1724) and various other pamphlets argue for a national imperative to control prostitution. Cleland's *Memoirs of a Woman of Pleasure* (1748–49), probably written in India, serves as a case study for the erotic mapping of a woman's body and the affiliation of her manly body parts—specifically the enlarged clitoris and woman's alleged capacity to ejaculate—with the uncontrollable and unclassifiable sexuality of the other women of empire.

Chapter 5 focuses on women's sphere of influence, the empire of love, as contrasted with men's empire of adventure. Charlotte Lennox's *Female Quixote* (1752), Samuel Johnson's *Rasselas* (1759), and Frances Sheridan's *History of Nourjahad* (1767) provide examples of the connections between the blush (the embarrassed recognition of male dominion in the domestic realm) and the veil (the sign of the hidden sexuality of the harem and of the colonial empire abroad). These texts locate the veil and the seraglio as potential sites of rebellion against virtue and domesticity. Encouraging antagonisms among women, they also erase differences among women and equalize them in their veiled anonymous confinement. The veil Arabella wears is the unfashionable analogue to the Other woman, and it teasingly imitates her. Lennox distinguishes between the ideal Englishwoman and her Others by placing them in a rejected genre and in the past, though the novel's sexual, class, and cultural exclusions keep resurfacing to disturb the heroine's reabsorption into the world of domestic virtue and reason that ultimately renders her silent. In my discussion of polygamy in *Pamela* II, I emphasize the embodiment of ideology in cultural practices through metaphor; similarly, in this chapter I discuss the practices of veiling and blushing to elucidate the figural connections between the political and the domestic as they shape human consciousness and its perception of reality.

Johnson's *Rasselas* and Sheridan's *History of Nourjahad* have in common a utopian vision set in exotic territory. Chapter 6 focuses on another feminotopia, Sarah Scott's *Millenium Hall* (1762), as an instance of the alignment of deformity with womanhood and the novel's connection of domestic confinement to eunuchs, dwarves, and mutes in the seraglio. The associations between physical and sexual "deformity" turn Turkey into a site of homoerotic fantasy. The descriptions of the baths and the harem in the travel narratives of Lady Mary Wortley Montagu and Elizabeth Craven reveal the desire of woman for woman even as Englishwomen struggle to maintain dominance through the aesthetic.

The title of Chapter 7, "An Affectionate and Voluntary Sacrifice," is the phrase the heroine uses to characterize *sati* in Phebe Gibbes's *Hartly House, Calcutta* (1789), and this construction parallels other descriptions of that cultural practice in travel narratives of India at the end of the eighteenth century. *Sati,* the practice by widows of self-immolation, is likened to the Englishwoman's sacrifice of herself to marriage and domesticity, thus negating the Indian woman's actual pain and death in the interests of female community and sorority. In *Hartly House* colonial India serves as a mirror for the display of the Englishwoman's sexual desire and her command of love's "empire" abroad. Love's empire and the power it brings are most easily flaunted in romance, in the past, or in the empire abroad, since its exercise at home is severely restricted by convention and civility.

My point in recognizing the contests and connections among eighteenth-century women is to take account of the various contradictions and asymmetries. The epilogue to the book moves in the direction of finding traces of resistance among women of the empire and among contemporary postcolonial feminist theorists, locating their conflicts within a collectivity, and contributing to the materialist feminist "worlding" of the eighteenth century. Postmodernism has persistently questioned the validity of master narratives of history, among them the assumption that Enlightenment ideas such as human perfectibility, rationality, and liberty can be realized. While I have considerable intellectual alignment with postmodernism's anti-Enlightenment sentiments (articulated by Jane Flax, Sandra Harding, Aihwa Ong, and Cornel West among others), these sentiments may oversimplify the past and condescend to it as a ground against which the difference of the present may be asserted. Enlightenment contradictions abound: the age of scientific revolution paradoxically laid the foundation for scientific racism, the rise of feminism was the premise and occasion for newly fixed models of sexual difference, and the French Revolution altered class hierarchies but failed to grant full political rights to all. The uncanny result of establishing the Enlightenment as the ground of postmodernism may be the eclipse of histories of feminism and of Other women (however troubled these histories may be) as well as the assertion of simplistic periodization. My goal in the epilogue and throughout the book is to explore literary history as a catalyst for a new global feminist collectivity and thus to move toward a historical consciousness that extends beyond the current conceptual horizon and toward a "worlding" of our understandings of the eighteenth century.

CHAPTER ONE

Torrid Mothers

Domesticating the Erotic

I cou'd by no means think of ever letting the Children know what a kind of Creature they ow'd their Being to, or giving them an Occasion to upbraid their Mother with her scandalous Life, much less to justifie the like Practice from my Example.

Daniel Defoe,
Roxana (1724)

There are two ways in which a mother can be of use to her daughter: the one is by instilling into her mind virtuous principles, and by setting her a virtuous example: the other is, by being to her in her own person an awful warning, a melancholy proof of the dangers which attend a deviation from the path of virtue.

Amelia Opie,
Adeline Mowbray (1805)

I

An apparent constant throughout history is that women (though not all women) bear children and men as yet do not. The crux of sexual difference rests in the reproductive capacity, as feminist anthropologist Henrietta Moore points out: "Whatever cultural elaborations may exist in family forms and gender roles, [only] women everywhere give birth to children."[1] The questions posed by universal motherhood remain as vital to the late twentieth century as they were in the mid-eighteenth century. The maternal is a "conceptual impasse"; it is a metaphor for female difference that is difficult to displace because the maternal has often been configured as instinctually determined and intrinsically biological.[2] Yet feminist biologists and historians of science offer alternative paradigms for thinking about the construction of human nature as the complex shifting effect of social, historical, and biological forces upon each other. For example, the body, which we often take to be a given, may be radically changed by diet, drugs, economic resources, and environmental factors. This interactionist approach assumes that gender is culturally constructed at the same time that science, or biology in particular, is brought into the equation of sexual difference.[3] In short, there is no predetermined or fully realized material body onto which gender is mapped because the way we conceptualize it is itself part of its constitution.

Sexual difference as historical and cultural configuration allows us to analyze its manifestation in various historical moments and to imagine its reconfiguration because the meaning of a biological "fact" changes through time. As a result, rather than confusing the metaphors of science with objective truths, biology emerges instead as a powerful representational model that avoids claiming to be an essential reality.

The feminist project, as I would like to engage it here, interrogates the prevailing concepts of maternity and sexuality in order to rearrange them. In short, rather than simply adding feminism to traditional biology, new grids of meaning transform the scope and paradigms of science in order to rethink motherhood and reproductive politics. A postgender world of beings, as Donna Haraway imagines her utopia, might be constituted of cyborgs, beings that combine machines with animal and human organisms so that gender differences will be translated into "the partial, fluid, sometime aspect of sex and sexual embodiment," "contradictory" and "unclosed" and continuously reinventing and regenerating rather than reproducing themselves, agents rather than victims.[4] Such a vision, and others like it, begin to recode the very terms that we use to imagine reproduction and make available new and currently unthinkable subject positions that would be disentangled from essential sexual or racial embodiments.

The fact that only women, though not all women, give birth would seem to be a universal, but that universal may at some point be an artifact of the past. A recent *New York Times* report suggested that in the future men might be able to serve as incubators for fetuses; in an episode of his television sitcom, Bill Cosby donned a maternity corset to experience firsthand the effort of carrying a child in the womb; and we know that in species such as the Australian tube fish, the mouth of the father fish acts as incubator for the fish eggs. If human males cannot give birth vaginally, they may perhaps eventually carry the child internally in the abdominal cavity and have the child extracted at term. Birthing would then lose its status as the most powerful marker of sexual difference.

Reformulating the maternal to separate the reproductive body from mother care and to recognize the way maternal power is distinct from (re)productive activity allows us to question maternity as the central metaphor for female difference and to consider the uses it serves in a particular historical formation. If this concept relies on certain similarities among women, naming its multiple manifestations enables us to think again about reproductive politics across gender, race, and species differences. What, we might ask, is the significance of cultural fixation on the mother as the locus of sexual difference? My focus here is on eighteenth-century England, a historical site that reflects a distinctive and historically nuanced fascination with the maternal. We may recall, for example, Joseph Warton's poem "Fashion," satirizing mothers who give over the care of their children to nurses; Pope's "Mighty Mother" of Dulness; or Joseph Andrews' revelation of his maternal origins through a birthmark.[5] At mid-century mothers become the object of numerous pediatric manuals providing advice on the care and nursing of children. New attention to the management of children, and to the affectionate bond between mothers and children, idealized women's socializing and educational role over their children while recruiting those women to a domesticity associated with the national destiny.[6] New ideologies of maternal affection and sentiment between mothers and children, conflicting with the nascent doctrine of feminist individualism, encouraged women to adjust to a domestic life compatible with the pursuit of empire.

At the same time England also experienced the rise of the market economy and—especially relevant to women—a shift from cottage industries to wage labor. During the century the number of men and women who never married dropped from 16 percent to 6 percent, and as noted by G. J. Barker-Benfield, "Women's age at marriage dropped with it, increasing their production of children (especially after 1740), an increase crucial to industrial capitalism's take-off."[7] Women of the nascent middle class devoted themselves to reproductive labor and to the private realm of the house instead of wage labor. As women contributed less directly to the family economy, the emancipatory power of domesticity and parturition for eighteenth-century women came into question and is still being debated. Ros Ballaster has argued recently that until the cult of domesticity prevailed in about 1740, sexual language and content afforded the woman writer an opportunity to veil political discourse under the guise of the erotic. Domesticity thus quelled women's expression of both the erotic and the political.[8] At mid-century maternity and femininity displaced overt sexual display and the racy language of writers such as Behn, Manley, and Haywood, and replaced them with tales of the proper lady. Yet Nancy Armstrong finds in the domestic novel new agency for the middling woman, and Irene Q. Brown links domesticity to feminism because she believes it promoted rational morality and placed cultural stress on sociality rather than sexuality.[9] For both Armstrong and Brown, domesticity became a cultural force that women mobilized in their own behalf. Others, however, have maintained that domestic power is always compromised because of its containment within the private sphere, its association with the middle class, and its failure to provide access to genuine economic power or political sway.[10]

The emphasis on the maternal seems to function in contention with the sexual. Maternity and sexuality divide women's reproductive and nonreproductive labor into two often incommensurable categories. Most obviously, prudes are pitted against coquettes and virtuous women against whores, but at least as powerfully divisive are the class antagonisms between women of privilege and women of the streets, and between wives and mistresses. Breasts matter so much that they divide mammals from nonmammals, but they also matter because the maternal or sexual use of female body parts is claimed for conflicting purposes. The lactating breast entered scientific discourse as a categorizing organ when Linnaeus somewhat arbitrarily chose it in 1758 as the defining term in the category *Mammalia*.[11] Ruth Perry contends convincingly that a separation between erotic and maternal functions was effected by the end of the century and that the breast became the locus of their mutually exclusive definition.[12] The contest over maternity and sexuality set women as rivals against each other, as when middle-class mothers joined men in regulating women's sexual practices by refusing to socialize with women of questionable sexual character. Further, women of different classes took up compensatory aspects of maternal and sexual labor, since middle- and upper-class women relied on cadres of working-class wet nurses to free them to be sexual partners for their husbands. Pediatric manuals and conduct books urged these same women to breastfeed their own children to safeguard the babies' health against diseases transmitted in breast milk.

Conflicts between maternity and sexuality extended to the emerging empire as metropole was set against periphery. A crucial consequence was that women, both within England and throughout the globe, were alienated from each other because of imperial demands. The torrid zones were not, of course, confined to foreign lands, nor were the domestic zones confined to England. One permeated the other through the lower-class woman, the prostitute, and the homo-erotic as margins that were most visible in the metropole. Because sexuality in all women was associated with the Other, and the domestic female servant and prostitute were likened to the savage, the category of the Other woman became perplexing and problematic in its definition.

Prostitution, illegitimate children, and profligate sexuality bore a material connection to empire: they increased because of the economic pressures that came to weigh on women when large numbers of men who were engaged in soldiering in foreign parts deserted their mistresses or wives, or were killed in the interests of maintaining England's sovereignty abroad.[13] In addition, a larger population was needed to man ships, establish trade, and attend to civil service matters abroad. Yet M. Dorothy George labels the period from 1720 to 1750 a period of "waste of life" in London because of the high burial rate, high infant mortality, the inebriated lower class, and the pauperization of women.[14] In the later eighteenth century, the age of marriage declined, and the number of marriages and pregnant brides increased, as did the number of illegitimate children. The result was a "sudden spurt in population from roughly the middle of the eighteenth century, after a hundred years of minimal growth."[15] In a further twist to the relation between maternity and empire, male convicts were sent to the American colonies and to Australia without regard for the devastating effects on the convict's wife and children. Women were left in the home country to beg, to rely on charity, or to starve, and the disruption to family life provided justification for bigamy and illegitimacy in the colonies. The number of women convicts transported was disproportionately small in relation to men transported, and the combined effect of scarce jobs for women and the difficulty of regularizing marital relationships in the colonies encouraged women to become prostitutes and men to claim that they were naturally driven to seek women's sexual labor.

By most social historians' accounts, the infant mortality rate was extraordinarily high in the period before 1750 and dropped off considerably after that time. Jonas Hanway, the Foundling Hospital's chief advocate and administrator, drew explicit connections between saving the nation's children from abandonment and starvation and creating sufficient troops for the Seven Years' War.[16] A curious pamphlet written in the manner of Swift's *Modest Proposal*—*The Benefit of Procrea-*

tion (1739)—justifies the expense of establishing foundling hospitals and carries the concept of rescuing children and expanding the population to a feverish millennial pitch. Its rationale, so extreme as to seem satirical, is that increasing the number of children will improve trade and production, and build the empire: "Thus we should always find our Strength and Wealth increase in a Geometrical Proportion! Thus in a little time we should be in a Capacity to pay off our national Debt. . . . We should . . . soon become the Terror of all *Europe*, and the most formidable Power upon the Face of the Globe." *The Benefit of Procreation* argues that the future of the nation is intimately bound to the welfare of its children. Initially proposing that foreigners should be admitted to increase the population, the narrator reneges when faced with the ensuing pollution of pure British blood. Instead, its author, Thomas Man, contends, "since 'tis thought impracticable to increase the People to the Land, I fell immediately to consider how much would be gained to the Prince by increasing the Land to the People."[17] Children are commodified and encoded with economic meaning for the nation. But the actual connections between maternity and empire, between illegitimate or abandoned children, English expansion, and imperialism, seem somewhat different from the cast that Hanway and others assigned to them when understood from the perspective of the mothers involved.

The Foundling Hospital petitions written or dictated by mothers eager to place their children in that institution testify that these children were often treated as detritus in spite of the fact that empire favors reproductive sexuality over nonreproductive forms.[18] Empire required women's dedicated reproduction, but it also failed to provide an ideology and an economic structure that would allow working women to support the children they bore. The cult of domesticity, and of a maternal love that saves its children instinctually and at all costs, excludes from its nurturing womb the issue of working women. There is, it would seem, an economics to "maternal instinct" that has largely escaped analysis. Women were left without companionship or support because empire called their partners to war.

Examples abound in the Foundling Hospital petitions. One petitioner to the Foundling Hospital, Mary Brown, whose husband, James Brown, is a mariner on board "his Majestys Ship the Rainbow on the Philadelphia Station," testifies that she must give up her child because she is unable to care for it alone, and her brother can no longer assist her (March 14, 1764). Mary Dorrell is "widow of Robt. Dorrell, late Lieutenant of Adjutant in General Duroures Regiment of Foote, who died of a malignant Fever at the reduction of Guadaloupe, and left your said petitioner with three small Children" (January 4, 1764). Sarah Whitfield (c. 1795), a menial servant who was seduced by a "Private of the 11th Regiment of Light Dragoons," testifies to her "great affection for her child" and says she "cannot bear the thought of placing it entirely within the care of the parish." Another petitioner, May West, also was seduced and gives evidence that a widow, Mrs. Moffat, will take her on as a servant only if the child is accepted. Harriet Williams' lover is a soldier in the 113th Regiment, and Hannah Chendlin testifies that the father of her child is an officer in East India. Elizabeth Wingrove's lover, William Corbett, died "in his majesty's service" in Bombay. Ann Hartland hopes to be a servant if her female infant is accepted, "your Petitioner having had the misfortune of falling a Prey to the persuasions of a false man who is gone abroad and left her with an infant for which she is totally unable to provide for." Several petitions from the end of the eighteenth century report that the women's lovers had gone off to America.

The women who put their children in the Foundling Hospital are generally laborers who anticipate being unable to continue their work if forced to maintain their children. Engaged in productive though ill-paid labor, they are wet nurses, mantua makers, washerwomen, cooks, domestic servants, and charwomen who resist the undesirable alternative of sex work. Sarah Duke, like Daniel Defoe's fictional heroine Roxana, explicitly declares that she is giving up her child in order to avoid prostitution. Several petitioners indicate that their children were the result of seductions under promise of marriage. Judging from the scrawled comments of those evaluating the petitions, the sins of the mother were visited on the child, since the mothers had to be certified as being of good character in order for the child to be taken into the Foundling Hospital. Jane Reeves, characterized as a "very turbulent woman" and "very squalid," was rejected. Children of women who were known to have had more than one lover were turned away, as were children of women who were chronically pregnant. The criterion for admission was supposed to be distressed economic circumstances alone, but the overwhelming majority of these petitions were rejected because the Foundling Hospital was badly overcrowded, and the children were sent instead to the parish for care.

The petitions often reflect the fact that the person currently supporting the child has fallen on a changed situation. Clearly, these women represent themselves as the prey of men. Having sold their clothes in order to survive, they are usually supported by someone who witnesses to their destitution and isolation. Rachel Brimson, deserted by her child's father, writes a plaintive plea for the hospital to accept her eighteen-month-old child, "since by Hard Labour have I struggled to maintain it by which I have Distrest myself of common necessaries finding it not in my power to Maintain it any longer" (c. 1800). Sarah Bruce laments that she cannot gain sufficient support for her children by the day-labor of washing. Elizabeth Brewery also seeks employment and writes that the acceptance of her child might free her to make a "Living at Mr. Langland Bull head Court facing the Free Mason's Tavern." On May 1, 1797, Elizabeth Smith provides a typical personal history and testifies to the importance of wet-nursing as providing subsistence: "I left my Parents in Devonshire, who are hardworking people with a large Family, to come up to London for a place." After a footman seduced her, she was unable to continue work: "I then came to know pain and want and was obliged to sell my Cloaths to support myself and child. As soon as I was able to go out again my late Mistress recommended me to a Lady as a Wet Nurse with whom I have been ever since. The good wages I receive have enabled me to pay for my Child at nurse, but as I cannot expect to be much longer in the situation of wet nurse, I have no prospect when these wages cease of being able to support my child. I shall be reduced to despair."

The problem for all these women is not that they are devoid of maternal feelings, but that they are unemployed and left without the support of the fathers of their children, often because the nation has demanded their husband's or lover's service in the cause of empire. The economics of the situation meant that while the nation needed to produce children to perform its labor and populate the empire, it rendered itself virtually helpless when confronted with the inequities endured by women engaged in reproductive *and* productive labor. The Foundling Hospital apparently refused admission to the children of the majority of these women, and the records indicate that the chances of survival for such infants were in any case quite small.

The petitions of the Foundling Hospital hint at a submerged tale of the elusive intertwinings of maternity, sexuality, and empire. Though the nation needed its children in order to create an empire and thus encouraged maternal domesticity, the demands of mercantilism and territorial expansion paradoxically contributed to working women's economic deprivation and to their necessary abandonment of children in order to secure nonsexual wage work. The eighteenth-century history of empire is deeply entangled in the history of mothering, and we are only beginning to probe the connections.

II

Gayatri Spivak has written that J. M. Coetzee's South African novel *Foe*, inspired by Daniel Defoe's *Robinson Crusoe* (1719) and *Roxana* (1724), "may be gesturing toward the impossibility of restoring the history of empire and recovering the lost text of mothering *in the same register of language*."[19] The implication, she continues, is "that feminism (within 'the same' cultural inscription) and anticolonialism (for or against racial 'others') cannot occupy a continuous (narrative) space" (168), a space that Coetzee attempts to open up by combining elements of *Crusoe* and *Roxana* in *Foe*. The two frames of reference are incompatible, and the *aporia* that is opened up is represented by the daughter-narrator Susan in *Foe*. Coetzee makes Susan the guardian of the margin or the other as she attempts to "rescue mothering from the European patriarchal coding and the 'native' from the colonial account" (165).

Because these two ways of accounting—feminist and postcolonial—seem incompatible, Spivak explores the deconstructive uncertainty, the silences and gaps, as examples of the inadequacies of a politics that would seek an alliance between them. But when the "native" is a mother, I suggest, she is bound within the patriarchal coding of both the European patriarchy and the colonialist of both sexes; and at that point perhaps mothering and the anticolonial may be held, however fleetingly, within the same register. Such a native mother mediating between feminism and anticolonialism does not at first glance appear within *Roxana* and *Crusoe*, though I argue here that traces of such women connect Englishwomen to women of empire and that these traces help construct the missing history of feminism's relationship to anticolonialism by raising its complicity *and* its common interests to the level of visibility. Marginalized mothers at home and abroad complicate colonial relations, foreground its economics, and gesture toward the absent narrative of mothering in an imperial context.

The status of feminism in *Roxana (The Fortunate Mistress)* is surely compromised when one considers that Roxana's "feminism" is associated with an economic and sexual independence purchased at the cost of her daughter's life, and that women resort to murdering each other in the novel's tragic ending. For Roxana, economic freedom and libidinal freedom exclude mothering. The division of labor operating here is tripartite: maternal labor, sexual labor (sometimes for wages, sometimes not), and other kinds of productive labor. Both *Roxana* and the foundling mothers' petitions testify to the mutually exclusive nature of reproductive and productive labor in the eighteenth century; those who have children are most often unable to engage in wage labor.

But the question of the connection between feminism and anticolonialism in the text is worthy of pursuit. Laura Brown, for example, finds in her recent study that Roxana's feminism is "derived from a passionate advocacy of mercantile capitalism," and that women are thus complicit in imperialism's "male acquisitiveness."[20] According to Brown's formulation, misogyny may be aligned with anticolonialism and a critique of imperialism (as in Swift's *Gulliver's Travels*), thus suggesting that a feminism based on extending mercantile individualism is racist and colonialist and can be at least as violent as an antiimperialist misogyny. Englishwomen are also implicated in empirebuilding and in pleasurable participation in trade, but at the point when feminism makes possible an antagonism to empire, it parts company with colonialism. Certainly, the children who survive the Foundling Hospital will man the nets and sew the uniforms of the merchant marines; the Foundling Hospital helped shore up the imperial effort by providing its labor force. Yet women petitioning the Foundling Hospital want economic independence *and* care for their children. They are telling examples of the way working-class women seek resolution of the conflict between maternal and wage labor. Petitioners seek to change the division of labor by calling attention to the difficulty of combining productive labor with mothering. Roxana testifies to that struggle and complicates it in her seeking to amass a fortune through sexual labor, the very kind of labor from which the mothers of the foundlings recoil.

To examine the cross-hatchings of maternity and sexuality within the context of emergent empire in eighteenth-century England involves, I believe, recognizing feminism's internal struggles and its "Othering." By shifting the venue of imperial relations away from England's colonization of the New World, which Defoe had explored in *Robinson Crusoe*, to the Turkish empire and the Orient (which England did not command), *Roxana* masks the relations between the cultural text of mothering and the cultural text of colonialism. As I suggest throughout this book, this masking or displacement facilitates the division of women's labor into incommensurable categories of sexuality and maternity, on the one hand, and into wage and reproductive labor on the other, divisions important to the political and economic demands of imperialism, in order to distinguish clearly the Englishwoman from her sexualized others as well as to foster maternal domesticity.

At the conclusion of this chapter, I turn to another story of maternity and sexuality, Amelia Opie's *Adeline Mowbray: The Mother and Daughter* (1805), which provides a paradigmatic instance of the conflicts between Englishwomen as they are mediated through a racialized Other woman at the end of the century. Again maternity, feminism, and empire are linked. In *Adeline Mowbray* the West Indian servant Savanna negotiates the troubled relationship between Adeline and her estranged mother; the novel also, in an objectionable way, establishes the sexually renegade Adeline as superior to the "savage" woman, Savanna, the former slave. The role of this former slave in *Adeline Mowbray* provides a useful point of contrast to the function of the Other woman in *Roxana*, in which Roxana's impersonation of a Turkish dancer, her pretense at being a woman of the Ottoman Empire, ostensibly signifies her sexuality but paradoxically becomes the marker of her maternal identity and the point of a fatal contest with her daughter. In *Roxana*, pretending to inhabit the body of the sexualized Other breeds violence within the domestic sphere.

In *Roxana* the private arena of bourgeois maternity and the torrid zone of sexuality cannot be reconciled in the person of the heroine without serious economic consequences because the heroine's livelihood depends on erasing the history of her maternity. As the working-class women's petitions to the Foundling Hospital make clear, the emphasis on maternal feeling in the eighteenth century is a luxury available to the middling class and indicative of its self-definition. Roxana's attitude toward her children varies from indifference and neglect to the overwhelming passion she feels for daughter Susan and ultimately to the desire for Susan's death. The affective nature of this range of attitudes toward the children produced by sexual labor, sometimes outside marriage, cannot be adequately coded by the general term "maternal affection."[21] When Roxana gives birth to a boy on the Grand Tour, it dies—"nor, after the first Touches of Affection (which are usual, I believe, to all Mothers) were over, was I sorry the Child did not live"—and she fears that frequent breeding will spoil her shape and beauty.[22] What is ultimately at stake in determining maternal feeling is the mother's economic viability, rather than her individual liberty or identity. Roxana declares, "I saw nothing but Misery and the utmost Distress before me, even to have my Children starve before my Face" (14). She makes an economic argument for giving the children away: "We had eaten up almost every thing, and little remain'd, unless, like one of the pitiful Women of *Jerusalem*, I should eat up my very children themselves" (18). Displacing the violence aroused by hunger upon the allegedly barbarous Other, Roxana alludes to the ultimate savagery of cannibalistic infanticide.[23]

It is generally acknowledged that Defoe's historical point of reference in *Roxana* included the libertine court of Charles II, as well as the more contemporary reference to the licentiousness of George I; Roxana's character may well derive from a combination of both kings' various mistresses.[24] Rachel Weil has suggested that (male) sexual narratives, satires, and poems on Charles II enabled writers to speak politically through sexual fictions in ways unavailable in any other discourse.[25] Weil draws links between tyranny, absolutism, and Catholicism during the Restoration to show Charles's sexual dissipation and the court's attachment to popery; but, more pertinent to our purposes, Charles's debauchery also connected his reign to Turkish tyranny, his court to a seraglio, and his royal scepter to a sovereign penis. Typical of descriptions of this time, *An Address to the Honorable City of London . . . concerning their choice of a New Parliament* (1681) displays the rampant fear that England would turn into an unruly seraglio, "like the Turkish Empire under a weak Grand Signior, by the prevailing concubine of the seraglio, who is perhaps herself managed by no higher dictates than that of her chief eunuch, or she-slave."[26] The Turkish empire as represented by a sexually ambiguous and powerful concubine Roxana is not so much one threatened to be colonized by England as a greatly weakened empire that threatens England's conception of itself through negative analogy to it.[27] Charles II's pursuit of prostitutes and his reputed bisexuality linked his court with the risk of dissolving into Turkish chaos: in the sense that England is embodied in the king, the nation comes to represent profligate male sexuality. Turkey, a country with which England conducted considerable trade, is imaginatively linked to sensual dissipation and male tyranny, but its torrid zones also provoke envy and desire. Sexuality, which was confusedly incorporated into the nation in the person of

Charles, metamorphoses into an Other who is a transgressive woman at home and abroad.

Roxana, a name synonymous historically with the interference of harem women in state matters in Turkey, recalls the Reign of Women and the considerable power women possessed from 1541 to 1687.[28] The Roxane of Racine's *Bajazet* is the commanding ruler of the seraglio who in Amurat's absence wields both sexual and political authority. In a sexual inversion, she has the prerogative to decide the fate of Bajazet, whom she passionately desires though he prefers another member of the harem. There are many other antecedents to Defoe's Roxana, such as Roxalana in Sir William Davenant's *Siege of Rhodes*. Drawing analogies between the various Roxanas, Katie Trumpener writes, "Roxane, the historical figure (the seventeenth-century mistress of Amurat and Bajazet), had by the early eighteenth century become Roxane [, who] . . . embodied ambition, sexuality, revenge, exoticism; in fact, in the eighteenth century she came to personify womanhood itself: mysterious, sensual, resentful."[29] The name "Roxana" signaled a sexual, public, and exotic persona with influence over political decisions, although in Defoe's novel the political has been much diluted.

After Roxana gives up her children because of the economic strain of caring for them, sexuality overshadows maternity in the novel, and she engages in polyandry and prostitution. For men, prostitution is a threat to the social, economic, and sexual order; for women, prostitution is an economic necessity.[30] Roxana intones, "Necessity first debauches me, and Poverty made me a Whore" (202)—though her love of money eventually makes her forget her abhorrence of whoring. The heroine of *The Fortunate Mistress*, given the birth name of Susan, is proclaimed "Roxana" by the cheering crowd that delights in her dress and enticing dance. Roxana travels as the French prince's mistress on a Grand Tour, an activity usually confined to men, which allows her to make "very diverting and useful Observations in all these Places; and particularly, of the Conduct of the Ladies" (102). Her Grand Tour, then, provides a peculiarly female means of learning the ways of women and the means to imitate the Other once she is possessed of a "little Female *Turkish* Slave" who teaches her dressing, dancing, and a bit of the language. But Roxana's troublesome and suspect identity *as Roxana* is based on a vague mimicry of empire, and the terms of the novel keep it distinct from her maternal life.

In addition to the conflicts between sexuality and maternity in *Roxana,* the manifold differences among women are negotiated through women of empire. Roxana is compared in passing to a Native American king and taken for a woman who gained wealth in the Indies, but her dominant Othered identity is a sexually ambiguous blend of the Turkish dancer she impersonates and the Amazonian man-woman, a refutation of the Other woman as subordinate. As an Amazon located geographically in Scythia in southeastern Europe and Asia, Roxana declares that her freedom derives from her sexual ambiguity: "Seeing Liberty seem'd to be the Men's Property, I wou'd be a *Man-Woman*; for as I was born free, I wou'd die so" (171). At least one travel narrative, Major John Taylor's *Travels from England to India, in the Year 1789*, remarks on the author's belief that Amazons existed among the Kurds and Turks.[31] In travel narratives Turkish women are frequently characterized as engaging in manly activities such as pipe-smoking, and the homoerotic potential of the harem is considerable.[32] Roxana is an exemplum of insurrection against male dominance and political tyranny through sexual and economic freedom because her property is her own and she cannot be construed as property herself: "I return'd, that while a Woman was single, she was a Masculine in her politick Capacity; that she had then the full Command of what she had, and the full Direction of what she did; that she was a Man in her separated Capacity, to all Intents and Purposes that a Man cou'd be so to himself; that she was controul'd by none, because accountable to none, and was in Subjection to none" (148–49). The woman who governs is like the "prevailing concubine of the seraglio" feared by the Restoration Parliament because of her influence over the king, usurping labor that cannot be confined to the sexual and maternal, and embodying a sexually desirable yet manly Other. But Roxana's feminism is always realized through an *imitation* of women of empire rather than an Other with a subjectivity and culture of her own. Other women represent the unknown, the not yet tangible; they are present, yet not really present, in the text. As England's caricature of the Turkish harem woman, Roxana is imagined to be subject to the imperial dominance of the sultan yet exerting subversive sexual power that may extend to political authority. Crucially, Roxana's investment in the other woman is to extend her own freedoms through camouflaging her identity as "Susan" within "Roxana." Roxana's impersonation gives that Other woman comprehensibility in terms of English femininity, at the same time that the assumption of the Other woman's alleged sexual ambiguity and libidinal freedom liberate Roxana from her confinement to certain gendered regimes.

Most central to the novel is the familiar scene in which Roxana, attending a masquerade, dresses "in the Habit of *a Turkish Princess*" (173), her clothes cast off from women who were to be enslaved en route from Turkey to Egypt: "And as the Ladies were made Slaves, so their fine Cloaths were thus expos'd; and with this *Turkish* Slave, I bought the rich Cloaths too" (174). Her sexual liberation is based upon the exploitation of these other women.[33] Dancing a French dance (before the disguised king) that people imagine to be Turkish, she represents the *new*, exportable Turkey rather than the old barbarism: the dance, "being perfectly new, . . . pleas'd the Company exceedingly, and they all thought it had been *Turkish*" (175). Outdoing the two "authentic" women from Georgia and Armenia, Roxana expresses her contempt for their dance that has "something wild and *Bizarre* in it, because they really acted to the Life the barbarous Country whence they came; but as mine had the *French* Behaviour under the *Mahometan* Dress, it was every way as new and pleas'd much better, indeed" (179).[34] Roxana's colonizing novelty supersedes the other women's barbarous nativism. The assembled company prefers Roxana's imitation of the exotic, and she relishes her superiority of complexion, habit, and dance and delights in being the "Queen of the Day" (179). The Turkish dress and public masquerades produce enormous revenue for her during two years' time; the Other woman is commodified and denigrated. The cost to Roxana is self-alienation (she is "very far from knowing myself" [177]), and she begins to speak of herself in the third person.

The sexualized Other woman also encroaches on the domestic sphere. In a repetition of the earlier public dancing scenes, this time within a private marital tête-à-tête, Roxana teases her Dutch merchant husband with the oddity of her Turkish disguise: "I believ'd I was able to dress me so, in one kind of Dress that I had by me, that he wou'd not know his Wife when he saw her" (246). Astonished at her putting on the Turkish dress, which is "not a decent Dress in this Country," he recognizes her only because she had prepared him but does not recognize her maid, Amy, who dresses as the Turkish slave Roxana had owned. The dress, meant for torrid zones, is thin "and so open before" she must sit by the fire, "and it was by the help of that Slave that I learn'd how to dress in it, and how every-thing was to be worn, and many of the *Turkish Customs also, with some of their Language*" (248). Both Roxana and Amy, then, are imitating in the private arena the seductive woman of the public space. In that private realm

Roxana engages in polygamy herself, thus taking on the role of the master of the seraglio as well as that of a member of the harem.

But the dancing Roxana personifies only a limited kind of woman-hood—sexuality and seduction—and this does not encompass her former life as a mother and a wife of a brewer.[35] The actual connection between abandoned children and empire, so poignantly revealed in the women's petitions to the Foundling Hospital, is obscured in *Roxana*. Having returned to England, Roxana belatedly remembers the five children she had deserted and sends Amy to seek information about them. Finding her seventeen-year-old son, she determines to make him into a Turkey merchant, a child of empire; and she sends another son to become rich in the Indies so that both will join the colonial mercantile class. Her daughter, on the other hand, has been employed as her servant—as a cookmaid—in Pallmall, and Roxana is in danger of being recognized. Roxana's need for disguise consequently increases: she faces "the Difficulty of concealing myself from my own Child, and the Inconvenience of having my Way of Living be known among my First Husband's Relations, and even to my Husband himself" (197). The only time that Susan has seen her mother recently, however, has been when Roxana was dressed in her Turkish habit. The sexually charged Turkish dress—the material means to making a living—sufficiently disguises Roxana's maternity for a short time.

Soon, however, Roxana begins to be haunted by the contradictions between her public identity as a Turkish dancer in the "seraglio" of the king, her maternal identity in the person of Susan, and her life as a brewer's wife; her history of motherhood eventually interferes with being a prostitute.[36] It is *sexual* labor rather than other kinds of wage labor that interferes with her mothering. Roxana can resolve maternity and sexuality only through the sacrifice and death of her daughter, who carries life-threatening knowledge of her mother's deceptions. Yet at the same time, the murder of her child is a fantasy of self-destruction, since both mother and daughter are named Susan.

By the conclusion, the novel transforms the French-born Roxana into a wealthy, married Englishwoman who is too old for whoring or childbearing. Just as she had impersonated the sexual and profligate woman of the empire, her life of crime was analogous to the colonialist merchants' having travelled the empire and gathered its spoils: "I was like a Passenger coming back from the *Indies*, who having, after many Years Fatigues and Hurry in Business, gotten a good Estate, with innumerable Difficulties and Hazards, is arriv'd safe at *London* with all his Effects, and has the Pleasure of saying, he shall never venture upon the Seas any-more" (243). Having used up the Other woman, benefited from her enslavement, and bested her in performing, she no longer needs to explore the empire. Roxana and her husband intermingle their portable wealth, her whore's spoils with his mercantile earnings.

Sexuality and maternity also intermingle in the relationship between Amy and Roxana, a team of whores who are sexually ambiguous. Early in the novel Amy is taken for a male bedfellow when Roxana's lover arrives unexpectedly, and he teasingly suggests Amy's gender ambiguity: "Yes, *says he*, 'tis Mrs. *Amy*, but how do I know what *Amy* is? It may be Mr. *Amy*, for ought I know; I hope you'll give me Leave to be satisfy'd" (186–87). The intense homoerotic desire between women in this text may be considered, in the case of Amy and Roxana, to be an exchange of one kind of female labor for another, sexual for maternal. Amy here embodies maternal labor, freeing Roxana to continue to be the object of desire for their mutual lover. The interdependence between Amy and Roxana begins when Amy pretends to be the mother of Roxana's children in attempting to parcel them out, and soon after, when she indicates she would whore for Roxana: as Roxana says, "The Girl lov'd me to an Excess, hardly to be describ'd" (31).

The lack of boundaries between the two women is most memorably enacted in Amy's desire to bear a child for Roxana's landlord lover. The idea that Roxana must produce a child to keep the landlord, while plausible, is odd, and the idea that Amy's child would be equivalent to her own in the landlord's eyes is odder still. Roxana, the "wife of affection," assists Amy, "the wife of aversion," as a bawd would initiate a whore, woman against woman, undressing her and voyeuristically observing the sexual act. Amy becomes the adulterous other woman, but that act enables them to bond together as whores and as mothers once Amy bears the child of the union, a daughter, for "we had it nursed." Their apparent cobirthing of the child anticipates their mutual relation to another child, Roxana's daughter Susan by the brewer.[37]

That Roxana is being haunted by images of Susan might also be interpreted as the spectral appearance of homoerotic desires.[38] Deeply troubled by ghostly visions of a phantom figure who disappears and then reappears as her servant on a boat to Holland, Roxana curiously feigns pregnancy in order to avoid her daughter Susan, now called a slut, a "wicked Jade," "this impertinent Girl, *who was now my Plague*," "Tormentor," and "that vexatious Creature." Violence ensues as Amy threatens to kill Susan, and Roxana Amy. Yet Roxana resists killing her own child, who possesses the secret of her name. Even as the haunting becomes more intense and Susan seeks out Roxana in the house of the Quaker, Roxana refuses to entertain murder. The first encounter between Roxana and her grown daughter arouses a passionate visceral response:

> It was a secret inconceivable Pleasure to me when I kiss'd her, to know that I kiss'd my own Child; my own Flesh and Blood, born of my Body; and who I had never kiss'd since I took the fatal Farewel of them all. . . . No pen can describe, no Words can express, *I say*, the strange Impression which this thing made upon my Spirits; I felt something shoot thro' my Blood; my Heart flutter'd; my Head flash'd, and was dizzy, and all within me, *as I thought*, turn'd about, and much ado I had, not to abandon myself to an Excess of Passion at the first Sight of her, much more when my Lips touch'd her Face; I thought I must have taken her in my Arms, and kiss'd her again a thousand times, whether I wou'd or no. (277)

Female erotic bonds fairly sizzle in Roxana's extreme response, the "Excess of Passion . . . when my Lips touch'd her Face," and hint at an uncontrollable desire that cannot be articulated, a breaking of an incest taboo, and a recognition of sameness within Susan the mother and Susan the daughter. Unconventional desire and illegitimate maternity are buried, since for Roxana, "upon my concealing [motherhood], depended the whole of my Prosperity" (277). Killing Susan, then, also murders homoerotic desire and alienates Roxana from the other female object of her desire, Amy, who takes on the "savage" infanticidal violence.

The vague boundaries between the women in the novel make them seem almost interchangeable at times. On the boat to Holland the dance of death begins in the strange female family of Amy, Roxana, Susan, and the Quaker woman. Amy and Roxana both wear Turkish dress, both fear the power of the Turkish habit to reveal their "true" identities, and Susan's recounting of the tale of Roxana's Turkish dance eventually requires her death. When the story of Roxana's dancing is retold, this time by the captain's wife, Roxana becomes uneasy: "I was oblig'd to sit and hear her tell all the Story of *Roxana*, *that is to say*, of myself, and not know at the same time . . . whether she knew me or no; or, *in short*, whether I was to be expos'd or not expos'd"

(285). Truth—a sexual truth—rests unspoken in the mouth of the daughter, who recognizes Roxana as her mother.

In both *Roxana* and *Adeline Mowbray*, as we shall see, the torrid mothers' excessive passion is judged harshly, and repentance is demanded. *Roxana* represents the transgressive power of the mother's acknowledged sexuality and the impossibility of linking domesticity and sexuality. In addition, her domestic labor is unharnessed by her affinity to the Other woman. Most dramatically, torrid mothers, refusing to bear children within the expected patterns of bourgeois domesticity, lay bare the uneasy yoking of maternity to nation and violate the nation's definition of femininity. Roxana's sexual freedom is inextricably tied to her double threat of political power (impersonating a harem woman) and economic power, and both run counter to appropriate maternal behavior.

In the early eighteenth century, convictions were less likely for infanticide than for the murder of an older child, making Roxana's and Amy's crime seem even more heinous.[39] The loss of children is figured as a loss to the entire nation at a time when there is hardly "an Assizes or Sessions where some unhappy wretch is not executed for the Murder of a Child."[40] In the end, Susan's death, engineered by Amy but tacitly encouraged by the mother, effectively kills the daughter's truth. Insisting on sexual liberation grants Roxana an identity, but that identity is severely compromised, for the novel ends abruptly when the suddenly repentant Roxana falls into terrible calamities.[41]

In *Roxana* the nation does not so much have to conquer that which is represented by the Englishwoman dressed in Turkish habit as to domesticate its menace of female sexual, economic, and political power and thus bring it into alignment with acceptable conduct for the woman at home. The impossibility of reconciling maternity with sexual freedom is painfully clear in *Roxana*. Through Roxana's identification with unnatural and exotic sexualities, that otherness in the "self" seems to require the eradication of the unseemly evidence of maternity. In the last analysis, Roxana's eroticism is not domesticated but explodes in violence. This trace of the Other in Roxana's impersonation, even in her distorted depiction, vitally demonstrates a longing to usurp the Other woman's imagined political power that is most often figured as sexual liberation, as well as the threat to English domesticity that she poses. Roxana's "unveiling" as Susan, abandoning her position as a politically powerful and sexually liberated courtesan who dons the costume of the Turkish woman, would necessitate her heeding the appellation of "mother." To establish the connection to her daughter, to honor kinship bonds, she would have to relinquish her attested connection to other women around the globe because in the terms of the novel, they are the displacement of the sexuality she wishes to possess yet keep distinct from maternity in the interests of economic independence. In the terms *Roxana* offers, bonds with the daughter preclude bonds with other women, Turk or Amazon, and reduce them to a figural connection rather than a link to actual women of empire.

III

In Amelia Opie's *Adeline Mowbray: The Mother and Daughter* (1805), Adeline's mother, Editha Woodville Mowbray, susceptible to new-fangled theories herself, connects Turkish dress with fashionable novelty, freethinking, and loose sexuality, which even she rejects: "Little did I think that you were so romantic as to see no difference between amusing one's imagination with new theories and new systems, and acting upon them in defiance of common custom, and the received usages of society. I admire the convenient trousers and graceful dress of the Turkish women; but I would not wear them myself, lest it should expose me to derision."[42] The Turkish women in their fanciful dress are a middle term that negotiates the difference between savage and civilized, woman and man. In *Roxana* the whore usurps the clothing and sexual freedom of the exotic woman; the daughter who recognizes the English mother and her mimicry of the Other as imitation is eradicated from the narrative. In *Adeline Mowbray*, a novel modeled on the life of Mary Wollstonecraft, the woman of empire is represented in the sympathetic if somewhat cartoonish Savanna, a West Indian servant, but like *Roxana*, the novel also employs the trope of Turkish dress. The savage woman, represented in Savanna, rather than being murdered, acts as an agent in the plot to bring about Adeline's domestication into marriage, her successful economic independence, and the final reconciliation with her mother. In the later novel, the Other woman strengthens female community, though it is severely compromised by her status as a domestic.

In *Adeline Mowbray* it is not only Turkey that is associated with excessive and misguided passion. Women's failure to be proper ladies who conform to conventions of dress and behavior connects them to a more broadly generalized Other in Turkey, India, and "savage" nations. Further, Adeline's mother, Editha Mowbray, though clearly the object of satire in the early portions of the novel, speaks with authority in connecting free inquiry and free sex with the savage: "I agree with the savage nations in the total uselessness of clothing; still I condescend to wear clothes, though neither becoming nor useful, because I respect public opinion; and I submit to the institution of marriage for reasons equally cogent" (46). In the language of the novel, refusing to marry is a "savage" decision. Adeline's refusal to marry is likened to an Indian woman's misguided willingness to commit *sati*: "I can't help admiring you, but no more than I could a Malabar widow, who with fond and pious enthusiasm, from an idea of duty, throws herself on the funeral pile of her husband" (93). Adeline Mowbray's actions threaten the notion of English womanhood necessary to national identity, which includes monogamous marriage and bearing legitimate children. Marriage, in spite of the gendered hierarchies and unfair property relations that ensue, is equated with European civilization. To disrupt these relations is to align oneself with the "savage."

Adeline Mowbray's knowledge of domestic economy consistently allows her to escape utter condemnation from other women for her unconventional practices. She is able to "unite various and opposing excellencies. Though possessed of taste and talents in literature, she was skilled in the minutest details of housewifery and feminine occupations" (16). Mrs. Norberry bites her tongue when confronted with Adeline's peculiar combination of sexual freedom and domestic powers: "Mrs. Norberry could not make these pertinent remarks, as Adeline was as conversant with all branches of housewifery as herself; and, though as learned in all systems as her mother, was equally learned in the component part of puddings and pies" (95).[43] At times, the extent of Adeline's domesticity, a practical gift taught her by her grandmother, is almost comical. She caters to the culinary wishes of her husband, Berrendale, as she had for her lover, Glenmurray: "Adeline was so assiduous to anticipate her husband's wishes, and contrived so many dainties for his table, which she cooked with her own hands, that Berrendale, declaring himself completely happy for the first time in his life, had not a thought or a wish beyond his own fireside" (181).[44] In *Adeline Mowbray*, domesticity is distinct from sexual freedom, yet Adeline harbors both, just as she delights in reading an incongruous combination of romance and political tracts (a combination of genres that the novel itself attempts to unite).

In the terms of the novel, politics interferes with appropriate mothering. Adamant in representing herself as an independent woman capable of making her own choices rather than being a kept woman, Adeline is united with the freethinking "enlightened," who, according to the sympathetic Mrs. Pemberton, "disregarding the customs of ages, and the dictates of experience, set up their own opinions against the hallowed institutions of men and the will of the Most High" (126). Adeline's eventual rejection of unconventional principles is predicated on the contagion spread by her lack of virtue: "I am convinced, that if the ties of marriage were dissolved, or it were no longer to be judged infamous to act in contempt of them, unbridled licentiousness would soon be in general practice" (243). But it is the fear for her daughter's future as an illegitimate child that leads Adeline to ponder marriage seriously: having a daughter means that the mother must follow convention, marry, eschew independence, and avoid freethinking. Adeline also wishes to avoid having her sexual errors visited upon her child as her mother's had rested on her. In the midst of the novel's many conflicts among women, there is recognition that victimization unites the two generations: "The mother and daughter had both been the victims of female treachery and jealousy" (247). Mother and daughter in *Adeline Mowbray* are also both shockingly transgressive. The novel blames Mrs. Mowbray, a Shandean eccentric, for fostering Adeline's bizarre beliefs. Mrs. Mowbray's maternal neglect because of her own reading and philosophizing becomes the narrative explanation for Adeline's misguided life. Had Mrs. Mowbray not been distracted from child-rearing by the American Revolution, the reader is told, she could have countered Glenmurray's pernicious influence over her daughter's views on marriage.

Mother-daughter roles are reversed when Mrs. Mowbray's suitor, Sir Patrick O'Carrol, attempts to seduce Adeline even as he professes love for her mother. Adeline perversely accedes to offering a maternal wedding benediction for her mother and Sir Patrick in spite of the sexual attack: "Instead of your mother giving the nuptial benediction to you, the order of nature is reversed, and you are giving it to her" (54). As in *Roxana,* the mother is criticized for having sexual desires; maternity and sexuality, again tortuously entangled, are incompatible. There is also a doubling of Adeline (similar to that of Roxana and Amy) when Colonel Mordaunt falls in love with Adeline and then transfers his affections to Emma Douglas, one of the few women who has defended Adeline: "Colonel Mordaunt declared that every day

seemed to increase her resemblance to Adeline in expression and manner; and in conduct his reason told him that she was her superior";
eventually he comes to admire Emma on her own terms (240–41).

Savanna, a mulatto woman whose husband is being taken to debt-
or's prison, mediates the opposition between women's sexual and maternal labor by embodying both. Introduced as the mother of "Tawny
Boy," Savanna is also yoked together in maternity with her mistress in
the pleasure of Adeline's giving birth: "The mulatto was wild with joy:
she almost stifled the babe with her kisses, and talked even the next
day of sending for the tawny boy to come and see his new mistress, and
vow to her, as he had done to her mother, eternal fealty and allegiance"
(185). Later, the term "wild" is used again to describe Savanna's praise
for Editha (Adeline's child), an excess that calls to mind the associations with Savanna's supposed primitive feelings. The child's birth
also reiterates and seals the hierarchical relationship between the
white female babe and the youthful male mulatto servant. The loyal
youth later conveys knowledge of Adeline's true character to Langley,
a man who had previously assumed she possessed loose morals.[45] The
boy, like his mother Savanna, possesses the "truth" of Adeline's identity; the "savage" is imbued with extraordinary moral and sensory
power.

Savanna, in spite of her class and racial subjugation, exercises powerful agency in the story. After Glenmurray's death, Adeline founds a
short-lived day school, partly because Savanna cleverly solicits students by informing the town that the death of Adeline's fiancé has left
her in need of earning a living. Of course, Savanna's economic well-
being depends on that of her mistress. On the other hand, Savanna
urges Adeline into traditional domesticity and a marriage to Berrendale that she once spurned. When Savanna recognizes that Berrendale
puts his own welfare ahead of his wife's, she determines to thwart his
ends and figures even more importantly in the plot. Savanna defends
Adeline's domestic management against Berrendale's criticism, testi-
fying to the legitimacy of her claims in language reminiscent of Crusoe's Friday but very different in its import: "'You man!' she cried at
last, 'you will kill her; she pine at your no kindness;—and if she die,
mind me man! . . . You marry, forsoot! You marry a lady! true bred lady
like mine. No, man!—You best get a cheap miss from de street and be
content—'" (188–89). This speech intones a register that unites feminism and anticolonialism as Savanna revolts against her "master" to
recognize and name Berrendale's abusive behavior. Marriage to Ber-

rendale also is complicated by his bigamy with a woman slave[Jamaica, a woman whose position is consonant with his malevolent politics.

Adeline's death scene both includes Savanna in the intimate circle of women and subordinates her. Adeline declares her familial fondness for Savanna: "'Love you! Indeed I do, next to my child, and,—and my mother,' replied Adeline, her voice faltering" (196). As Adeline is dying, Dr. Norberry chides Savanna for her penetrating stare. The doctor protests: "'I'll trouble you, mistress, to take those formidable eyes of yours off my face,' cried the doctor pettishly; 'for I can't stand their inquiry!—But who the devil are you?'"(272). Savanna is represented here as a kind of alien being, even animal-like in her desperation, and when she weeps she is called a "blubberer," though from Savanna's perspective her terror must at least in part be predicated on her economic dependence on Adeline. Mrs. Pemberton promises that she will join Adeline's mother in caring for Savanna after Adeline's death. In dying, Adeline grasps her mother's hand to her lips and lays her head on Savanna's bosom. Savanna is clearly the domestic who acts as surrogate mother for privileged women who delegate maternal responsibilities to their social inferiors, and as such she replicates racial stereotypes. In *Adeline Mowbray* colonialism *and* anticolonialism incorporate their dissonances with feminism into a soothing, if highly unsatisfactory, narrative of the colonized Other. Mother and daughter are reconciled through the nurturing breast of the servant woman who is dependent on their benevolence.

IV

In *Roxana* the child possesses knowledge concerning the mother that threatens the mother's economic welfare. As a consequence, the daughter, a version of the mother who shares her name, comes to a violent end. In both *Roxana* and *Adeline Mowbray* women's transgression through sexual freedom, economic independence, and political influence is equated with the exotic and savage, as well as with disruptive forces at home that work against national stability. Marriage and domestic maternity function to define civilization. Domesticating the erotic means displacing it onto the "savage," or exotic, woman—in Roxana's case onto the *imitation* of the Turkish harem, the emblem of sexuality. In *Roxana* women are alienated from each other's sexual, maternal, and wage labor, an alienation exacerbated by the demands of empire; but women may also be reconciled to each other through the racially other woman. In *Adeline Mowbray* the Other woman is very much in evidence, an actual character influential in the plot rather than a phantom of the imagination or an impersonation. Savanna provides wage and affective labor on Adeline's behalf and reconciles the mother to her sexualized, political, and economically independent daughter, though in that novel too the young mother must die.

Roxana and *Adeline Mowbray* display the hierarchies and oppressions that *women* exert on each other, in addition to the usual feminist agenda of examining patriarchal structures. In both cases the status of the Other woman is crucial to the mother-daughter relationship. In *Roxana* the wealthy mother cannot coexist with her common laboring daughter, and her masquerade as the Other woman is lethal to their relationship. The advance in *Adeline Mowbray* is that the Other woman possesses some agency and creates the potential for aligning feminist and anticolonial interests. In the female community of Rosevalley a renegade Englishwoman, a failed mother, and a mediating mulatto woman unite. The difficulty in this utopian vision, however, is all too apparent, for Savanna's capacities for action are severely delimited by her social position and her racial Othering. Yet although the utopian moment at Rosevalley is relatively isolated, it allows us to interpret that female community's fallen woman, its surrogate maternity, and its imperfect attempt at inclusiveness as a harbinger of a feminist collectivity. Feminism connects with nationalism and colonialism, but it also forges connections among all the women of empire who countermand patriarchy and, in the character of Savanna, a "native" mother, find agency in that endeavor.

CHAPTER TWO

"Savage" Mothers

Johnson's *Life of Savage*

A colony is to the mother-country as a member to the body, deriving its action and its strength from the general principle of vitality, receiving from the body, and communicating to it, all the benefits and evils of health and disease; liable in dangerous maladies to sharp applications, of which the body however must partake the pain; and exposed, if incurably tainted, to amputation, by which the body will be mutilated.

The mother-country always considers the colonies thus connected, as part of itself; the prosperity or unhappiness of either is the prosperity or unhappiness of both; not perhaps of both in the same degree, for the body may subsist, though less commodiously, without a limb, but the limb must perish if it be parted from the body.

Samuel Johnson,
Taxation No Tyranny (1775)

Ye cruel Mothers—soft! these Words command—
So near should *Cruelty* and *Mother* stand?

Richard Savage,
The Wanderer (1729)

I

In the eighteenth century motherhood is a trait associated with women, but its procreative power is increasingly compromised and awarded, in a figurative guise at least, to men. In a profound historical contradiction, eighteenth-century Englishmen defined themselves as fully outside the scope of the maternal yet eager to intervene within it.[1] In the case of Samuel Johnson's *Life of Savage* (1744), a biography I discuss in some detail, the production of life in text and the mother's capacity to identify her own offspring are insistently (and paradoxically) determined to be masculine activities. In addition to the complicated figuring of gender distinctions between men and women, sexual difference also sets out significant implications for relations among women of various classes and "races." Through a doubling and even tripling of difference, women of the upper and middle classes are pitted against lower-class women, and "civilized" English mothers against "barbaric" mothers—with their difference offered as proof of racial and class superiority, and their sameness an indication of their gendered inferiority.

The cult of domestic maternity in the eighteenth century, especially intense at mid-century, encouraged the belief that females of every culture and species should be imagined as loving and nurturant mothers heavily invested in the care of their children, an assumption that bred dissonances in the narratives I examine here—scientific documents, accounts of voyages, and the *Life of Savage*.[2] That cult of motherhood disguised the way that middle-class Englishwomen, formerly producers of things as well as of life, were encouraged to limit themselves in the newly emergent money economy to producing life. At the same time, the domestic woman gained power to shape the public realm, particularly the nation, through procreation and education of her children. If the "natural" instinct for motherhood is somehow absent or twisted, the "unnatural mother" refuses these duties and is instead capable of heinous acts that threaten lineage and even civilization itself. This perverse mother is a center of energy and violence rather than nurturing love, and her excesses, as we have seen in *Roxana* and *Adeline Mowbray*, are made akin to the "barbaric" or "savage" of both sexes. England, the colonizer, is frequently likened to the benevolent mother of its colonized children, who are the limbs of its maternal body. The crisis of authority over England's mothers is sometimes deflected onto its "children"—the territories outside the mother country—and it has implications for women of all races and species.[3]

One location of these various differences within eighteenth-century motherhood appears in the *Life of Savage*, which takes as its central object of attack a spectrum of women, especially Savage's mother. The metaphors of mother country and the associations of maternity with nationhood elevate the woman to mythic heights, whereas in reality we find, for example, that women have less authority over birthing, since the female scientific profession of midwifery is somewhat displaced by male physicians. At the same time women's maternal function supersedes all others. As Londa Schiebinger points out, representations of wombs in medical texts of the period become bigger and those of heads become smaller as the reproductive capacity of woman overshadows her ability to do intellectual labor.[4]

At this pivotal point in the representations of sexual difference, the

Galenic model of woman as an incompletely developed and imperfect man gives way to representations of distinctly female skeletons and anatomy. This concept of woman's incommensurable corporeal difference from man joined with a new model of reproduction in which woman's sexual pleasure is newly imagined as unnecessary to reproduction, orgasm unnecessary to conception, and sexuality as separate from motherhood. In addition, while Aristotle had contended that male emissions bore the sperm enabling conception and that women were simply passive receptacles, Hippocrates (and Galen) believed that the two fluids, male and female, mixed with each other to produce life.[5] What would seem to be a feminist model in the eighteenth century, in which women are equal participants in procreation, is instead one in which woman's sexual pleasure was no longer believed necessary for conception, although she is still regarded as contributing a necessary element to produce life. The notion that women contribute a seed to reproduction persisted, but the nature of that "seed" was a matter of dispute between the ovists (who believed that a fully formed miniature was in the mother's egg) and the animalculists (who believed a similar being existed in the sperm). In both cases, even when the theory acknowledged that the mother contributed the egg, her sexual pleasure was no longer important to conception. And the passive egg is described as activated by the aggressively mobile sperm. Women became the objects of impregnation rather than participants in reproduction. The difference, however, is in sexual difference. Both sexes produce seed, according to dominant eighteenth-century theories, but increasingly, these seeds are seen as different (and thus not equal) in kind. This *difference* in the seed made possible new models of sexual difference compatible with establishing a respectable middle-class motherhood (sexuality being assigned to the lower-class woman). Is it merely coincidence that as scientific theory granted woman an egg and some agency in participating in the creation of the fetus, her participation was defined in such a way as to eclipse that agency?

Natural "dominion is in the mother," argued Hobbes. "For in the condition of mere nature, where there are no matrimonial laws, it cannot be known who is the father," he continued, "unless it be declared by the mother: and therefore the right of dominion over the child dependeth on her will, and is consequently hers."[6] Hobbes may have believed that because the child emanates from the female body, maternal authority exceeds the paternal, but this argument ignored the fact that women did not have right to custody of their children under age seven until the Infant Custody Act in 1839. Mothers may have had dominion over their children in the sense of identifying their paternity but not in the sense of possessing them. As the material conditions of maternity changed at mid-century and infant mortality decreased, attitudes toward mothers shifted as well.[7]

Clarifying sexual difference also involved eradicating any ambiguity that might be suggested anatomically. The population was increasingly encouraged to think of itself as divided into two and only two sexes, and sexual definition cohered around the generative organs. The question of hermaphroditism, for example—of a third sex that combines generative organs and sexual functions of both sexes—is thoroughly examined in James Parsons' taxonomy, *A Mechanical and Critical Enquiry into the Nature of Hermaphrodites* (1741), which concludes that sex cannot be ambiguous: hermaphroditism (in spite of historical evidence to the contrary) is pronounced a hoax.[8]

The impetus for Parsons' study was the well-advertised arrival in Bristol of an Angolan woman with genital anomalies; Parsons attempts to explain these anomalies. He is at pains to disprove the possibility of hermaphroditism, sex changes, and sexual ambiguity. Though he is insistent that hermaphrodites do not exist, he asserts that the hermaphroditical tendency, uncommon in Europe, is "common enough in *Africa* and *Asia*, in all those Places especially that are nearest the Equinoctial Line" (153). He seems to suggest that the best English women are absolutely distinct from English men, yet joined by their genitals to women of the colonized worlds and other species. Parsons' treatise apparently equates strict binary gender differentiation and the ability to bear children with civilization, and gender ambiguity with the Other. It is the implicit task of the English colonizer to control and appease the maternal power of the African slave, of the Caribe, of the English mother, and of the ape to maintain the gender economy at home and abroad as it becomes increasingly complicated by race. These renderings of sexual difference distinguish the English mother from other women around the globe. Though specific sites of colonization evoke various applications of the maternal trope, the similarities among indigenous peoples as represented by British travel writers are most relevant here. This lumping together of all exotic peoples was one of the conditions enabling the contradictory and complex notion of the noble savage.

The travel narratives of the period convey a maternal trope that bolsters and controls women in England through the imagined (m)Other and renders the savage mother both like them and different from them. In the narratives I discuss here, the savage mother serves this dual purpose. Like the English mother, she too is both adulated and rendered incompetent, though with different material consequences. Rather than being merely displaced, she is enslaved and rendered silent. She is the worst and best of "nature," supposedly capable of eating, killing, or giving away her child. She supposedly experiences little pain when bearing children: "The women of savage nations seem, in a great measure, exempt from painful labours."[9] But she may also typify a gentler mother unspoiled by culture's claims. The category of the "natural" encompasses incompatible versions of the mother as ideal, innocent pastoral caretaker, and as elementally violent, erotic, and primitive, as instinctual caregiver and as civilizer of man. The tensions that result from this attempt to hold "native" mothers, English mothers, and animal mothers within the same assumptions about maternal feelings may be read to reveal the logic of gender relations and Eurocentricism in the Enlightenment.

In short, these stories of English and savage mothers in the eighteenth century may be woven together to reveal the ways in which race complicates notions of sexual difference and is systemically linked to it. In *An Account of South (or West) Barbary* (1713), Simon Ockley wishes to demonstrate that Englishwomen are much more equitably treated than women elsewhere: "I reckon we are generally more secure of the Chastity of our Women in *England*, where their Vertue and Innocence are their only Guards, than these *Barbarians* with all their Suspicion and Jealousie." Diderot too speaks of the superiority of the European male's treatment of women: he warns in "On Women" (1722) that "there is no manner of vexation which the savage doesn't exert against his woman: the unhappy woman in the cities is far unhappier still in the midst of the forests." On the other hand, James Adair in *The History of the American Indian* (1775) finds Amerindian women to be models of virtue, "of a mild, amiable, soft disposition: exceedingly modest in their behaviour, and very seldom noisy, either in the single, or married state."[10] Whether to their advantage or disadvantage, favorably or unfavorably, the voyagers explicitly draw comparisons, sometimes aligning the women in terms of gender and sometimes setting them against each other as class or racial antagonists.

The early nineteenth century has recently been characterized as the moment when maternal instinct was first assumed to be "woman's definitive characteristic."[11] Whether this was the dominant view in the nineteenth century or simply one view among others in circulation, I am not convinced that most eighteenth-century philosophers, or women themselves, thought of maternal feelings as instinctual or innate. Locke, in fact, is quite explicit in arguing that there are no innate principles and that mother care is a duty.[12] Not surprisingly, Mandeville declares in *The Fable of the Bees; or, Private Vices, Publick Benefits* (1728): "Women have no Natural Love to what they bear; their Affection begins after the birth: what they feel before is the result of Reason, Education, and the Thoughts of Duty."[13] Similarly, Samuel Johnson is at pains to explain that natural affection is nothing, while affection from principle is all. (Savages in particular, Johnson points out, are often bereft of natural affection and must be schooled in duty.)[14] And in his *Memoirs of the Reign of Bossa Ahadee, King of Dahomy* (1789), Robert Norris believes the same when he reports that Dahoman mothers accede to giving their children to the king: "Here, paternal affections, and filial love scarcely exist. Mothers, instead of cherishing, endeavour to suppress those attachments for their offspring which they know will be violated."[15]

The savage mother need not, then, be exemplary of the universal law of female difference—a crucial move because savages must sometimes be figured as genderless children in order to enable Mother Britain to exercise her duty over the colonized. The question of maternal instinct similarly complicates the distinctions that might be drawn between women of different races. Are primitive women, allegedly more closely bound to nature, more or less attached to their offspring than the ideal doting English mother?[16] The difficulty in reconciling the accounts of savage mothers capable of infanticide and child homicide is to explain how civilized English mothers could reject or kill their children. Though all women are united in their reproductive capacity, maternal instinct does not seem to be the definitive sexual difference. But its absence does seem to figure as a sign of the Other when it becomes visible in the English mother.

Johnson, though he abhorred slavery, tolerates no sentimental notions of the primitive. Savages are always cruel, he maintains, and he is adamant in his insistence on the superiority of civilized life.[17] An Englishwoman enraptured by the savage life must be captured and dragged back to civilization from the colonies, for she mistakes pleasure for happiness: JOHNSON. 'You may remember an officer at Fort Augustus, who had served in America, told us of a woman they were obliged to *bind*, in order to get her back from savage life.' BOSWELL.

'She must have been an animal, a beast.' JOHNSON. 'Sir, she was a speaking cat'" (*Life of Johnson* 3:246). The bestial and sensual Other may tempt Englishwomen into forgetting their own superior nature. Savages of past and present are collapsed into each other, the savage of the past remaining in a timeless zone. The eighteenth-century Englishwoman climbs on the back of the savage woman to her pedestal. In short, the eighteenth century marks the formation of an English and civilized notion of motherhood that is contrasted with a savage motherhood capable of infanticide and cannibalism yet at the same time described as "natural." The paradox of the noble savage is reconciled in the body of the mother, idealized yet colonized.

While the Englishwoman is protected within the cult of domesticity from economically productive labor and confined to reproductive labor, the primitive woman's labor of both kinds is harnessed to the interests of empire. These narratives participate in readjusting England's relations of reproduction when slavery silently and violently disrupts African kinship relations and denies enslaved women the issue of their own bodies. In these attitudes toward domesticity and maternity, we can locate the historically particular intersections of race and gender, the uses of feminism and antifeminism for colonialism, the contests between women of different classes, and the internecine wars among the oppressed.

II

In another eighteenth-century travel narrative that considers maternity, *A New Account of Some Parts of Guinea and the Slave Trade*, Captain William Snelgrave begins his 1734 account of Guinea (after a caveat about its inappropriateness for an introduction) with a first-hand description of "a sad Instance of Barbarity" in which a ten-month-old child was sacrificed to speed the recovery of the king of Jabrue: "I saw the Child after it was killed, hung up on the Bough of a Tree, with a live Cock tied near it, as an addition to the Ceremony." He then offers a tale of his *saving* another child when, invited by King Acqua to come on shore, Snelgrave agrees in spite of believing the people to be "fierce brutish Cannibals." Finding "a little Negroe-Child [to be sacrificed to a god] tied by the Leg to a Stake driven in the Ground, the flies and other vermin crawling on him, and two Priests standing by," Snelgrave threatens the king with a pistol and orders him to release the child, accompanying the command with a lecture on Christian morality and with appeals to "the grand Law of human Nature," and convinces him to trade the child for some beads. He continues to recount the story:

> It happened, the day before I went on Shore to see the King, I had purchased the Mother of the Child (tho' I knew it not then) from one of his People; and at the same time my Surgeon observing to me, she had much Milk in her Breasts, I enquired of the Person that brought her on board, whether she had a Child when he bought her from the Inland Trader? to which he answered in the negative.
>
> But now on my coming on board, no sooner was the Child handed into the Ship, but this poor Woman espying it, run with great eagerness, and snatched him out of the white Man's Arms that held him. I think there never was a more moving sight than on this occasion, between the Mother and her little Son, (. . . for 'tis to be noted, the Negroe-Women generally suckle their Children till they are above two year old) especially when the Linguist told her, "I had saved her Child from being sacrificed." Having at that time above 300 Negroes on board my Ship, no sooner was the Story known amongst them, but they expressed their Thankfulness to me, by clapping their Hands, and singing a Song in my praise. This affair proved of great service to us, for it gave them a good Notion of white Men; so that we had no Mutiny in our Ship, during the whole Voyage.[18]

Finally, Snelgrave reports that he sells mother and son to a kind master.

In this short account the colonizer portrays himself as the mediator between mother and child, the civilized intervener in barbaric infanticide. Of course, the slave buyer and trader represents himself as the savior of the mother-child bond rather than its destroyer in the interests of economic gain. The Englishman prevents the (male) savage from killing his progeny; he becomes the surrogate father to the native mother and son. The apparent idealization of maternity turns instead into an assertion of paternity. The native mother, driven by her supposed maternal feelings, claims her child immediately and, in so doing, guarantees its identity. There is for the native mother, however, no possibility of establishing legitimacy or political authority. She, like the slaves who literally applaud the slave trader, is represented as grateful for deliverance from her barbarous country, its religion, and its customs in the name of "the grand Law of Human Nature" that, among other things, compels her to nurse her children until they are two. This native mother, then, serves as an indictment of the upper- and middle-class English mother who sends her child to the wet nurse, as well as a telling reminder of what they are alleged to share—maternal feeling and the female organs of reproduction.

A distraction from the evils of slavery, Snelgrave's version of the reunion of mother and child leads the slaves to take pleasure in their enslavement, and the mother's identity is melded together with the three hundred happy slaves who willingly yield their freedom. The crying child of colonialism must be silenced—returned to the mother, adopted, or even killed, but by the white man. The story obscures the fact that slavery, of course, removed mothers from children rather than brought them together, and that the technique of stealing the child to capture the mother was not an uncommon enslavement tactic. At the same moment that slave mothers are urged to accept the idea that maternity is bodily rather than social or emotional, Englishwomen are imbued with the belief that motherhood involves complete physical and emotional commitment. As Hortense Spillers has pointed out, "The 'romance' of African-American fiction is a tale of origins that brings together once again children lost, stolen, or strayed from their mothers."[19] Snelgrave's colonialist version evokes ideas about manumission, though the cruel vignette promises a freedom that it renders a mockery. The mother's regaining her infant masquerades as freedom and substitutes for it in the text. The mother country, England, promulgates an ideology of itself as a loving, caring mother and its colonial agents as benevolent in order to keep its children closely bound rather than allowing their independence. The virtue of the Britons is consolidated in the intervention between mother and child.

III

This trope of the male interloper who unites child and mother is also the subject of the *Life of Savage*, the first major English literary biography, though in this instance mother and child are English, the mother aristocratic and the child of uncertain class. In both Snelgrave's vignette and the biography of Savage, identity rests in the special knowledge the mother possesses. The narrator, Johnson, positions himself as the restorer of the child to the mother. An anonymous *Life of Savage* published in 1727 served as a source for Johnson's 1744 biography of his friend and companion. Johnson apparently later changed his mind about his vitriolic condemnation of Savage's mother in the *Life*, but Johnson published the biography again without substantial revision in 1781 along with the *Lives of the Poets*.[20]

The text that Boswell aptly called "one of the most striking narratives in the English language" was highly conjectural, since Johnson's suppositions and invention substitute for rigor in researching the details or corroborating anecdotes of the early version of Savage's life (*Life of Johnson*, 1:165). The *Life* is in many ways a fable. Johnson is wrong about Savage's birth date and the fact that Lady Macclesfield attempted to conceal rather than proclaim her affair with Earl Rivers. He also neglects to mention that Savage's sister is illegitimate as well, and he is mistaken in believing that an anonymous poor woman first cared for Savage, therefore confusing a Mrs. Lloyd with the nurse. Johnson is also simply inaccurate about the timing of Savage's published attacks on his mother and the date of his quarrel with Lord Tyrconnel. But the *Life* may be a fable in yet another way, for Savage may have been simply an aspiring shoemaker's son whose fictional reclamation of his birthright was designed to advance him in the world. Though the text has been read as a manifestation of Johnson's psychological ambivalence toward his mother, I am interested instead in the text's complicated interweaving of the cultural discourses of motherhood at a moment of significant historical change in reproductive politics.[21]

Johnson's narrative finds Savage's "mother" disturbing in that she violates assumptions about motherhood as well as assumptions about the English nation, and the two metaphoric fields become linked. The *Life of Savage* depicts a broad array of women. Most horrid is the countess of Macclesfield, the alleged mother, whose "implacable and restless cruelty continue her Persecution from the first Hour of his Life to the last" (6). Equally heinous is Mrs. Read, who had Savage arrested for the eight-pound note he owed her at the coffeehouse on Princes Street. Savage calls her "Madam Wolf Bitch, the African Monster," using this epithet to turn her into a monstrous animal mother who eats her own children. In the *Life* these ravenous women are the bad mothers who contrast to the good women in Savage's life: his nurse; his maternal grandmother, Lady Mason; his godmother, Mrs. Lloyd; the countess of Hertford; and his patron, Anne Oldfield, who granted him a pension of fifty pounds a year. The famed actress Anne Oldfield (1683–1730), herself the mother of two illegitimate sons, possessed a considerable fortune and earned a panegyrical epistle in return for her alleged generosity to Savage: "At her Death, he endeavoured to shew his Gratitude in the most decent Manner, by wearing Mourning as for a Mother" (19). Moving between these good and bad women is Queen Caroline (1683–1737), the influential wife of George II, who reigned from 1727 until her death on November 20, 1737, whom Savage solicits as surrogate mother and patron, and who grants him a small pension but neglects to award him the coveted poet laureateship.

Savage, then, is a man defined, at least in Johnson's imagination, by his relationships to women. He is a "prostitute Scribler" and a "Bastard" because of his mother's action, a volunteer laureate because of the queen's mistreatment.[22] Savage's definition of himself as a poet relies on a somewhat antiquated notion of patronage that allows him to play out the family romance with his queen. Johnson's version turns on unraveling the mystery of the countess of Macclesfield's unnaturalness, the inexplicable failure of maternal desire, particularly in a woman of the aristocracy. He writes, "It is not indeed easy to discover what Motives could be found to overbalance that natural Affection of a Parent, or what Interest could be promoted by Neglect or Cruelty" (6). Savage was, by his own account, the son of the countess and Earl Rivers (the elder Richard Savage), with whom she had an adulterous affair. Once her marriage to her husband, Count Macclesfield, was annulled through parliamentary act (she later married Colonel Bret), Savage became illegitimate in the eyes of the law. According to Johnson's version, when Earl Rivers inquired about Savage's whereabouts with the intention of leaving him a legacy, his mother declared him dead in an unprecedented unmotherly act: "His Mother, who could no longer refuse an Answer, determined at least to give such as should cut him off for ever from that Happiness which Competence affords, and therefore declared that he was dead; which is perhaps the first Instance of a Lie invented by a Mother to deprive her Son of a Provision which was designed him by another" (8–9). Johnson speaks of Lady Macclesfield's "barbarity," her monstrous inhuman shape, her acts of wickedness in denying Savage his birthright. Further, she is supposed to have arranged for Savage's being secreted away to the American plantations. His status, then, is made parallel to that of a slave, a criminal, or at best, an apprentice shoemaker, denying him the status Johnson (and Savage) felt he merited. Because of his mother's neglect, he had to become an author, and he uses his writing to shame her publicly.

The *Life of Savage* repeatedly calls the countess of Macclesfield "Mother" rather than "Countess," the word "Mother" occurring on almost every page:

This Mother is still alive, and may perhaps even yet, though her Malice was so often defeated, enjoy the Pleasure of reflecting, that the Life which she often endeavoured to destroy was at least shortened by her maternal Offices; that though she could not transport her Son to the Plantations, bury him in the Shop of a Mechanick, or hasten the Hand of the publick Executioner, she has yet had the Satisfaction of imbittering all his Hours, and forcing him into Exigencies, that hurried on his Death. (39)

She is a bizarre instance of the other, the marginal human, a monstrosity. She stands accused of using her social position to banish her son to a life as a manual laborer or to an untimely death.

In Johnson's account there is implicit contrast between Savage's mistaken murder of a man in a drunken brawl and his mother's willful neglect. Johnson would seem to support Savage's plea that, because the murder was unpremeditated, Savage ought not to be held accountable. Johnson manages to explain away Savage's complicity and the fact that despite an eloquent self-defense, he was judged guilty of murder. In December 1727 and into 1728 Savage appealed to the queen for pardon, "obstructed only by his Mother" (36), who used the incident of Savage's entering her home without invitation as a mark of his criminal character. The queen, convinced by the evidence, responds that "she could not think that Man a proper Object of the King's Mercy, who had been capable of entering his Mother's House in the Night, with an Intent to murder her" (37). But Savage—the murderer of Sinclair and the potential murderer of the countess—is transformed in Johnson's narrative into a victim of his mother's lie: "Thus had *Savage* perished by the Evidence of a Bawd, a Strumpet, and his Mother, had not Justice and Compassion procured him an Advocate of Rank too great to be rejected unheard" (38). Savage was pardoned, but his mother, through narrative association, becomes a murderer and a whore. Johnson implicitly contrasts the two mothers—the countess of Macclesfield and the queen—but eventually makes them seem more alike than different.

The highest and most public woman in the land is also enfolded within the definition of motherhood that I have been describing. At mid-century, motherhood as both duty and fashion finds its public representation in Queen Caroline, devoted consort of the king, who commands the public realm and exerts considerable influence over affairs of state, yet allegedly prefers the private sphere as the exemplary noble mother of nine who rears and educates her own children. *An*

Essay Towards the Character of her late Majesty (1738), an essay by Alured Clarke published shortly after Caroline's death, praises her recognition of "this great duty of nature" because of her education and conversation with her children, "who were almost always under her eye," and laments that her mode of devoted motherhood is not more pervasive:

> What a misfortune is it to our country that so illustrious an example, which has been publickly known, and universally admired amongst us for above twenty years together, should not have had weight enough to bring an employment of the greatest importance into more fashion and credit; an employment in itself the most honourable, and in its consequences the most usefull of any in the world. And it is impossible not to reflect, with the utmost degree of grief and indignation on the melancholy state of such times, when Parents of rank are grown so degenerate and have so little regard to their own honor, or the happiness of their children, by leaving them in the hands of their Servants, to suffer them to receive their earliest impressions from those, who are commonly taken from the dregs of the people.[23]

Queen Caroline personifies the new ideal mother who welcomes the work of child care as a privilege. The erotic or virginal is submerged in the figure of the nurturing parent; her antagonism toward her first-born son, the Prince of Wales, is ignored; and her political influence and her acting as the king's regent on four occasions is subjugated to her private maternal identity.

This essay on Queen Caroline was itself attacked for its fawning flattery in a series of satires. One of these, *An Essay Towards the Character of the Late Chimpanzee Who Died Feb. 23, 1738–9*, associates Caroline with an Angolan female chimp, actually displayed at Randall's Coffee-House dressed in latest Parisian fashion, who is anthropomorphically defined as a bluestocking and a deist. Soon after, the work of Linnaeus and Lord Monboddo would make it possible to identify the chimpanzee as a relative of the human species. This particular chimp, visited by Sir Hans Sloane while on display, was connected to Queen Caroline through satire. Racism and misogyny, implicit throughout the essay, are complicated by the chimp's exhibiting maternal instincts or affection for a similar childish creature. A response to the *Essay* in the *London Magazine* remarks on her tenderness for a human child: "She walks upright naturally, sits down to her food, which is chiefly Greens, and feeds herself with her Hands as a human Creature. She is very fond of a Boy on board, and is observed always sorrowful at his Absence. She is cloathed with a thin Silk Vestment, and shews a great Discontent at the opening her Gown to discover her Sex."[24] The satiric similarities among queen, savage, and ape are drawn in the interest of maintaining the sexual difference of maternal feeling. The universalizing trope erase racial and species distinctions.

The representation of Queen Caroline as a mother makes an early appearance in Savage's 1728 poem, *The Bastard*. In the argument preceding the poem, he draws an explicit analogy between his mother, now called Mrs. Bret, and the queen: "Indeed, if I had not been capable of forgiving a *Mother*, I must have blush'd to receive Pardon *my self* at the Hands of my *Sovereign*."[25] Mrs. Bret, refusing to acknowledge Savage as her son, stands accused as an "unnatural" mother while he is "Nature's unbounded Son," energetic and free from traditional restraints. In an apparent compliment turned sour, the poet first thanks his mother for defying "Nature's narrow Laws," and then condemns her for the launch "into Life without an Oar." She does not deserve the name "mother," and the queen in the final stanza becomes the adoptive mother who more richly deserves the name:

> *New-born* I may a nobler mother Claim;
> But dare not whisper her immortal *name*;
> Supreamly lovely, and serenely great!
> Majestick *mother* of a kneeling *state*!
> *Queen* of a people's hearts, who ne'er before
> Agreed—yet now with one consent *adore*!
> One contest yet remains in this desire,
> Who most shall give applause, where all admire.
> (*Poetical Works*, 92)

It was literally the pension from the queen that enabled Savage to survive, but the good mother analogy gives way to the bad as he wears "out his Life in Expectation that the Queen would sometime recollect her Promise" (102).

When Savage was passed over for poet laureate in 1730, he began plying Queen Caroline with poems. A substitute mother muse, Caroline inspires his poetry. Savage attempts to arouse Caroline's maternal feelings in his annual unsolicited poem on the queen's birthday in 1732, "The Volunteer Laureat, No. 1":

You cannot hear unmov'd, when Wrongs implore,
Your Heart is *Woman,* tho' Your Mind be *more.*
. . . .
Nor dare I groan beneath Affliction's Rod,
My Queen my Mother and my Father God.
                    (*Poetical Works,* 171).

In the vituperative poem he writes to his alleged mother, Mrs. Bret, "Nature in Perfection; or, The Mother Unveiled" (1728),[26] Savage compares his mother to the mad Euripidean misguided mother, Agave:

Thus old *Agave,* mad, denies her Boy,
Possess'd with frantic, *Bacchanalian* joy,
Knows not his Form, but with distracted Roar,
Mistakes her offspring for a Forest-Boar,
Runs to compleat his Death, exulting on,
And slays a Monster, while She kills her Son.
                    ("Nature in Perfection," 8)

This contrasts to the natural queenly maternal instinct which he earlier links to birds and chicks:

So Birds, by Instinct taught, supply with Food,
And chear, with genial Warmth, their callow Brood,
And oft their kind maternal Breasts expose,
To guard the helpless Young from Threatening Foes,
Fearless, and fierce, unequal Fight maintain,
And dye themselves, e'er see their offspring slain.
                    ("Nature in Perfection," 5)

Mother is pitted against mother, the one an erotic murdering mother who misconstrues that nature, the other a maternal protector whose breasts become the weapons of war in providing safe haven—woman against woman to win the prize of the ideal good mother, lower-class women made incapable of attaining the prize that upper-class women are urged to strive for. Savage's quarrel with his mother is displaced to seem to be a quarrel between women, classes, and races.

In the preface to Savage's *Miscellany of Poems* that Johnson mentions in the *Life,* Savage's mother becomes an exotic instance of a monstrous and primitive female inhumanity. Johnson is explicit in condemning the countess for being worse than an infanticidal parent because she "rejoices to see him overwhelmed with Calamities" (*Life,* nd allusions to infanticide lurk in his frequent use of the word "exposure" (see, for example, pp. 10, 20, 75, 109). It was "the Design of a Mother to expose her Son to Slavery and Want, to expose him without Interest, and without Provocation" (10). Even when Savage is an adult, there is an implication that his mother starved him as he walked the streets without food or home. In fact, throughout the biography, Savage remains the injured child rather than the independent adult: "He may be considered as a Child *exposed* to all the Temptations of Indigence, at an Age when Resolution was not yet strengthened by Conviction, nor Virtue confirmed by Habit; a Circumstance which in his *Bastard* he laments in a very affecting Manner" (75).

Citing Locke, who (in an argument against the innate principle of maternal affection) claimed that whole nations subjected their children to exposure and infanticide, Savage charges that his mother is worse than those barbaric peoples. She, like a member of a bizarre cross-bred sect called the Mengrelians, "may be said to have buried me alive." Worse, she did so without scruple, Savage writes,

> for she is a Woman of Spirit, and can see the consequence without Remorse—*The* Caribees (continues my Author) *were wont to castrate their children in order to fat and eat them*—Here indeed I can draw no Parallel; for to speak but Justice of the Lady, she never contributed ought to have me pampered, but always promoted my being starved: Nor did she, even in my Infancy, betray Fondness enough to be suspected of a Design to devour me; but, on the contrary, not enduring me ever to approach her, offered a Bribe to have had me shipped off, in an odd Manner, to one of the Plantations. (*Life of Savage*, 29)

Locke groups "Children, Ideots, Savages, and illiterate People" together as those who lack general principles. There are no innate moral rules, he suggests in *An Essay Concerning Human Understanding*, because whole nations have engaged in "exposing their Children and leaving them in the Fields, to perish by Want or wild Beasts" or have put live children in the same graves as their mothers who have died in childbirth or have had children who killed their parents (I.iii.70–72). In addition, Locke remarks, "It is familiar amongst the *Mengrelians*, a People professing Christianity, to bury their Children alive without scruple." He continues, "Where then are those innate Principles of Justice, Piety, Gratitude, Equity, Chastity?" These are instances of breaking moral laws that prove to Locke's satisfaction that moral laws are not innate: "For, *Parents preserve your Children*, is so far from an innate Truth, that it is no Truth at all; it being a Command, and not a Proposition, and so not capable of Truth or Falshood" (74).

Savage's mother—who should be operating in accordance with "natural" laws—defies them. She is, in fact, judged to be *worse* than a murdering mother. Johnson writes: "If they deserve Death who destroy a Child in it's [*sic*] Birth, what Pains can be severe enough for her who forbears to destroy him only to . . . make it miserable; and who exposes him without Care and without Pity, to the Malice of Oppression, the Caprices of Chance, and the Temptations of Poverty; who rejoices to see him overwhelmed with Calamities" (20). Women are capable of exposing children, burying them alive, castrating them, eating them, starving them, and abandoning them to their unhappy stars, but the example of Savage's mother demonstrates that maternal instinct is not an innate principle.

Savage's views on the naturalness of these inhabitants of colonized lands in the Americas, the Caribbean, and Africa display contradictions between his political views and the analogies he uses to describe his mother. In his poem *Of Public Spirit in regard to Public Works* (2nd ed., 1739), Savage's strong antislavery and anti-imperialist sentiments are made explicit:

> Let by *My* specious Name no *Tyrants* rise,
> And cry, while they enslave, they civilize!
> . . . .
> Why must I *Afric's* sable children see
> Vended for Slaves, tho' formed by Nature free,
> The nameless tortures cruel Minds invent,
> Those to subject, whom Nature equal meant?
> If these you dare albeit unjust Success
> Empow'rs you now unpunish'd to oppress
> Revolving Empire you and your's may doom,
> (*Rome* all subdu'd, yet *Vandals* vanquish'd *Rome*),
> Yes, Empire may revolve, give Them the Day,
> And Yoke may Yoke, and Blood may Blood repay.[27]

In the *Life of Savage*, Johnson especially commends this conclusion for its original sentiments and draws on it to discuss the distinction between a public politician and a retiring poet. Johnson congratulates Savage for asserting "the natural Equality of Mankind" and rejecting the notion "that Right is the Consequence of Power." The contradictions persist.

In short, I am arguing that in the *Life of Savage*, a mother, positioned in these contradictions, usurps a power she is not entitled to—the right to deny a son identity, property, and class status. According to Johnson, the countess of Macclesfield refused her reproductive function and her "natural" bond to her child, refused to be a woman, and refused to give birth to Savage's identity. Savage—"nobody's son at all," dispossessed of name and property by an Amazon who rejects and destroys him—is conveniently made the one who honors natural bonds. Sympathetically aligned with the colonized, he is also contemptuous of the "savage" mother. The narrator in this "mournful Narrative" becomes the surrogate mother who weeps over the lost child and, at the same time, gives him the lasting identity his mother refused to grant.

IV

Perversely, the logical effect of this attention to the proper English mother is to focus on the white man's burden. By the end of the century, this is made explicit in Mungo Park's account of his travels, published in 1799. The African women tending him composed a song about him, which he translates: "The winds roared, and the rains fell—The poor white man, faint and weary came and sat under our tree—He has no mother to bring him milk; no wife to grind his corn." The chorus, sung by the young women, repeats, "Let us pity the white man; no mother has he / Let us pity the white man; no mother has he" (198).[28] In usurping the words, translating them, and rendering them legible to the European reader, Park mediates the subjectivity of the colonized through the colonizer. His gaze and his words, not theirs, predominate. The words are further sentimentalized, albeit in the progressive cause of abolition, when Georgiana Cavendish, duchess of Devonshire, later writes an odd little antislavery ditty in imitation of this song *thanking* the "Negro" for surrogate care when the white man has no wife or mother. In so doing she erases its irony and makes the "Negro" genderless.[29]

The enslaved mother in Snelgrave's account, the countess of Macclesfield, and even the chimpanzee would seem to be joined in a universal sameness of sexual difference and passivity that variously requires their reproductive and emotional labor for the colonial travels of the exhausted male European bourgeoisie. These disparate narratives have in common the vision of reuniting mothers and children, but in intervening they also attempt to usurp the reproductive and legitimating function they had displaced. The European man wants to be mothered by the women he would offend, enslave, save, or colonize.

As Michele Wallace has written, "The problem of silence, and the shortcomings inherent in any representation of the silenced, needs to be acknowledged as a central problematic in an oppositional black feminist process."[30] The lonely examples of Phillis Wheatley, Lucy Terry, and Mary Prince testify to the public presence of women of color from the turn of the eighteenth century into the nineteenth century; the African woman's voice can barely be heard and is heavily inflected with the dominant discourse. At another level of reading, however, the irony and agency of these women's ventriloquated song, even in the colonizer's translation, may be recaptured. The women empower themselves in making him the central object of their song; they would seem to mock Mungo Park's dependence on them and simultaneously absolve themselves of the responsibility to mother him or to serve him sexually. His exhaustion renders him impotent. British men, defined by themselves as unable to be mothers in the slightest way, are victims of their own vision of sexual difference. Savage's resentment, as Johnson construes it, is directed against his mother's ignoble behavior, which prevents him from occupying the place she pollutes.

What remains unrecognized in the *Life of Savage* are the oppressive conditions that Savage, his mother, and the "savage" share—the mother because of the sexual difference that renders her voiceless and associates her with whore and adulteress, Savage because of illegitimacy, Johnson and Savage because of impoverishment, the "savage" of both sexes oppressed because of enslavement and colonization. All are unable to see their association, their alignment within domination. Instead, the emphasis on difference yields psychic and cultural misery, as well as mutual desire alternating with antagonism and violence.

This mid-century fascination with the mother as a "natural" category may also be a response to the increasingly prolific women writing publicly. Johnson seems to imply that because of the mother's cruelty and neglect, Savage had to succumb to being an author: "But all his Assiduity and Tenderness were without Effect, for he could neither soften her Heart, nor open her Hand, and was reduced to the utmost Miseries of Want, while he was endeavouring to awaken the Affection of a Mother: He was therefore obliged to seek some other Means of Support, and having no Profession, became, by Necessity, an Author" (12). In short, women may in some significant way be held responsible for men's economic need to support themselves through writing. The patronage system made female entry into writing difficult, and the rites of passage necessary to enter its privileged circle—university education and classical learning, the Grand Tour, acquaintance with political and literary leaders—eluded most women. As William Epstein has written, "Hierarchical patronage gradually lost its influence over literature not because it ceased to support authorship . . . but because the size of the reading public and the number of authors or potential authors increased dramatically."[31] What has not been fully considered is the effect of the shift to an increasingly female reading public and female authorship that strained the patronage system. It is not so much that Savage seeks his mother in order to gain patronage, but that he is allegedly driven to writing because he is disinherited. That is, writing—unnecessary if he were not a bastard—becomes oddly synonymous with bastardy, the motherless child, and it is the seemingly inevitable occupation of those without fortune. In Savage's pamphlet, which was later published with other pieces relating to the *Dunciad,* the parallel becomes explicit through Iscariot Hackney, the hack scribbler who is "The Author to be let." The biographical narrator in Johnson's *Life* metaphorically assumes the position of substitute father by giving Savage life in the text, appropriating the mother's birthing, and becoming the mother muse of this new intimate form of literary biography. The world of letters and biography is the masculine domain, and the unnatural mother who refused her primary function as a conduit of lineage and wealth is chastised and excluded from it. The male narrator impersonates the reproductive body to give birth to Savage('s life). European men, not women, legitimate bastards; and producing life—in text, at least—is reclaimed as mental rather than material labor, a masculine prerogative.

FIGS. 1–3. Graphic images of eighteenth-century stereotypes of women representing the various regions of the world. In Fig. 1 the crowned Britannia, seated holding her sceptre, is surrounded by attendants America, the East, and Africa.

In Fig. 2 naked Africa, flanked by the emblems of lion, pyramid, and the devil looks toward beckoning Enlightenment.

In Fig. 3 admiring men in the marketplace encircle the woman representing
the East but her body, unlike her African counterpart's, is beautifully draped.
Frontispieces by G. Child to *A New General Collection of Voyages and Travels*,
vols. I–III, respectively [compiled by John Green?] 4 vols. (London, 1745–47).
Reproduced by permission of The British Library.

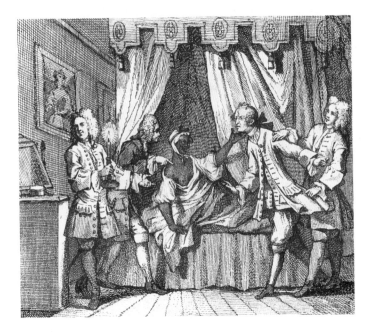

FIG. 4. The conflation of the prostitute and the racial Other. It refers to a practical joke played on Highmore, manager of Drury Lane, and perhaps comprised part of the pranks encouraged by the "Sublime Society of Beef Steaks." William Hogarth, "The Discovery." From Ronald Paulson, *Hogarth's Graphic Works*, 2 vols. (New Haven: Yale University Press, 1965). Courtesy of Fine Arts Library, Cornell University.

FIG. 5. The woman of Barbary whose rich veiling is lifted in partial exposure. Veiling, out of fashion in England in the eighteenth century, was associated with the sexualized Other and the romantic past. "Full Dress of A Lady of Quality in Barbary in 1700." From *A Collection of Dresses of Different Nations, Ancient and Modern*. Vol. 1 of 4 vols. (London, 1757–72). Reproduced by permission of The British Library.

CHAPTER THREE

Polygamy, Pamela, and the Prerogative of Empire

Nay, don't give us India. That puts me in mind of Montesquieu, who is really a fellow of genius too in many respects; whenever he wants to support a strange opinion, he quotes you the practice of Japan or of some other distant country, of which he knows nothing. To support polygamy, he tells you of the island of Formosa, where there are ten women born for one man, and so make a marriage between them.

Samuel Johnson
in Boswell's *Journal of a Tour
to the Hebrides* (1785)

I

If maternity and domesticity of a particular kind signify civilization in contrast to foreign barbarity, monogamy too figures importantly in defining English identity in contrast to the non-Christian world. In this chapter I turn to another aspect of the power relations between nations. Here I treat the Other woman of empire both geographically and sexually—that is, the African woman who is the "'other' of the 'other,'"[1] doubly colonized, *and* the other woman of polygamy, women at home and abroad who make others of each other in competition for the male prize. The domestic monogamous Englishwoman, who personifies chaste maternal womanhood, frequently contrasts to the wanton polygamous Other. "Colonial power produces the colonized as a fixed reality which is at once an 'other' and yet entirely knowable and visible," Homi Bhabha argues.[2]

The African woman, of course, was even less likely than the Englishwoman to speak for herself. Africa was frequently visually figured as a naked woman, a scorched mother under the heat of the sun, flanked by devil and lion, carrying gifts to Europe, with a pharaoh's head and pyramids shown in the background and tropical trees behind (see Fig. 2).[3] Certainly, "Africa" was invented for European consumption in the eighteenth century, but what has been less recognized is the way in which the African *woman* (and other women of empire) was invented as well as made coherent and consistent, yet represented as inscrutable and sexually polymorphous in relation to the European domestic woman. "Woman," like other colonial territories, is treated as something to be defined, charted, probed, exploited, and overcome. Metaphors of seduction, penetration, and conquest permeate the language of colonialism to tame the wild exotic and the imagined unbridled sexuality of the Other.

"Africa is indeed coming into fashion," Horace Walpole wrote to Sir Horace Mann in July 1774 upon James Bruce's return from Abyssinia.[4] In January 1799 Mungo Park's *Travels in the Interior Districts of Africa* was a best-seller.[5] Its 1,500 copies sold out within a few months, and three other editions were issued before the end of the year. Translated into French and German and published in an American edition as well, the book testified to the appetite for consuming Africa, including its representations, its raw goods, and its human commodity, slaves. As Robin Hallett has written, "By 1750 no countryhouse library could be reckoned complete without one of those great multivolumed *Collections of Travels*,"[6] and Africa, the unknown continent, nearly always figured prominently in these collections. European ignorance about West Africa persisted until increased trade prompted penetration beyond the coast; and Mungo Park's narrative especially sparked the imagination of layperson and merchant, scientist and missionary, Joseph Banks. Banks, himself a voyager and the treasurer of the African Association, wrote that Park had opened a road "for every nation to enter and extend its commerce and discovery from the west to the eastern side of that immense continent."[7] And the preface to a book that was part of Joseph Banks's library, *A New Voyage to Guinea* (1744), acknowledges that it aims to satisfy the public's appetite for the foreign: "The present Curiosity of the Publick for whatever may contribute to the rendring the Produce of distant Countries and the Manners of Foreign Nations, fully and certainly known, was what encourag'd the Publication of this Work. . . . There is no part of the World with which we are less acquainted than the interior Part of *Africa*."[8] Willem Bosman anticipated these ideas in the description of his voyage to New Guinea, written earlier in the century: "But 'twas an ancient Saying among the Romans, that *Africa* always produces something *New*; and to this day the Saying is very just."[9] Africa and its products, material and human, sold well in the expanding market, and it was regarded as a welcome producer of the new and the novel.

These travel accounts encouraged commerce deep into the unmapped interior, and European manufactures were sent to West Africa in exchange for African slave labor in the Americas.[10] As was characteristic of the larger print world in the eighteenth century, explorers' accounts were seldom dependent on patronage for publication and more exactly aimed at writing for an anonymous market. As "Africa" was invented, its description in the printed word gained a commodity status. Africa was increasingly included in the extraordinarily popular collections of travels in spite of the fact that the same accounts were often simply reprinted or slightly altered, since very little new information emerged after the travels of Labat in 1725 and Moore in 1738 until Park undertook his monumental voyages at the end of the century.[11] Apparently, the urge to exploit Africa's wealth was not sufficient to overcome the obstacles to penetration. Though the struggle for power over West Africa (colonized by the Portuguese, French, English, and Dutch) was intense in the eighteenth century, Africa's interior remained largely unmapped by Europeans. In short, the commercial market, especially in the middle and late eighteenth century, gave evidence of a passion to consume the unknown and uncharted, the "new" blank space of Africa.

When the human object of obtaining something "new" from Africa speaks, however, as in the case of Ignatius Sancho, an African living in England, it is with incredulity, anger, and contempt for the misuse of his land and people. Sancho writes in his letters (1782):

> The grand object of English navigators—is money—money—money
> —for which I do not pretend to blame them—Commerce attended
> with strict honesty—and with Religion for its companion—would be
> a blessing to every shore it touched at.—[But in] Africa, the poor
> wretched natives—blessed with the most fertile and luxuriant soil—
> are rendered so much the more miserable for what Providence meant
> as a blessing:—The Christians' abominable traffic for slaves—and the
> horrid cruelty and treachery of the petty Kings—encouraged by their
> Christian customers. . . . But enough—it is a subject that sours my
> blood.[12]

The European pleasure in consuming Africa exacted a high cost, and its apparent "blankness" to the European eye veiled massive human suffering.

II

Polygamy is often treated in remarkably benign ways in the African travel accounts written before missionary zeal began to preach monogamy as a tenet of civilization. At home, polygamy includes a multiplicity of practices that may set women against each other or, contradictorily, may bond them together in collective pleasure or to their mutual benefit. In the eighteenth century, polygamy was defined variously as a husband's taking more than one wife, marrying after the death of his first wife, or even seducing a woman while married to another and therefore being held responsible for her ruin.[13] Johnson's *Dictionary* (1755) explains polygamy as "a plurality of wives," but polygamy could also mean simply having sexual commerce with more than one woman on an ongoing basis. As Caleb Fleming writes in *Oeconomy of the Sexes . . . the Plurality of Wives* (1751), "I shall use the term, *polygamy*, for a man's having more than one wife at one and the same time; without any regard to the term bigamy or digamy [a second legal marriage after the death of the first spouse]: because monogamy be transgressed, for the same reason that a man has two wives, he might have twenty."[14] Here, I will explore some of the profound historical contradictions that emerge when polygamy, a crux of desire and domination, is invoked in British travel narratives of West Africa, the polygamy tracts of eighteenth-century England, and Samuel Richardson's *Pamela* II, the sequel to *Pamela*. England's national imperative to manipulate and control women's sexuality in the later eighteenth century derives in part from the increasing demands of colonization, and polygamy serves as a crux to negotiate the erotic and the exotic.

Discussions of polygamy in England were nearly as common as discussions of divorce because of its religious and political implications, and William Cowper, Lord Chancellor of England, was among those who defended polygamy in order to vindicate his own *ménage à trois*. Bishop Burnet, Bernardino Ochino, Lord Bolingbroke, Patrick Delany, and the Deists also took up the pressing questions surrounding the timely issue.[15] In *Reflections upon Polygamy* (1737) the pseudonymous P. Dubliniensis writes, "Polygamy is a doctrine daily defended in conversation, and often in print, by a great variety of *plausible* arguments."[16] One popular pamphlet compares polygamous practices in England to participating in a seraglio: "Polygamy, according to the *spirit* of the law, is still punishable; but the *dead letter* lets it every day escape with impunity. There was a time when a man, who openly kept one mistress, though a bachelor, was considered as a very bad man; but a man of fashion now should be ashamed of not keeping three or four mistresses, even under the nose of his wife."[17] In England the issues focused on establishing scriptural authority for or against polygamy, as well as determining whether seduced women would significantly benefit from it.

The various African narratives nearly always mention polygamy or, in a few instances, its remarkable absence. Most notable is the narrative of the former slave Olaudah Equiano, who reports of his native Ibo tribe that "the men . . . do not preserve the same constancy to their wives, which they expect from them; for they indulge in a plurality, though seldom in more than two." Jerom Merolla da Sorrento comments about the Congo that "every one of these Negroes takes to wife as many women, be they slaves or free, it is no matter, as he can possibly get: these women, by his consent, make it their business to charm men to their embraces." Moore and Stibbs remark that in the Gambia every man may take as many wives as he wishes, even up to a hundred; and Barbot says that "as many wives as he can keep" enhances a Guinean man's reputation. Grazilhier comments that every man in Guinea "may have as many Wives as he pleases." William Smith reports that men may take as many wives as they want in Barbary and as many as they can maintain in Cape Monte, that there is much polygamy in Dahomey, and that wives are a measure of status, ranging from the ordinary man's forty to fifty to the king's four thousand to five thousand. Smith believes, following Alexander and Millar, that such practices are vestiges of an earlier time.[18]

Sometimes distinctions between wives and concubines are reported, though not always. In some instances, polygamy is presented as commercially sound, and the wives are treated as inheritable property. The women work excessively hard in the field and in the bed, and all the wives except the rich man's foremost two may prostitute themselves to other men. In other cases, a wife's infidelity is grounds for selling her to the Europeans. John Millar's treatise draws distinctions between polygamy in "opulent and luxurious nations" and in "barbarous countries." In the former, women are reduced to slavery by polygamous practices. Further, children are so numerous that paternal affection is severely diminished, wives demonstrate great jealousy among themselves, and they are strictly regulated by the father/husband. On the contrary, "in barbarous countries, where it [polygamy] is introduced to a great measure from motives of conveniency, and where it is accompanied with little or no jealousy, it cannot have the same consequences."[19] According to Millar, when combined with luxury, polygamy is clearly destructive to women, but the terms of evaluating it differ in "barbarous" countries.

William Smith's *Voyage to Guinea* follows the popular assumption that African women are excessively sexual, the climate rendering the African coast and interior a torrid zone: "As for all the rest of the king's women, they may be accounted little better than his Slaves, neverthe-less they live in Peace together without envying each other's Happi-ness, and he in their Turns, renders to them all, if able, due Benev-olence: But if that be not sufficient for those hot constitution'd Ladies, they very well know how to supply such Defects elsewhere, without fearing any check from the Husband, who generally makes himself easy in those Cases, provided he duly receives such Profits" (146). According to Paul Lovejoy's recent findings, women slaves for export apparently cost up to one-third more than men in spite of the greater supply of women. Lovejoy's explanation for this disparity is that women were in greater demand in the colonies as sexual objects: "The extraction of surplus labour is certainly a factor in explaining why the price of female slaves was greater than that for males. . . . Women worked hard at most tasks, and sometimes they could be made to work harder than males. But women's 'work' also included sexual services."[20]

William Smith also comments that polygamy helped propagate sufficient numbers for slavery and allowed explorers to take sexual advantage of the indigenous population: "A man sometimes in one Day [may] . . . have Half a Dozen Children born to him" (202) because polygamous men do not cohabit with pregnant or menstruous wives. Francis Moore and Captain Stibbs witness the apparent will-ingness of Gambian women: "The Girls would have People think they are very modest, especially when they are in Company; but take them by themselves, and they are very obliging. . . . If any White Man has a Fancy to any of them, and is able to maintain them, they will make no Scruple of living with him in the Nature of a Wife, without the Ceremony of Matrimony" (121). Smith adds, "Most of the Women are publick Whores to the *Europeans*, and private ones to the *Negroes*" (213). The women "miss no Opportunity [for sex], and are continually contriving stratagems how to gain a Lover. If they meet with a Man they immediately strip his lower Parts, and throw themselves upon him, protesting that if he will not gratify their Desires, they will accuse him to their Husbands" (221). Claiming this kind of seduction, Smith, of course, takes an African woman for his own. Polygamy, Smith suggests, varies not so greatly from European practices under the guise of courtship: "We often spend several Years therin [in courtship]; in which we at one Time, address this young Woman, write to that, and keep criminal Conversation with a Third" (260). Smith elides the differences among sexual practices, his point being to show the superiority of Europeans while allowing for the strange excellence of "savage" ways. Smith concludes his account with a description of a paradisial liaison: "At Midnight we went to Bed, and in that Situation I soon forgot the Complexion of my Bedfellow, and obey'd the Dictates of all-powerful Nature. Greater Pleasure I never found" (254). Portraying African women, especially the wives of other men, as unabashedly seductive and unclaimed for monogamy provided a legitimating rationale for European travellers who were impregnating African women and fathering illegitimate children of mixed race.

The sexual traffic between European men and African women is much remarked upon in the British travel voyages, as is the troubling question of color. For John Barbot, too, the women of Guinea are also proud and lascivious, seeking to attract Europeans even at a small profit: "Such manner as might prove sufficiently tempting to many lewd *Europeans*; who not regarding complexions, say, *all cats are grey in the dark*" (239). (Barbot also notes that most Europeans keep three or four women "as if they were marry'd to them," 36). This trope of the European male congratulating himself for ignoring the color of his female bedmate in the dark is common in these accounts. Color is very much on the minds of the travellers, who give fantastic reports of spotted or mottled women, children who are half black and half white, twins of which one is black and the other white, and children born white who turn tawny or black in a matter of time—all presented as accurate history. Male sexual desire erases the color of the bedfellow, and men's sexual oppression of women is justified by their assertion of the absence of racism.

Similarly, the issue of polygamy becomes grimly relevant when we remember that white slaveowners participated in unacknowledged polygamy and used the slave woman's womb for increasing slave population. Harriet Jacobs' *Incidents in the Life of a Slave Girl,* though written in the nineteenth century, gives voice to a slave woman's perspective: "Southern [white] women often marry a [white] man knowing that he is the father of many little slaves. They do not trouble themselves about it. They regard such children as property, as marketable as the pigs on the plantation."[21] In short, one threat of public polygamy is that it makes legal and visible that which has transpired all along—serial monogamy and especially adultery by white men, who claim African women as their sexual property and who wish to bring to market their progeny in such unions. Polygamy is further justified as a practical solution to slavery's disruption of family life in *Some Historical Account of Guinea, Its Situation, Produce, and the General Disposition of its Inhabitants* (1788) when male slaves are wrenched from their wives and children and taken to another state.[22]

In Henry Neville's popular erotic novella, *The Isle of Pines,* the political rule of the polygamous protagonist is also a sexual monopoly. First published in 1668, and reissued thirty times in six languages during the eighteenth century, the novella recounts a prince's tale of shipwreck and being left with four women. His polygamous relationship with all of them repopulates the island. Polygamy here is figured as male magnanimity in spreading the sexual wealth to his sex-starved female companions. He writes: "Idleness and Fulness of every thing begot in me a desire of enjoying the women, beginning now to grow more familiar, I had perswaded two Maids to let me lie with them, which I did at first in private, but after, custome taking away shame (there being none but us) we did it more openly, as our Lusts gave us liberty; afterwards my Masters Daughter was content also to do as we did; the truth is they were all handsome Women when they had Cloathes, and well shaped, feeding well. For we wanted no Food, and living idly, and seeing us at Liberty to do our wills, without hope of ever returning home made us thus bold."[23] Racial difference becomes something to reckon with, though class seems less significant: "One of the first of my Consorts with whom I first accompanied (the tallest and handsomest) proved presently with child, the second was my Masters Daughter, and the other also not long after fell into the same condition: none now remaining but my *Negro* who seeing what we did, longed also for her share; one Night, I being asleep, my *Negro*, (with the consent of the others) got close to me." "I," he continues, "willing to try to difference, satisfied my self with her" (12). The shipwrecked group enacts the ultimate male fantasy as the women become the breeders and the protagonist a stud: "So that in the year of our being here, all my women were with child by me, and they all coming at different seasons, were a great help to one another" (12). The women produce the community of workers he needs to populate the island. Race and class, subordinate to fulfilling the fantasy of male sexual desire and voyeurism, are erased as the sexually available women become interchangeable in the hero's mind. These and other discourses of polygamy locate the libidinal energy needed to colonize the Other in the body of the woman.

Polygamy in these travel narratives works both as a male fantasy and as an economic rationale for dealing efficiently with excess women. Eroticizing having more than one wife tends to obscure polygamy's economic uses. If one considers these matters within the context of nascent empire, rather than simply the English domestic scene, Martin Madan's massive 1780 vindication of polygamy, *Thelyphthora*, ostensibly written to protect seduced women, becomes nuanced in surprising ways.[24] Madan, who was William Cowper's cousin, incited a controversy that evoked over two dozen responses. Madan's ill-received book espoused the views published a decade before by his great uncle, Lord Chancellor Cowper. In spite of having been an enormously popular preacher, Madan was forced to resign as the chaplain of the Lock Hospital because of the resulting controversy.

Those who argue in defense of polygamy, and those who argue against it, often claim to have the women's interests at heart. *Thelyphthora* proposes polygamy as a serious solution to an epidemic of seduction or female ruin; polygamy in England would be a means to deal with excess females and to dispose of their living carcasses, which simply become wastage after sexual consumption. Prostitutes are visible everywhere: "Our streets abound with prostitutes and our stews with harlots at present, and the crimes of *adultery* and *seduction* are grown to an enormous height."[25] Richard Hill believed that Madan's proposal would actually *increase* the number of prostitutes. "Prostitutes swarm in the streets of this metropolis to such a degree," wrote Saunders Welch, "and bawdy-houses are kept in such an open and public manner, to the great scandal of our civil polity, that a stranger would think that such practices, instead of being prohibited had the sanction of the legislature, and that the whole town was one general stew." Polygamy resolves "the woman problem" and is a way to deal with the public embarrassment of unmarried and ruined women who show themselves in the street.[26] Yet paradoxically, *Thelyphthora* was crucial in fixing the monogamous family and in claiming private property. Madan proposed to control women's superfluity of desire in the purported cause of alleviating women's oppression, while those who opposed him also cited emergent feminist sentiments in defense of women's investment in monogamy.[27]

Another important justification for polygamy was to relieve the
sexual deprivation of men, especially when eighteenth-century middle-class Englishwomen were being urged to suckle their own children for long periods of time. The practice of women's nursing their
children, rather than giving them over to a wet nurse, was firmly
reinstituted during the eighteenth century. Sexual intercourse was discouraged during nursing as spoiling the milk, men's sexual deprivation
became the object of concern, and sexuality was separated from maternity. (Not surprisingly, the question of women's sexual deprivation
during this time seldom arose.) These matters became subject to comment when British voyagers represented foreign practices as exemplary or instructive to Englishwomen. John Matthews, for example, in
his *A Voyage to the River Sierra-Leone* (1788) commends the domesticity and attentive maternity of the African women: "They never
wean their children till they are able to walk . . . for, during the time a
child is at the breast, the woman is not permitted to cohabit with her
husband, as they suppose it would be prejudicial to her milk."[28]

David Hume's essay on the subject, while it finally argues against
polygamy, also treats it as potentially releasing men from extreme
passions for women by indulging them to the fullest.[29] Hume openly
acknowledges the political nature of sexual mores. Dividing and con-
quering the women who quarrel for his favors, the polygamist resembles a sovereign who politically manipulates one group against another
in order to maintain his power. By analogy then, the best ruler is the
monogamist, who maintains authority over his wife because he need
not confront the difficulties of conflicts between wives or of one faction against another. Similarly, Mungo Park, in his *Travels in the
Interior Districts of Africa*, sets up a paradigm of benevolent colonialism through the metaphor of polygamy. Park observes that although
African husbands hold complete command, the wives do not resent it,
and in fact remain cheerful and compliant. The husband is not cruel,
but the community supports his right to mete out punishment. Polygamy encourages women to quarrel; and the husband rules, judges, and
punishes. "When the [African] wives quarrel among themselves, a
circumstance which, from the nature of their situation, must frequently happen, the husband decides between them; and sometimes
finds it necessary to administer a little corporal chastisement," he
writes. In these public hearings, the wife's complaint is seldom taken
seriously, and if she protests, "the magic rod of *Mumbo Jumbo* soon
puts an end to the business" (268).[30]

British travellers in Africa and elsewhere had considerable investment in reporting that polygamy was completely acceptable to the
women involved. As I will suggest, among the benefits of polygamy
were that it fostered female companionship and allowed an excess
population of women to be protected through marriage. However, it
seemed especially tied to patriarchal practices in most of its manifestations, though women's resistance within polygamy was possible. England's toying with and ultimate rejection of polygamy near the end of
the eighteenth century was part of a nation's defining itself both as
distinct from and morally superior to the polygamous Other. Monogamy became instituted as part of England's national definition, and
whatever practices its explorers might have found to tempt them in
other worlds, England asserted its public stance that marriage meant
one man, one wife, at least in law. As David Hume wrote, "The
exclusion of polygamy and divorces sufficiently recommends our present European practice with regard to marriage" (195). Yet polygamy
of one sort or another was common practice in eighteenth-century
England.

III

I want to turn now to Richardson's *Pamela* II (1741), a hastily composed sequel to the popular *Pamela*, as a local instance of the tensions
between women set in play to sustain monogamy's public face, before
turning finally to three Englishwomen's views of the Other woman. In
Pamela II, a penchant for polygamy is one of Mr. B's tendencies.
Pamela's scenes of seduction are replaced by threats of polygamy. By
"polygamy" Mr. B seems to mean an adulterous affair—sexual relations with more than one woman—and the tantalizing possibility of
keeping both available to him. *Pamela* II is a response to the commodification of *Pamela* I and the need to purchase another book when
the first has been consumed. According to Richardson's biographers
Duncan Eaves and Ben Kimpel, "By January 1741 the whole town had
read *Pamela* I and by the summer Richardson had determined to write
a sequel to counter a spurious continuation."[31] The first version, like
the first wife, is somehow not sufficient to the desire—though of
course Pamela proves her virtue and sufficiency at the cost of the
sauciness that enlivened and complicated Part I.

The Pamela of the sequel, an other woman to Mr. B's countess
works out the difficulties of Otherness on the domestic terrain; the
polygamous woman abroad is remarkable for her absence from the

novel and its sequel. Pamela II is as unchanging in her maternal virtue
as the Pamela of the first part is volatile, maddening, and uncertain in
her sexuality. Part II, as Terry Castle has shown, offers "a paradoxical
kind of textual doubling" to its predecessor.[32] Part II revises and refutes Part I's empowering of Pamela and places her within a more
familiar sexual traffic, in which women are a form of exchange between men. Pamela II, a polygamous second wife to Mr. B, is a
realization of the driving fantasy of providing different women for
different functions. In *Pamela* this was already displayed in Mr. B's
liaison with Sally Godfrey and manifested in the embodiment of his
illegitimate daughter. In *Pamela* II Mr. B meets Pamela's demand for
breastfeeding with his own threat of "that vile word *polygamy*."[33] This
debate centers on Pamela's belief that it is her natural duty, and thus a
divine duty, to nurse her child, but "if the husband is set upon it, it is a
wife's duty to obey" (3:48). Appealing to scriptural, legal, medical,
natural, and parental authority, she musters considerable argument to
insist on her duty to the child. To do otherwise, she believes, would be
to indulge in "the sin of committing that task to others, which is so
right to be performed by one's self" (3:50). But Mr. B defines the
question as one of hierarchy and priority. Is the husband's will to be
honored as superior to divine or natural law? How much authority
over his wife does a husband have? Pamela wonders to her friend Miss
Darnford, "Could you ever have thought, my dear, that husbands,
have dispensing power over their wives, which kings are not allowed
over the laws?" (3:5). Male sexual desire is encoded as male sexual
prerogative boldly intertwined with the political. Mr. B's sovereignty
rests on his authority over Pamela.

In the sequel, Pamela (Mrs. B) becomes the ideal wife who limits
the demands of maternity in order to remain sexually available to her
husband. The wet nurse assumes those aspects of the maternal that
threaten Mr. B's sexual prerogative, and she keeps the two functions of
the breast distinct. Pamela is tormented everywhere she turns by other
women who are under Mr. B's control. He flirts with Pamela's nemesis, the countess, with whom he travels, dallies, and converses in Italian. Pamela daily confronts a reminder of Mr. B's sexual liaison with
Sally Godfrey in the presence of their child, Miss Goodwin; and
Pamela herself is confined within Mr. B's increasingly intense strictures to submit her will to him. No longer the feisty Pamela of the first
book who can withstand male prerogative, she decorously withdraws
into the tempering of her "self."

For Mr. B the issue of breastfeeding involves both class privilege and male prerogative.[34] He wishes to prevent Pamela's descending to her origins. He fears that she will become "an insipid, prattling nurse . . . a fool and a baby herself" (3:56), absorbed in the nursery instead of learning French and Latin. Calling on patriarchal authorities, Mr. B teases Pamela with the threat of polygamy but then retreats: "The laws of one's own country are a sufficient objection to me against polygamy: at least, I will not think of any more wives till you convince me, by your adherence to the example given you by the patriarch wives, that I ought to follow those of the patriarch husbands" (3:53). When Pamela intones, "*Polygamy* and *prerogative!* Two very bad words! I do not love them," Mr. B demands that she be angelic about the matter rather than a "*mere woman*" who despises competition from other women.

Until Pamela becomes pregnant in *Pamela* II, there is little to say about the virtuous domestic married woman, no story to be told. Polygamy seems to be inextricably linked to pregnancy as an assertion of male prerogative when men find themselves faced with the female authority that women's pregnancy releases: "For ladies in your way," Mr. B argues, "are often like encroaching subjects: They are apt to extend what they call their privileges, on the indulgence showed them; and the husband never again recovers the ascendant he had before" (3:63). Pregnancy paradoxically enables her to invade his "province." Mr. B's patriarchal retort here and elsewhere is a physical reminder of his authority: a tap on her neck as he says, "Let me beat my beloved saucebox." Later, Mr. B commands, "Speak it at once, or I'll be angry with you; and tapped my cheek" (3:153). The community of readers, just as in the case of Mungo Park's Africa, supports the husband's right to mete out physical punishment and to regulate the women who quarrel over him.

For Pamela, the issue is a woman's authority over her own body, her child, and her will; and she perseveres though Mr. B finds her saucy and perverse: "Upon my word, he sometimes, for argument's sake, makes a body think a wife should not have the least will of her own. He sets up a dispensing power, in short, although he knows that the doctrine once cost a prince his crown" (3:153). Her parents do not hear her plea, "But do you take it *indeed*, that a husband has such a vast prerogative?" (3:56). Pamela succumbs, and the two are reconciled. But Mr. B has been duplicitous throughout the sequel in becoming involved with the countess, who is dressed as a bold Italian nun at the masquerade, even though the reader is encouraged to believe that they indulged only in a harmless platonic flirtation. Mr. B expresses the longing upon which monogamous marriage in the eighteenth century is based, the longing that *love* will mask the power relations that guarantee male prerogative.

Mr. B's alleged affair with the countess occurs near the time of Pamela's first lying-in. The rest of the novel is, after all, about polygamy, the production of a redundancy of female desire directed toward Mr. B, and the regulation of that desire. Mr. B is able to take plural "wives" in the sense of one sexual Pamela and one maternal Pamela, but more literally both a former chambermaid and a countess. The sympathetic Lady Davers reports to Pamela: "What vexes me is, that when the noble uncle of this vile lady [the countess] . . . expostulated with her on the scandals she brought upon her character and family, she pretended to argue, foolish creature! for polygamy; and said, 'She had rather be a certain gentleman's second wife, than the first to the greatest man in England'" (3:171). The wily Pamela, who had survived the wicked Mrs. Jewkes, now discovers herself to be a meek domestic cowering at the prospect of meeting her nemesis, the countess. Again, as in the first volume, the reader remains uncertain if Pamela is overreacting. If *Pamela* I has links with pornography, *Pamela* II roots out the connection between debauchery and male tyranny to foster benevolent monogamy.

Mr. B plays the two women against each other after arranging for them to meet. The countess excels at the harpsichord when each plays, and her equestrian skills are also reported to be superior to those of the class-bound Pamela. Seldom is a comparison between women so blatant except in misogynous satire. Mr. B reports the countess's questioning concerning the superiority of face, hair, forehead, brows, complexion, eyes, cheek, nose, lips, smiles, teeth, chin, and ears; but the lady calls a halt when he threatens to move lower. No need, however, for the facial features may easily be read as codes for sexual parts.[35] In the second telling of this twice-told tale of the encounter between Pamela and the countess, the beauty contest between the "incomparable" ladies is made very particular: "For black eyes in my girl, and blue in your ladyship, they are both the loveliest I ever beheld.—And, Pamela, I was wicked enough to say, that it would be the sweetest travelling in the world, to have you both placed at fifty miles distance from each other, and to pass the prime of one's life from black to blue, and from blue to black; and it would be impossible to know which to prefer, but the present" (3:229). The countess cuffs him in response, and he "kissed her in revenge." Pamela cries out in disgust, "Fine doings between two Platonics!" which leads Mr. B again to exercise his physical authority and tap her neck.

The former chambermaid and the countess, reduced to body parts as they compete for the polygamous male, are interchangeable women in spite of social class differences. Mr. B, like the weak sovereign of David Hume's essay "Of Polygamy," "must play one faction against another, and become absolute by the mutual jealousy of the females. *To divide and govern*, is an universal maxim" (185). Hume says polygamy means male prerogative, male governance, and male authority. Masculine privilege is integrally connected to the territorial prerogative of empire. Pamela is Mr. B's territorial domain to conquer as the power relations of *Pamela* I are reversed, and she fully submits her will to his. Pamela wins out over the nobility through the display of her superior beauty and virtue, but we can imagine Mr. B's continuing to produce polygamous rivals throughout their marriage only to be once again chastened by the moral order of monogamy.

The progress of *Pamela* II reveals Mr. B's apparent libertinism yet supposed fidelity. In the unsatisfying resolution of the plot, Pamela rather than Mr. B is put on trial. The countess, it turns out, was quoted out of context, and the entire epistolary affair may now be reread and reinterpreted to free Mr. B from imputation. He unequivocally rejects polygamy as outside the bounds of his country. He claims that it was only advanced "in the levity of speech, and the wantonness of argument" (3:223). In sum, *Pamela* II reestablishes an order in the world made topsy-turvy in *Pamela* I. It replaces the first Pamela with Pamela II, a maternal Pamela who strains at sexuality. One nursing breast is equal to another, one sexual organ substitutes for another. But Mr. B recognizes that polygamy is un-English. It is an exotic tease more suitable for masquerades than real life, and *Pamela* II becomes finally a triumphant assertion of monogamy at Mr. B's expense. Richardson, like Hume, seems to argue that the best ruler, in the home as well as the state, is the monogamist, who does not need to pit factions against each other in order to maintain authority. He rules by the willing submission of woman's will, which relies on her sexual competition with other women—her signaling a new class status by relinquishing nursing to the working-class woman, the Other.

Polygamy operates on two fronts at once—the domestic and the colonial. At home, its imagined possibility maintains a husband's sovereignty over his wife's body and its parts by threatening to replace it with another female body. Yet to legalize its practice, even for the benevolent purpose of providing husbands for ruined women and taking up a surplus of useless women (as Martin Madan's *Thelyphthora* proposed), proves too disturbing for England's sense of itself as moral, Christian, Western. On the colonial front, polygamy involves men's control of women as property. The colonizers penetrate and possess the African continent; they may also take pleasure in penetrating another man's property. The sovereign male, the counterpart to the woman who realizes her civic duty in mothering, freshly expresses his patriotism and his Englishness in public monogamy at home at the historical moment when private property and the monogamous family form are linked.[36] Mr. B's threats of philandering in order to prevent Pamela from breastfeeding play out on the domestic front the issues of maternity, sexuality, and male monogamy purchased through the profoundly tedious declaration that Pamela (and even quite literally her body) is his private possession. These apparently domestic issues have larger political implications in an emerging empire and help to define the differences between the European and his polygamous others—the African, the Indian, the Turk, and the Pacific Islanders. The use of the exotic for Mr. B, as in the passage from Montesquieu that Samuel Johnson cites in the epigraph to this chapter, is to make the strange practice of polygamy familiar. Thus, Mr. B justifies polygamy to a credulous wife who, in ultimately refusing to accept Mr. B's Other woman and rejecting a foreign pollutant to her marriage, remains the firm moral center of the domestic English novel.

IV

For the Englishwoman, the attitude toward polygamy is even more intensely fraught with contradictions. In this context I want to turn briefly to the responses to polygamy of three Englishwomen: Anna Falconbridge, Lady Mary Wortley Montagu, and Mary Wollstonecraft. In tension with the cult of domesticity represented in *Pamela* was an increasingly strong female voice, readership, and authorship—a tension between empowerment and domestication. The profound historical contradiction revealed is that Africa and other countries of the emergent empire provide the justification for exotic practices, but also present a threat that the Other may be too similar to the European for comfort if the practice was justified and shared. The polygamous, sensualized, yet supposedly ugly African woman stands in contrast to the monogamous, domestic, and lovely Englishwoman.

Falconbridge, Montagu, and Wollstonecraft, all women with feminist sentiments, voice both admiring and antagonistic reactions to women of empire. In this context we might well ask what use pitting women against each other might serve at a time of emergent feminism, of newly rigidified differences between the sexes, and of the formation of empire. Both Falconbridge and Montagu focus on the female body of the Other in their accounts of polygamy, while Wollstonecraft concerns herself instead with polygamy's social implications. In the three accounts discussed here, the Other is the self displaced in a veiled and even skewed recognition of its own colonization under domestic patriarchy.

Anna Falconbridge, writing a narrative of her voyages to Sierra Leone, where she traveled with her Abolitionist husband, comments on how unusual it is for an Englishwoman to visit Africa. In conversation with a Portuguese woman who envies Englishwomen, Falconbridge acknowledges her similarity to the European lady and their mutual oppression: "I thanked her in behalf of my country women, for her good opinion, but assured her they had their share of thorns and thistles, as well as those of other countries."[37] Falconbridge also befriends seven outcast Englishwomen, whom she found dirty and diseased. These prostitutes—taken to Wapping, made drunk, and married to African men—she says, will "practice their inequities more brutishly in this horrid country." But her initial reaction to the African women she finds is to remark on her distance from them: "Seeing so many of my own sex, though of different complexions from myself, attired in their native garbs, was a scene equally new to me, and my delicacy, I confess, was not a little hurt at times" (21). She champions "my own sex" yet considers their "different complexions"; she positions herself as the delicate and squeamish one, for they are not yet mapped in terms of gender because of the difference in color.

Falconbridge, like other travellers, locates racial difference in the fetishized breasts of the Other, the exposed breasts of the polygamous king's many wives. These breasts place the women in a conjunction of the sexual and maternal that is difficult, if not impossible, to reconcile in the Englishwoman. The way she reconciles this disjunction with the African woman is by judging the women to be aesthetically repellent. Breasts, like pudenda, mark racial differences between European and

African women. Their breasts—large, long, stretched by nursing, "disgusting to Europeans, though considered *beautiful* and ornamental here"—are reminiscent of the near-constant invocation of the legendary Hottentot breasts that women supposedly threw over their shoulders for the comfort of the nursing child on their backs. Most of the women, Falconbridge believes, are attached as mistresses to the various English gentlemen, and their appearance of occupying "superior rank" stymies the conventional response of assuming their inferiority to her. Polygamy, she notes, "is considered honorable, and creates consequence" (77). She reports that the number of wives is a measure of wealth: "When an African speaks of a great man, he or she will say, 'Oh! he be fine man, rich too much, he got too much woman.'"

When faced with these naked African women, Anna Falconbridge also records her frustration in attempting to convince Queen Clara, the oldest of the king's wives, to dress in the European manner. Instead, the queen—"impetuous, litigious, and implacable"—tears the clothes off her back, and Falconbridge, "finding no credit could be gained by trying to new fashion this *Ethiopian Princess*, . . . got rid of her as soon as possible" (62). Falconbridge, attempting to wash the Ethiop white, resists the recognition that her body resembles the body for which she has contempt; the bond of the female body, which transcends race, is instead made the unmistakable marker of conflictual difference. The European woman's Other cannot logically possess a female body, so Falconbridge wishes to rid herself of its sight and clothe it in the spoils of empire.

Lady Mary Wortley Montagu's Other is exotic and various in the Turkish embassy letters extracted in part from her journal and published after her death.[38] The preface by Mary Astell angrily dismisses men's travel narratives as inaccurate and "stuft with the same Trifles." Unlike men's travel narratives, Montagu's remarkable letters probe the private women's quarters in Turkey and offer "a new path."[39] Women travellers were contemptuous of exact descriptions from male travellers because men were unlikely to have been eyewitnesses to these private quarters. In a recent history of women travellers to the Middle East, Billie Melman writes, "The Third Court with its women's quarters and the quarters of black eunuchs were the most impenetrable territory in the Ottoman Empire and, before the nineteenth century, were hermetically sealed to adult males other than the Sultan himself, his sons and the black eunuchs."[40] European women travellers, disempowered by their gendered identification with the women confined, were empowered in their ability to describe a part of the world that could be conquered only by a woman's eye. The seraglio invited the description of women by women as did few other sites.

In Montagu's vision of the Other, a romantic vision of two hundred women of the Turkish baths, she admires their nude splendor and the nudity of the slaves who tend them, and they provoke her aesthetic and erotic pleasure, "their skins shineingly white" (1:314). She commends the ladies' "finest skins and most delicate shapes," and she wishes Mr. Gervase (Charles Jervas, the portrait painter) could share her voyeur's attitude "to see so many fine Women naked in different postures, some in conversation, some working, others drinking Coffee." In bold contrast to usual notions of the female tea party and other private domestic occasions, Wortley Montagu conjures up a vision of female community. She remarks on the women's resistance to mutual disdain and backbiting: "In short, tis the Women's coffée house, where all the news of the Town is told, Scandal invented, etc." In spite of polygamy, she believes the Turkish women to be the "only free people in the Empire." The veil allows them the freedom to move invisibly, flitting from one scene to the next without detection.

Crucially, liberty for the aristocratic Montagu is equated with *sexual* freedom to conduct intrigues rather than with Enlightenment principles of political liberty and equality: "You may guess how effectually this [clothing] disguises them, that there is no distinguishing the great Lady from her Slave, and 'tis impossible for the most jealous Husband to know his Wife when he meets her, and no Man dare either touch or follow Woman in the Street. . . . This perpetual Masquerade gives them entire Liberty of following their Inclinations without Danger of discovery" (1:328). She good-humoredly portrays herself as the one imprisoned, caught as she is in the "machine" the Turkish women assume her husband has locked her in, her stays. Yet there is also sameness: "Thus you see, dear Sister, the manners of Mankind doe not differ so widely as our voyage Writers would make us beleive [*sic*]." Polygamy is here synonymous with female collectivity, female beauty, and sexuality; and in a magnificent reversal, *her* body is imprisoned rather than theirs. The Other—not racially different, but different in kind—is free, and polygamy (because the women under its aegis are able to move surreptitiously within it) represents liberty rather than restraint.

In sharp contrast, when Montagu regards "the Companies of the country people" in North Africa "eating, singing, and danceing to their wild music" (1:425), class and race surface as more significant than gender. The creatures appear to her to be animal-like instead of human, and their ugliness and exotic tattooed ornamentation safely distinguish them from European women: "They are not quite black, but all mullattos, and the most frightfull Creatures that can appear in a Human figure. They are allmost naked, only wearing a piece of coarse serge wrap'd about them, but the women have their Arms to their very shoulders and their Necks and faces adorn'd with Flowers, Stars, and various sorts of figures impress'd by Gun-powder; a considerable addition to their natural Deformity" (1:425).[41] Later, "many of the women flock'd in to see me, and we were equally entertain'd with veiwing [*sic*] one another. Their posture in siting, the colour of their skin, their lank black Hair falling on each side their faces, the features and the shape of their Limbs, differ so little from their own country people, the Baboons, tis hard to fancy them a distinct race, and I could not help thinking there had been some ancient alliances between them" (1:427). These North African women, like Queen Clara of Falconbridge's account, refuse to wear the clothing of empire or to commodify themselves according to the imperial ideal of femininity and virtue. Here, the European woman narrator, Lady Wortley Montagu, wishes to claim as female the exquisite naked beauty of the Turkish harem while rejecting any gender, class, or racial connection to the near-naked mulatto women. Their nakedness in her eyes is bestial rather than evocative of the harem's homoerotic sensuality. Wortley Montagu is not unlike the male traveller she scorns in pitting the "shineingly white" Turkish women against the tattooed African women.

Mary Wollstonecraft, adamant in her opposition to polygamy, established the feminist position that was to prevail. "Polygamy," she writes in *A Vindication of the Rights of Woman* (1792), is another "physical degradation" of women by men and "a plausible argument for a custom, that blasts every domestic virtue. . . . If polygamy be necessary, women must be inferior to man, and made for him."[42] She cites John Forster's *Observations Made During a Voyage Round the World* (1778), which claims that in Africa, polygamy enervates men, while women "are of a hotter constitution, not only on account of their more irritable nerves, more sensible organization, and more lively fancy; but likewise because they are deprived in their matrimony of that share of physical love which, in a monogamous condition, would all be theirs."[43] Forster claims that this sexual deprivation for women leads to a hotter constitution, and the sex of the hotter constitution prevails in the population. In other words, in his representation Africa is a torrid zone of sexuality where large numbers of passionately sexualized women roam unsatisfied. Wollstonecraft does not explicitly contrast the cold and less desirous European woman to her lascivious polygamous African counterpart, but the implication is there. It is rhetorically unclear whether Wollstonecraft believes that polygamy protects seduced women in countries where more women are born than men and is therefore justified. Recognizing polygamy's social use in the cause of women's common feminist interests and arguing against those who find polygamy arises in response to some natural law rather than within a particular social formation, Wollstonecraft nevertheless demonstrates little interest in the situation of African women as she argues forcefully in behalf of European women.

The relation of feminism to polygamy and the Other woman is indeed a vexed one that is charged with unresolved contradictions. William Alexander points out in his history of women that polygamy works to limit women's property and thus her independence, since she is faced with rivals for that property.[44] Arguments in behalf of polygamy on the domestic front encourage providing economic support for seduced women, but both feminism and domestic femininity are united in their antagonism to polygamy. At the same time that Enlightenment feminism emerged in the West, claiming liberty and equality, differences among women made feminism's progress exclusionary. Western women attempted to supervise the Other woman abroad. The Other is undressed and dissociated, admired yet held fast in the voyeuristic and aestheticizing gaze, freed within confinement, a princess yet a slave, a noble female savage, superior yet inferior, various yet the same, erotic, repulsive, excessive. The Englishwoman abroad finds in the Other something that aids her in granting herself an identity and thus contributes to the now suspect liberal feminism—so closely bound up with monogamous marriage and motherhood—of the latter part of the century. Englishwomen are pitted against African women and other women at the emergence of empire, as colonizing men lay claim to the female body and to imperial territory. Monogamy, with the support of feminism, is established as a national imperative; the Englishwoman is contained within the boundaries of marriage and nation, and her superiority is confirmed by her difference from the sexuality of empire's polygamous women. The exemplar of the domestic feminine woman, Pamela musters her moral power to make a convincing, if tedious, case for monogamy at home.

European-American feminism may find in its eighteenth-century manifestations a harbinger of its current urgent need to produce alternative trajectories when confronted with the problems that African-American and Third World feminist theorists in the United States and elsewhere aptly reveal. In postcolonial feminism, polygamy also maintains a potential subversive power and threatens to become radically uncontained. Feminist theorist Trinh T. Minh-ha suggests that "difference" need not be opposed to "sameness, nor synonymous with separateness." She cautions against using difference as an attempt to locate racial essence: "When women decide to lift the veil one can say that they do so in defiance of their men's oppressive right to their bodies. But when they decide to keep or put on the veil they once took off they might do so to reappropriate their space or to claim a new difference in defiance of . . . standardization."[45] The Other woman of polygamy turns out to be, not surprisingly, both self and Other. What may be more surprising and less predictable, at home and abroad, is the way the Other woman's differences may instead be the occasion for unsettling "essences," sabotaging conflicts that arise because of those supposed essences and preserving the enigma of speaking at once as the domestic woman, the Other woman at home, and the Other woman abroad.

CHAPTER FOUR

Prostitution, Body Parts,
and Sexual Geography

From what has been said it is manifest, that there is a Necessity of
sacrificing one part of Womankind to preserve the other, and prevent
a Filthiness of a more heinous Nature. From whence I think I may
justly conclude (what was the seeming Paradox I went about to prove)
that Chastity may be supported by Incontinence, and the best of
Virtues want the Assistance of the worst of Vices.

Bernard Mandeville,
Fable of the Bees (1714)

I

England's fascination with and ultimate rejection of polygamy as a
legal practice at the end of the eighteenth century defines national
sexuality in opposition to the polygamous Other. The discussions
helped justify slaveowners' polygamy and explorers' free intercourse
with indigenous populations while turning women against women.
When Bernard Mandeville wrote in 1714 that "there is a necessity of
sacrificing one part of womanhood to preserve the other," the *part* he
had in mind was the English prostitute, but the sexual division of
labor had global implications, even in the eighteenth century. Colonial enterprises contributed to eroticizing and commodifying the female body, and unlicensed public sexuality in the London streets connected to the rest of the world, especially the "torrid zones." Body
parts, especially female ones, are located within global systems, and
their imagined nature varies according to their climatic location. By
the mid-eighteenth century, whole areas of the world were construed
as sexualized, as if to suggest that the world represented a human body
with its genitals in the lower southern climes.[1] The nation's interests
demanded that England be distinguished from its Other, and the
English "woman" from her sexualized other, in order to maintain
national identity and authority.

The eighteenth century has become increasingly marked as the
originary moment for modern definitions of sexual difference as they
are written on the body. While significant in reshaping our under-

standings of the present, I think this emphasis on fixed sex/gender differences interferes with our ability to consider the blurred edges of sexual practices, identities, and their representations within history, as recent work on transvestism, sodomy, and hermaphroditism suggests. Lyndal Roper acutely observes, "By treating heterosexuality as the key to understanding past patriarchies we have already transported our own notion of what is sexual into past societies whose delineation of the field of the sexual may be different."[2] While the sex/gender system in the eighteenth century may seem to reduce to simple biological binaries, its various cultural manifestations were diverse. To suggest otherwise—that sexual difference or the body as we know it was invented in the eighteenth century—holds considerable explanatory power, but it also sets up an Enlightenment ground that may encourage a launching of postmodernist projects from Enlightenment's inadequacies and a condescension toward the past.

While *bodies*—sexual anatomies—were increasingly described in the eighteenth century as being of one sex or another, and "biology" attempted to make this a simple distinction (so that, for example, hermaphroditism was described by at least one commentator as a false category in which women with enlarged clitorises were erroneously placed), sexual behavior and its encodings were extraordinarily various. If contemporary sexual identity involves physiology, anatomy, performance, and declared identity, eighteenth-century sexuality was at least as complex. Here, I would like to turn the focus away from the torrid or savage mother to the eighteenth-century prostitute, the transgressive sex worker whose sexuality was assumed to be uncomplicated by maternity.

At the same time that sexual passion was being displaced from one part of womankind onto another, and from the temperate English climates to other parts of the world, efforts to regulate sexuality at home in its more public manifestations urged a redefinition of femininity consonant with middle-class virtue. As we have seen, England's national imperative to control women's sexuality and fertility in the eighteenth century is connected to the formation of a national identity coincident with the emergence of its second empire. Prostitution was a *national* disgrace, an aberration, the reformers cried, but it was a naturally occurring phenomenon in the torrid zone: as Francis Foster wrote, "For my Part, I hold it incumbent on every Man to do his utmost to stop an evil, that is a Reproach to us, as a Nation—sullies our Name—and must, if not remedied, be our Destruction."[3] Prostitution was an internal disgrace, and controlling the permissive female at home would help to distinguish England from its less moral others. The representation of polygamous, torrid, and savage women made visible through British imperial designs enabled the consolidation of the cult of domesticity in England itself. Written on the body, on London, and on the world map, sexual geography established an analogy between prostitute and torrid zone, so that one was a geographical displacement (evoking a geographical equivalent in segregating prostitution into confined "stews"), and the other a socioeconomic and moral distinction (evoking a correlative categorization of the geographically displaced Other). The interrelation between these two displacements turned the English whore into the torrid zone's Other, and the Other into indolent whore.

II

When pornographic literature was first widely published in English in the later seventeenth century, usually in translations from French, it centered on the permissive female and her induction into erotic desire.[4] The widespread publication of pornography was coincident with the rise of the novel and its middle-class readership, women's increased entrepreneurial power, the expansion of empire, and the formation of mercantile capitalism.[5] The first full-length English novel explicitly and overtly engaged in arousing sexual desire in the reader was John Cleland's *Memoirs of a Woman of Pleasure* (1748–49), popularly if somewhat inaccurately known by the title of its later expurgation, *Fanny Hill*. The *Memoirs* was published on the cusp of the increasing privatization of middle-class women, their relegation to domestic and maternal life, and the separation of conception from women's sexual pleasure. In contrast, the permissive female attacked convention, authority, and national stability by her presence in the public sphere, her hanging from windows and doors to advertise herself as a commodity. The public display of the prostitute's body became an aesthetic problem because her presence was seen to be polluting the streets and creating an eyesore for proper ladies and gentlemen. Pornography helped to colonize the flagrantly sexual and to remap the legitimate space available to the prostitute. Nothing less than a self-contained worldview written by men for men about women, Cleland's *Memoirs* inscribes whores in the timeless other space where it "is always bedtime."[6] In the novel the prostitutes' specific and literal predicament is avoided; instead, the human geography of the erotic/pornographic body becomes the silenced ground for a nationalist and colonialist agenda.

Pornography—literally, writing about the prostitute—heightens sexual desire; in fact, by one definition, pornography is that which arouses the reader to orgasm through masturbation as well as other-directed sexual activity.[7] Of course, pornographic representations of prostitution largely mask the way that sexual work was motivated by economic exigency. Young girls who migrated to the city from the country, seduced women left without means of support, and impoverished mothers without the ability to support their children were increasingly characterized as bursting with sexual energy. In fact, eighteenth-century commentators Robert Dingley and John Fielding both believed that most prostitutes were the female children (ages twelve to fifteen) of the laboring poor sold to bawds by their parents.[8] Dingley envisioned a sexual war on the streets between "thoughtless girls" and "formidable Seducers," and as a remedy he proposed a place for girls ages twelve to fifteen "of the lower Class of people, who are often abandoned by their Parents, and even sometimes sold by them to PROCURESSES, names indeed too soft for such unnatural excrescenses of the human Species."[9] His benevolent design was to create a "happy Asylum" where the young women would distract themselves with useful work mending linen, scouring pewter, and making lace, mittens, garters, and children's toys. Spurred by religious principles, he imagined a Magdalen Charity House where young women could be supervised and inspired to productive lives.

Saunders Welch similarly placed the responsibility for wayward women on neglectful parents in his proposal to rid the streets of prostitutes. Like Dingley, he believed that children of the laboring poor were most at risk. Welch was much less sanguine than Dingley, however, about the long-term effects of providing shelter for indigent women. His principal concern was that the matrons within the shelters would become bawds to the girls who used the charity house as a convenient resting place before resuming their trade, rather than providing a haven that inspired conversion. By Welch's estimate, prostitutes in London numbered at least three thousand at mid-century, though the city's nearly doubling in size during the century probably increased that number considerably.[10]

Indeed, houses of prostitution proliferated sufficiently in the later eighteenth century to develop specialties. The Temple of Aurora offered girls as young as eleven to sixteen years of age; the Temple of

Flora, a luxury brothel; the Temple of Mysteries, sadomasochistic practices. All of these "temples" were run by a Miss Falkland in St. James's Street, Westminster.[11] Keeping a brothel was illegal (as was a man's sustaining himself from a prostitute's income), and bawds were subject to fines, imprisonment, and the pillory.[12] Anyone suspected of being a part of a bawdy house could be imprisoned for three days, and a second conviction could bring transportation for seven years.[13] The founding of Magdalen hospitals for penitent prostitutes and lock hospitals for treatment of venereal disease in the later eighteenth century is an indication of the extent of public concern, yet the tracts that condemned prostitution's effects were largely a middle-class attempt to prevent working-class sexuality from tainting bourgeois women.

Prostitutes, swarming in the streets in an "open and public manner to the great scandal of our civil polity,"[14] flaunted the public sexuality that was supposed to be kept hidden from the bourgeois mother and the chaste maiden. Alphabetical lists of available whores with their particular sexual talents were published openly, especially in the latter half of the century. Prostitutes accosted passersby in the streets: "they even surround them in crowds, stop and overwhelm them with caresses and entreaties."[15] Eighteenth-century men may have justified their demand for prostitution because they believed they had to forgo their wives' sexual attention while their children were nursed. Prostitutes allegedly encouraged crime and vice and, of course, produced bastard children. Whores were also accused of drawing tradesmen and apprentices away from business and into debt to support their sexual habit, and of leading them into "such a sort of Indolence, as is quite inconsistent with Industry, the main support of any, especially of a Trading Nation."[16] Demands to hide prostitution, to bury its evidence, helped obscure men's role in its perpetuation.

In tension with eighteenth-century efforts to regulate sexual behavior is pornography's apparent heterodoxy in locating its sexual object. The very definition of "woman" is at stake in pornography. Since by mid-century the class of female sexuality cannot be the middle class, sexual passion is displaced onto the transgressive, desiring bodies of prostitutes, which grotesquely parody the bodies of "women." Barbara Littlewood and Linda Mahood argue convincingly that "the 'prostitute' is not a simple observational category, with numbers to be counted, characteristics investigated and history documented. . . . Rather, the 'prostitute' and the 'magdalene' were characters constituted in significant part by the discourses in circulation and by the apparatuses designed to control them. Furthermore, the deployment of discourses is in this case most significantly embedded in material practices."[17] We might think, then, in terms of eighteenth-century sexual *practices* and *activities* rather than *identities*.

The prostitute is fluidly and ambiguously gendered, since she is a female embodiment; but sexuality itself, of which she is a cultural emblem, is gendered unfeminine. Defoe's Roxana, whose very name means "whore," is likened to an Amazonian *"Man-Woman."*[18] Anti-prostitution tracts often define whores as monsters, as something other than "women," who violate the boundaries of the female sex. Further, prostitutes were often assumed to be barren, incapable of performing woman's primary task of creating children.[19] The author of *A Conference about Whoring* (1725) emphasizes that a prostitute is not a fellow creature, but a "Monster and Dunghill": "Separate a Woman from Modesty, she becomes quite another Creature than God made her" (4). William Dodd's "Sermon Preached before . . . Magdalen House" claims that prostitutes are a species unlike any other, whose engagement in volitional, passion-driven activity requires their moral reformation: "Every man who reflects on the true condition of humanity, must know, that the life of a common prostitute, is as contrary to the nature and condition of the female sex as darkness to light."[20] In short, I am arguing that prostitutes, more various than a "third sex," are conceptualized in eighteenth-century England as a species set apart from women. Prostitutes, paradoxically, manage to incorporate all imagined sexualities and to exceed their allotted geopolitical space.

Penises, vaginas, sphincters, and nymphae (the labia minora) link body parts to global matters in Bernard Mandeville's remarkable treatise *A Modest Defence of Publick Stews*. By suggesting that prostitutes are the "part" of womanhood that must be sacrificed, the essay implicitly reduces them to expendable body parts. Men, according to Mandeville, when left to themselves prefer rubbing their own genitals to penetrating women: men "are every Day committing *Rapes* upon their own Bodies," thus becoming he-whores to themselves.[21] Preferring the vigor of their own hands to female parts, he believes that men court impotence by masturbation. Women, too, are discouraged from autoerotic friction. Enlarged clitorises were thought to indicate non-reproductive tendencies, and extreme measures were urged to protect women from themselves. In Bienville's treatise on nymphomania, for example, Leonora was diagnosed with "a considerable elongation of the *clitoris*, attended with tetters [pustular formations], and an abcess in the *matrix*, the malignity of which was but too apparent from the acrimony, and fetidness of the matter which ran from it. . . . The elongation, or turgescency of the *clitoris* was a little diminished; the tetters seem to have lost their acrimony." When Leonora began to recover, "the ulcer of the *matrix* appeared cicatrised, the turgescency of the *clitoris* was no longer observed, the tetters were absolutely healed, and, for some days past, her actions had been free from the least obscenity."[22] The narrator's fear of autoeroticism leads him to recommend that her body be hidden from her, literally swathed during the night. Discouraged from exploring their own bodies, women await "discovery" by another.

Mandeville develops a metaphor for the woman's body as a besieged town, and the sexual parts of a woman of virtue as rebellious citizens who open the gates to the (male) enemy. Her body is peopled with the easily aroused "members" against which she must struggle, and her "self" is at odds with her embodiment. Women's bodies, "like a Debtor's House upon the Verge of two Counties," are vulnerable to penetration from the front or the back, "*à parte ante, & à parte post*" (49); and in warm climates—in the torrid zones—they are more susceptible to attack because their dresses may be open or their thighs bare. Woman's "worldly Interest," strictly delimited, depends completely on retaining her chastity. When "world" is invoked in relation to women rather than prostitutes, it is confined to the world of chastity and specifically the body over which they reign; woman's empire is the constricted empire of love rather than the public world of adventure. In short, discourses about prostitutes in the eighteenth century afford an occasion for the rigidification of sexual difference *and* simultaneously arouse confusion in other cultural domains about male and female categories.[23]

In the older biological model that persisted into the eighteenth century, excess heat in women indicates potential masculinity, and the inverted penis may expel itself and become visible if women become too hot. But the enlarged clitoris is a second, already visible penis. The view that female orgasm was essential to conception underwent change during the century, and its struggle for dominance was complicated by the ejaculating clitoris that persisted in texts throughout the period. Following popular assumptions, Mandeville describes the clitoris as capable of erections and as provoking violent desire: "The whole *Vagina*, as one continu'd *Sphincter*, contracting and embracing the *Penis*, while the *Nymphae* and adjacent Islands have their particular Emissions at the critical Minute, either as a Vehicle to lubricate the Passage, or else to incorporate with the Masculine Injection" (41). These extreme physical responses must be countered, he contends, with strong moral injunctions.

The clitoris was a particularly vexing body part in the eighteenth century because of its refusal to remain within the feminine domain. It threatened national security and the body politic. "Discovered" by Renaldo Columbus and mapped by medical science in 1559, the clitoris is the body part that most resists male control.[24] The crucial question was how can a woman possess both a latent penis inside and an ejaculating organ without? At least one tract, *A Treatise on the Use of Flogging* (1718), confirmed the view that "tho' most Persons agree that women have the greatest Sense of Enjoyment in the Act of Copulation" because of the way their bodily parts are placed, the erection of the clitoris provided a way for the hermaphrodite to reveal a male sexuality when she or he had been taken for a woman.[25] In the pornographic *Teague-Root Display'd: Being some Useful and Important Discoveries Tending to Illustrate the Doctrine of Electricity, in a Letter from Paddy Strong-Cock* (1746), the gaping clitoris both ejaculates and consumes the male: "The Female Root is the same Way influenc'd by the Male: and it would divert you to see a Female Root, where it is highly electrical, how it will wriggle itself about, twist, squeeze, and gape, as if it would swallow the Male in its voracious Jaws, till the Electrical Fire is spent, in a Discharge of a similar Liquid, which moistens the whole Root" (16). Even the most extreme of these European clitorises, however, is not imagined to be as monstrous as the pudenda of the Angolan woman suspected of hermaphroditism or of the Hottentot women who are depicted as openly displaying this prized body part in travel narratives (often akin to pornography): "The women are distinguish'd from the men by their deformity . . . peculiar, among all other nations, that out of their privities you see two labels hanging down, like part of a man's yard (as now and then some of our *European* women are subject to the relaxation, or hanging out of the *Clitoris*) of these they are so proud, that if a stranger happens to come into one of their cabbins, or hutts (called *Krallen*) they will take aside the leathern apron, and shew them to the stranger."[26] These monstrous genitals, openly displayed, at once connect English prostitutes to the Other and dissociate them from the domestic woman whose genitals remain private, waiting to be discovered. It seems likely that the ejaculating clitoris survived longer on the bodies of the prostitute and the Other than on the feminine domestic woman.[27]

The enlarged or ejaculating clitoris, wiggling and gaping, resembling the penis but not equivalent to it, is a reminder that the distinctions between the sexes were not then, as they are not now, always already fixed, in spite of attempts to establish geographical empires of the sexual imagination. The whore is menacing because she is believed to be both a hypersexualized female and a man/woman who excites men to lose control. Further, even though her body is insistently female, at least one sexual body part threatens to produce its own ambiguous gendering in its assumed capacity for erection and ejaculation. The prostitute, passionately desired and condemned, titillates in part by impersonating and thwarting the available gendered categories. Her enlarged and sometimes ejaculating clitoris, at one level a certain sign of her femaleness, is connected to the monstrous hypersexualized man/woman at home and the Other woman abroad. Limiting the geographical space of the transgressive female and the exotic to the torrid zones—the clitoris, the stews, and the tropics—served to locate, regulate, and colonize the sexually ambiguous and disruptive.

III

Though the colonizing impulse has not before been connected to the first pornographic novel in English, *Memoirs of a Woman of Pleasure,* it is curious that at least part of the novel was probably written during John Cleland's stint in Bombay. Travelling to India first in 1728 as a common foot soldier at age seventeen (incidentally the age of several of the *Memoirs'* young lovers), Cleland soon joined the East India Company's civil service, in which he moved up through the ranks to the highest civilian office, senior merchant, in a matter of twelve years, returning to England in 1741. He would have been among the influx of young male employees in the East India Company whom Burke describes: "Animated with all the avarice of age and all the impetuosity of youth, they roll in one after another, wave after wave."[28] At midcentury the competition between France and England for India was clearly being won by Pitt's England, and the market for Indian goods burgeoned. Bolstered by successful trade since its founding in 1600, the East India Company's early interest in the subcontinent was primarily commercial. As is recorded in *Early Records of British India,* the civil servants "bought, they sold, they overlooked, they kept accounts, they wrote letters, they regulated establishments and expenditure. Large ships from Europe brought woolen goods, cutlery, iron, copper and quicksilver. The same ships carried away cotton piece-goods, fine muslins, silks, indigo, spices and Indian rarities."[29]

Buying and selling, trading and shipping, would have been Cleland's activities as he began writing the first volume of the *Memoirs*. In the *Memoirs* the looming white penis trades through the body of the prostitute, Fanny Hill, who is characterized as a ship that travels from man to man, country to country. Ships, a common trope for whores, were of course crucial to England's preeminence on the high seas and the success of its mercantilist policy. As an English merchant ship hired by men and loaded with freight by them, Fanny is described as a seaworthy means of exchange, a mediator between nations and a carrier of precious cargo. Her body transports commodities to and from trading nations during man's satisfying sexual journey. Amassing personal wealth is accompanied by sexual pleasure. At the end of the novel Fanny Hill, the ship, fits snugly into the English port of bourgeois love and morality, but the cost to her is that she dwindles into a "weak vessel."[30]

Making use of another commonplace, Cleland describes Fanny Hill's body as territory to possess. Into Fanny's "whole region of delight, and all the luxurious landscape round it," her lover attempted "to lay more open to his sign the secrets of that dark and delicious deep." Fanny's favored lover, Charles, explores her body: his "gleamy warmth . . . shot from it, made him feel that he was at the mouth of the indraught, and driving foreright, the powerfully divided lips of that pleasure-thirsty channel receiv'd him. He hesitated a little; then, settled well in the passage, he makes his way up the streights of it, with a difficulty nothing more than pleasing, widening as he went, so as to distend and smooth each soft furrow" (46). The image is one of mutual pleasure in the exploration and discovery, as the colonized is increasingly pleasured by the colonizer's intrusion.

At one level, *Fanny Hill* is an apocalyptic vision of the tumescent white male member controlling the world within the novel. The enormity of the giant "machine" swells so large that it obscures the female body represented there, both in recent criticism that has focused on the male machine, and in the text itself. Fanny Hill, whose very name signifies the female genitalia, possesses an ejaculating clitoris that figures importantly in the novel more than once, but Cleland also radically implies that Fanny Hill's body is both male and female. This implicit fantasy excites the reader of whatever sexual predilection by scattering the object of lust beyond familiar sexual divisions. Unquestionably, the novel puts at its very center the penis that subverts and emphatically displaces female body parts, but it also more subtly reinvents the contextualized embodiments to which those parts may be attached and the sexual activities in which they may be engaged.

The novel, I think, tolerates a sexual ambiguity not entertained or represented in eighteenth-century science. Fanny's clitoris in the *Memoirs* explicitly resembles a penis in its sexual journey from flaccidity to erection: it is a "soft fleshy excrescence, which, limber and relax'd after the late enjoyment, now grew, under the touch and examination of his fiery fingers, more and more stiff and considerable" (77).[31] Fanny's prominent clitoris indicates her hot and even aberrant sensuality, but sprouting a penis from her internal organs (one outcome we know is available within the biological frames of reference in the period) would seem comic in the terms of the novel's sexual economy. Fanny's hill, her *mons Veneris,* can possess only one ejaculating organ, the clitoris; for the alternative move to biological hermaphroditism through expelling a penis would make her indeterminate sex/gender identity visible and immoderately empower her. Though her clitoris is through most of the novel a lower-class one, her "rusticity" wears away as she gains Charles's love. By the conclusion of the novel it has been elevated to bourgeois status and fully domesticated.

The ambiguous gendering of the main character extends to the authorial voice as well. Nancy K. Miller has suggested that John Cleland writes in drag as the woman narrator in *Memoirs of a Woman of Pleasure,* and Julia Epstein argues that Cleland's female impersonation barely masks a homoerotic male voice.[32] We might think again, however, about the transvestite status of a male embodiment engaged in writing, to imagine him not as a "man" who puts on a "woman," but as an ambiguously gendered human embodiment that may resonate with recognized sexualities but may also invent others. While the narrative voice in the novel lends itself to assuming that the "real" author is homosexual, the text presents a tangle of sexual practices rather than a prior original and fixed identity.[33] The *Memoirs* makes available to its heroine, author, and readers heterosexual, homosexual, bisexual, autosexual, and omnisexual erotic responses from which the shopper for erotic novelty may choose. Cleland as narrator and character impersonates both a woman, reformed from her disreputable life, *and* a sexually ambiguous whore. Discursively constituted, Fanny's body is not only a sign of itself and a medium of exchange; it is an *effect* of its multiply gendered anatomical parts that have biological referents but are not synonymous with them or confined to one sexual practice.

Fanny's first love, Charles, a "manly beauty," takes her virginity with an air of gentility and maneuvers her escape from Mrs. Brown's brothel. A girl "fresh out of the country, and never before handled" (39), she is, unbeknownst to him, "still mistress of that darling treasure, that hidden mine, so eagerly sought after by men, and which they never dig but they destroy," and he is unable to penetrate at first. The *Memoirs* is replete with such *firsts*, from first kiss, orgasm, group sex, and homosexuality to Fanny's deliberate remaking of her virginity and the revising of the first volume through the second, as Fanny is repeatedly introduced to innovations in the repetitive act of sexuality.[34] Part of the sexual and textual pleasure of the *Memoirs* arises from the discovery of something new. Narratives multiply about the same event, but Charles's pleasure derives in part from the "discovery" of being first.

The *Memoirs* liberates female sexual desire in order to channel it away from autoeroticism and homoeroticism toward bourgeois heterosexual pleasure. Complicating the gender ambiguity of the novel is the erotic desire between women, explicitly described in Fanny's homoerotic initiation with Phoebe Ayres, and later alluded to in the caresses and gazes of the brothel sisterhood. From her female correspondent "Madam," her fellow traveller Esther Davis, and the intelligence officer who leads her away from other employment, to Mrs. Brown, Martha, and the seductive Phoebe, and eventually to Mrs. Cole's Covent Garden brothel, Fanny is teased and plagued by fellow women who encourage her to become a prostitute and join the brothel: "All the girls that compos'd her flock, were suffer'd to visit me, and had their cue to dispose me, by their conversation, to a perfect resignation of myself to Mrs. *Brown's* direction . . . insomuch, that the being one of them became even my ambition: a disposition which they all carefully cultivated" (22). Fanny's entrance into the erotic is an induction into heterosexuality through homoeroticism, enabled in part by creating antagonisms among plebeian women in the name of sexual possessiveness.[35] Cleland assigns the responsibility for a woman's being taken into prostitution to women themselves, both through the arousal of desire brought on by homoerotic pleasure, and through the necessity for employment as they learn the economic value of "that trinket of mine" (23). Women entice women; sexual desire for the same sex is necessary but must be rechanneled toward men in order to be fully satisfying. The *Memoirs* displays the way that women too may be complicit in colonizing other women's bodies (especially those of working-class women) and inciting same-sex desire through male cultural fantasies.

Fanny's body is also, of course, a medium of exchange among women as well as men. Mrs. Cole, a maternal figure who prides herself on refusing to seduce innocent women, is construed as someone who rescues women from potential ruin. She manages the intimate "little family of love," a "little Seraglio" (95) within the brothel that parodies the bourgeois family. In order to prepare Fanny for her sexual initiation with four men, the beautiful young prostitutes recount their histories, which are, of course, thinly disguised tales of arousal. The first is of Emily's deflowering by a sturdy plowboy; the second of Harriet, the daughter of a miller, succumbing happily to the son of a gentleman after he rapes her; the third of Louisa, the illegitimate daughter of a cabinetmaker and his maid, who masturbates without satisfaction from age twelve until she finds a man: "Here I gave myself up to the old insipid privy shifts of self-viewing, self-touching, self-enjoying, *in fine* to all the means of *self-knowledge* I could devise, in search of the pleasure that fled before me, and tantalized me with that unknown something that was out of my reach" (108). The girls of Mrs. Cole's brothel are "a little troop of love" who provide compliments, caresses, and congratulation for their fellow whores' erotic achievements. These are tales of pleasure and desire rather than tales of ruin, since sad, sentimental stories of economic hardship or disease have a stultifying effect on libido and are anathema to pornography. Their pleasure in sexuality, even in rape, confirms the myth of prostitution as motivated from desire rather than economic need.

Among Fanny's partners is Will, the liveried tenant's son, whom Fanny seduces in revenge for her lover Mr. H——'s seducing a female servant. Will's body as well as Fanny's is ambiguously gendered. In this incident, the emphasis is on the male servant's boyishness with "beardless chin." Except for the mention of Fanny's petticoats, the scene could be read as an instance of homosexual anal intercourse:

> I had placed myself with a jet under him, as commodious, and open as possible to his attempts, which were untoward enough, for his machine meeting with no inlet, bore and batter'd stiffly against me in random pushes, now above, now below, now beside his point, till burning with impatience from its irritating touches, I guided gently

> with my hand, this furious fescue to *where* my young novice was now
> to be taught his first lesson of pleasure: thus he nick'd at length the
> warm and insufficient orifice: but he was made to find no breach
> practicable, and mine, though so often enter'd, was still far from wide
> enough to take him easily in. (74)

The mixture of pleasure and pain, the resistance of the orifice to the
huge ivory machine, obscures the precise body opening involved and
allows the reader to imagine the receptor as either vagina or anus, male
or female.[36] Further, after the sexual encounter with Will, Fanny examines her body to discover that nothing "betray'd any the least alter-
ation, outward or inwardly" (79), in spite of the amazing encounter.
The disowned body of this first sexual encounter with Will was not
really hers, not even a woman's, it would seem. In fact, Fanny remarkably reports at the start of the second meeting with Will, that he "was
now in bed with a woman for the first time in his life" (81). This is
literally true, because their first intercourse did not take place in bed,
but if my reading of the fluid gender in the first encounter is plausible,
it may also be interpreted metaphorically to suggest that the intercourse between bodies was not solely marked as heterosexual. Indeed,
unlike the first encounter, Fanny's body in the second instance is quite
specifically female, with details of her "nether-mouth," legs encircled
round him, the furrows and folds of her gendered body delineated,
and the mixing of the male-female liquids of their bodies made explicit. Fanny's body is renewed yet again when, in the second volume
published three months after the first (1749), she creates her virginity
anew with the help of a bloodied sponge.

Gender fluidity also permeates the masquerade Louisa and Emily
attend as shepherdess and shepherd, when "nothing in nature could
represent a prettier boy than this last did" (154). Involved with a dom-
ino who assumes she is a boy, Emily, taken to a bagnio and her
breeches unbuttoned, reveals her female genitals to the great dismay of
her accoster: "But when they were alone together, and her *enamorato*
began to proceed to show extremities which instantly discover the sex,
she remark'd that no description could paint up to the life, the mixture
of pique, confusion, and disappointment, that appear'd in his countenance, which join'd to the mournful exclamation, 'By heavens a
woman!'" (155). Despite her exposure as a "woman," her androgynous
disguise misleads the client to believe he has a choice between sexes
"so, that the double-way between the double rising behind, presented
the choice fair to him, and he was so fiercely set on a mis-direction,

as to give the girl no small alarms for fear of loosing a maiden-head she had not dreamt of" (155). Her body possesses more virginities, it seems, than Emily wishes to reckon with.

This transvestite scene is prelude to the famous homosexual incident in which Fanny, piercing a peephole with a bodkin, witnesses two country lads engaged in sexual activity, one of whom possesses a "white shaft" poised for entrance into the boy who "was like his mother behind . . . like his father before." The name "Fanny Hill," as the homosexual vignette suggests, could also refer to a behind with a blurred gender status, the lusty seventeen-year-old youth, the "girl in disguise" (157) who is penetrated between "those globular, fleshy eminences that compose the mount-pleasants of *Rome*" (158). Critic Lee Edelman discusses Fanny's "heterosexual-male-identified" position as a viewer of the sodomitical scene which destabilizes "the binary logic of before and behind."[37] From Edelman's argument that Fanny's uneasy position (from which she falls and faints) "refutes the determinacy of positional distinctions," we may also consider that the inner-outer axis of sexual organs so fully represented in eighteenth-century medical treatises is complicated by another, the front and back, the axis Mandeville mentions as making women of the torrid zone doubly vulnerable to attack. In addition, along that axis from the back, men and women may share the same sexual function. Fanny's indignant response leads her to swoon, as if recognizing the dizzying implications of this incident, followed by Mrs. Cole's homophobic diatribe. Extending prostitution to the male experience of embodiment, to he-whores, beyond the body of the female prostitute, disturbs the sexual economy in reminding readers of the *Memoirs* that bodies of either sex may bear surprising resemblances from behind. The sexual ambiguity of women of the torrid zone along the front/back axis marks them as especially available to "discoveries" as diverse and as violent as the manifestations of colonialism itself; yet contradictorily, the sexually ambiguous or multiply gendered body would seem to be especially resistant to *discovery* as a prior existing entity awaiting colonization.

Near the conclusion of the novel Fanny herself voyeuristically shares with Louisa the pleasure of revealing to *Good-natur'd Dick* the half-remembered bestial passion which he happily possesses. A sexualized Other who is simultaneously manly and impotent, a tragicomic primitive whose penis is "positively of so tremendous a size," he has smooth, fair thighs which "seem'd the smoother and fairer for the coarseness, and even dirt of his dress; as the teeth of Negroes seem the whiter for the surrounding black" (162). After sex "the young savage" exudes "no meaning, and ideotism" as his flaccid manhood flaps pathetically, and Louisa takes command by paying *him* for the sexual encounter. Gaining temporary dominance in the sexual act itself, Dick afterwards "retain'd only a confus'd memory of the transaction." Defining Dick as subhuman and thus the act as a kind of miscegenation, Louisa and Fanny exercise power in the empire of sex that is denied them in the global hierarchy, and they erase from the memory of the colonized Other their use and mockery of his sexuality.[38] The prostitutes exploit and humiliate the exotic deformed through sexuality for their own ends, thus enacting the part of the colonizer, even while reversing the terms of the economic transaction.

In the final sexual scene, Fanny's first lover, Charles, returns with a more vibrant and visible masculinity, "riper, greater, and perfecter" (180) from his passage to the South Seas, displaying "the tant of his travels, and a beard somewhat more distinguishable . . . at the expence of no more delicacy than what he could better spare, than not, given it an air of becoming manliness, and maturity, that symmetriz'd nobly with that air of distinction and empire, with which nature had stamp'd it, in a rare mixture with the sweetness of it" (179). Now it is a mutual love that "refines, ennobles, and exalts" rather than sexual pleasure, a major reversal. In this final scene of love, this time "in quality of man and wife," Fanny's ejaculating clitoris figures significantly when she gushes "a convulsive grasp in the instant of my giving down my liquid contribution, [which] render'd me sweetly subservient at once, to the increase of his joy" (185).

The terms of Fanny's achieving this state of womanhood have not, however, been fully explicated. This sexual encounter marks the failure of the ejaculating clitoris to imitate the phallus within the sexual economy, and it infantilizes the vagina. In this bizarre description of Fanny's last recorded intercourse, ejaculating during orgasm makes her vagina literally milk Charles's penis dry, "moving me so as to make me exert all those springs of the compressive exsuction, with which the sensitive mechanism of that part thirstily draws and drains the nipple of Love, with such an instinctive eagerness, and attachment, as, to compare great with less, kind nature engages infants at the breast, by the pleasure they find in the motion of their little mouths and cheeks, to extract the milky stream prepar'd for their nourishment" (185).[39] In an extraordinary gender reversal, the penis becomes the

breast to which hungry infants (her vagina) attach themselves. Funda-
mentally altering the material effect of anatomy, the passage loosens
the penis from the male body, and the breast from the female, so
that the transmogrified penis is finally able to combine sexuality and
maternity in a maneuver which eludes the middle-class eighteenth-
century English breast. Man becomes maternal in a way that the
prostitute cannot be.[40] In granting the prostitute succor from the male
breast, the text releases Fanny to become a bourgeois matron who
transforms sexual pleasure into love. Charles appropriates the double
power of the ejaculating clitoris and the vagina, the internalized penis.

In sum, at the climactic relinquishing of her power to write, Fanny's vagina is metaphorically transformed into an infant sucking at the
male penis, which in turn is likened to a breast. If sexual transformations according to the Galenic model can take place only in one direction—up the hierarchical scale from female to male—then Cleland's
conclusion is indeed a radical inversion. When Charles wields "that
peculiar scepter-member, which commands us all: but especially my
darling elect from the face of the whole earth," it is the narrative point
when the penis becomes the breast and Charles appropriates her commodities, her traveling body parts. Fanny, having dropped her pen, is
no longer able to write, and her history is quite literally at an end.
Fanny changes into a bourgeoise, and thus a "woman" whose earnings
from prostitution are given over to Charles. No longer a sexual threat,
she is also no longer a writer/whore but becomes instead the subject of
a bourgeois matron's lovingly erotic tale rather than a whore's rhetoric.[41] If women are dangerous because men's desire turns men into
women, Cleland's novel manipulates this fear so that Charles con-
quers Fanny to achieve his manliness, not so much by becoming
a woman as by willing his body parts to take on female functions.
Charles, like the English nation, usurps the breast to claim that he
nurtures and supports his colonized domain rather than the reverse.
(After all, Charles and Fanny survive on Fanny's accumulated earnings rather than on Charles's inheritance.)

Pornography enables the repetitious "discovery" of what is already
available to be experienced in all its variousness by women themselves,
the female body. The *Memoirs* frees libido, elevates it to the aesthetic
realm, and undermines rigid sexual difference, but it also participates
in regulating the ambiguous body to remap its sexual nature into the
known. Charles and Fanny, freed from "firsts" through conjugal love,
play "over-again the same opera with the same delightful harmony

and concert" (185). Charles takes into his own human and worldly space the Other's body part and appropriates its capital. The geographical territory of the torrid zone and its (Other) body parts are annexed to the English/male/heterosexual body and contained within married love.

My point here is not, of course, to debate whether Fanny's inscribed body is actually male or female, or whether Cleland is gay, straight, or bisexual. Resisting discovery, Fanny's body contests the norms that determine its intelligibility; Cleland's sexual proclivities can only be the subject of speculation.[42] Good-natur'd Dick, the censored sodomite passage, the retreat from lesbianism, and the rejection of female community all guide the *Memoirs'* ostensible liberation of the libido and the enclosure of the female body as private property while the novel aligns sexual pleasure with the middle class and its mercantilist interests. If the English nation consolidates its national sexual identity through the Other, in an act that is deceptively benign and that even masquerades as an act of love, it also displaces the erotic onto the Other in order to "discover" its body.

IV

The problem of producing alliances between women in the later eighteenth century is acute when being a "woman" means disassociating one's self from one's sexualized body parts, relinquishing economic freedom, and fleeing communities of women. Creating contests among women as feminism was emerging, one "part" against another, made pornography and the inscription of whores resonate with the colonialist project when their very corporeality was being condemned as a disease to be evacuated in the national interest. Pornography contends that sexual desire is so pervasive that its omnipresence permits no space outside it. Everything and everywhere is sexualized within its world; in this configuration all zones are erogenous. Pornography threatens to unleash its sexual energy to claim any part, any body, any geographical space as torrid zone.

The undecidability of mixing genders ambiguously in the *Memoirs* nevertheless has decided material effects. In this case, as I have argued, these effects may contribute to the construction of the heterosexual/ homosexual binary, the oppression of women and the alienation of women from one another, and the colonization of the sexualized Other. Yet the pornoerotic violates taboos by its very definition and liberates sexual desire into a baffling array of disruptive possibilities.

The incongruities unleashed may allow the embodied whore to escape definitive corporeal and spatial mapping. This apparent undecidability, in contradiction to Enlightenment discovery and certainty, lends the pornoerotic its fluid, unsettling possibilities.

While all this undecidability in pornography extends the potential audience by making the various bodies appealing to a broad spectrum of readers and thus especially vulnerable to "discovery" from one or another axis, recognizing the pornographic body's ability to masquerade in multiple identities means that its sexual geography may indeed resist being mapped, penetrated, and colonized. In the *Memoirs* the pleasuring body obliterates the laboring body and the material conditions of the sex worker. Having relinquished her property, Fanny moves from the entrapment of prostitution to the prison of domesticity, in which her pen is silenced, her earnings appropriated, and her body parts remapped. Body parts move from sex to sex or class to class to unveil the way that erotic "pleasures" and sexual license are too easily equated with social and political freedoms, while the conclusion to the *Memoirs* claims the moral superiority of monogamous wedded love. Economic freedoms may enable women's independence but may not bring complete escape from gender boundaries or from exploitation. Resistance to equating libidinal liberation to other Enlightenment or feminist freedoms may be mustered through reading and critiquing the travel narratives of body parts in order to interrupt rigid notions of sexual identity and thus make possible a rearrangement of torrid zones, whether they are mapped onto the prostitute's laboring body, onto the streets where she plies her trade, or onto the world.

CHAPTER FIVE

The Empire of Love
The Veil and the Blush of Romance

The Empire of Love, said she, like the Empire of Honour, is govern'd
by Laws of its own, which have no Dependence upon, or Relation to
any other.

Charlotte Lennox,
The Female Quixote (1752)

They would by the charms of their beauty, and their sweet and insin-
uating way of conversation, assume that native empire over mankind,
which seems to be politically denied them, because the way to authority and glory is stopped up: Hence it is that, with their acquired arts
and languishing charms, they risk their virtue to gain a little contemptible dominion over a heart that at the same time it surrenders it
self a slave; refuses to bestow esteem upon the victor.

Delarivier Manley,
The New Atalantis (1714)

I

Romance, with its diffused, veiled allusion to sex, has been called
a woman's pornography.[1] Like pornography, romance encloses its
reader in a heightened utopian fantasy confined by its own rules. In
the case of Charlotte Lennox's *The Female Quixote: The Adventures of
Arabella* (1752), published only a few years after *Memoirs of a Woman of
Pleasure,* that idealized vision is also the object of satire. Just as Cleland's book denies that a world exists outside its pornographic realm,
The Female Quixote confines woman's empire of love to the solipsistic
world of the utopian romance. While men reign supreme in pornography's erotic labyrinths, women rule in *The Female Quixote*.

Much admired by Samuel Johnson, Samuel Richardson, and
Henry Fielding, the novel clearly struck a cultural chord. It reached a
second edition in English after three months; was translated into
German, French, and Spanish; and was much reprinted until 1820.[2] In
the novel Lennox mocks romance's self-delusion while employing its

techniques and requiring a dizzying double vision of her readers. Arabella, like Cervantes' hero, acts within romance conventions and attempts to convince others that her mistaken vision describes reality. Her fantastic assertions move others to convulsive laughter, but bound by propriety, they respectfully demur, chuckle behind raised hands, and sometimes enter into her illegitimate assumptions in the hope of leading her out of them. Like Johnson's mad astronomer in *Rasselas*, Arabella deludes herself into believing that she has cosmic powers. This appears most comically in her injunction to Mr. Hervey (and others later) to do what he cannot help: "I command you to live!" And similarly, when her cousin Charles Glanville seems to have decided to ignore her, she empowers herself to find self-validation in the snub: "I disclaim any empire over so unworthy a subject." Her perceptions are rife with hybristic error.

The Female Quixote begins with the failure of masculine authority when the Marquis of ——, banished by his enemies, retreats from society. Marrying a woman who was his inferior, he assumes responsibility for his young daughter's education after his wife's death. Arabella is completely entranced by the romances that her dead mother's library contains, especially the French romances of Madame de Scudéry and La Calprenède. In these romances women wield the power to organize and name the world so that love becomes "the ruling Principle of the World" (7).

In this text the concept of empire operates largely at the metaphorical level as a playful mockery of the more substantive issues of imperial and patriarchal domination. According to the rules of romance, the male and female empires of adventure and love are discrete spheres without relation to each other. The private empire of love titillates women with fantasies of escape, binding them ever more tightly to femininity, while the public empire of honor and adventure refuses women entrance. Arabella argues that the "independent Sovereignty of Love" (321) outweighs all other claims. Yet the source of Arabella's power, her ability to inspire loyalty in spite of her romantic delusions, rests upon her station and her inheritance (as well as the "majestic loveliness" that the peasants recognize), which lead others to believe that her state of mind is susceptible to a cure. Inevitably, the reader mocks Arabella, but the fact that Glanville pursues her in spite of her apparent insanity alerts the reader to judge her lovingly. The whole book is staged for a discerning reader, who must sort through the confusion to evaluate Arabella, though when she mistakes Hervey for a highwayman and believes the gardener Edward's catching carp from the stream is a suicide attempt, our opinion of Arabella as a dolt is confirmed. The authorial voice in *The Female Quixote* is carefully modulated to allow Arabella her enticing wit and beauty while unfailingly indicating the mistaken quality of her romantic notions. Finally, we are led to share Glanville's position that "her consummate Loveliness" justifies "his Passion . . . being in his Opinion more than an Excuse for all her Extravagancies" (346).

Delusions make adventures possible for a woman, while "reality" brings tedium. The tensions of *The Female Quixote* arise, however, when Arabella's highly suspect vision threatens to disrupt these neat divisions as romance intrudes on public life and shapes the "real." The novel posits that though Arabella may not have the influence she believes she possesses, the power of romance may indeed have material effects and substantial consequences.[3] In ruling through the illusion of romance, Arabella makes herself ridiculous yet manages to produce an antiromance in which she is both sexualized (in her willingness to imagine herself a queenly whore) and made modest (she turns her back on a prostitute she at first befriends, to relinquish abruptly the efficacy of romance tales). Her sexualized self is blushed over and veiled rather than overtly exposed, as in the case of the prostitute.

II

Throughout *The Female Quixote* Arabella naively flirts with prostitution as an imaginative model, if not a model for action, and she seems not at all troubled by her association with it. Imagining herself the princess Julia, judged "the most abandoned prostitute in Rome," she reinforces the novel's message that women who have "histories" are sexually dangerous yet compellingly, enticingly interesting. When Arabella, "who followed no Fashion but her own Taste" (269), dresses as Princess Julia, she adorns herself in blue and silver décolleté richly adorned with jewels. Her beauty prevails over her daringly absurd yet breathtaking choice of dress: "Upon the whole, nothing could be more singularly becoming than her Dress; or set off with greater Advantage the striking beauties of her Person" (271). By repeatedly comparing herself to Julia, and to Cleopatra as well, she prostitutes herself to romance, yet she narrowly manages to maintain her virtue while contesting the terms of its possession. Her empire rests on her beauty, and her peculiarity oddly sustains and complements the power that derives from her *imitation* of sexual transgression.

Arabella is, after all, a female quixote, and like Defoe's Roxana, a man-woman. One form of hybridity Arabella achieves in the novel, perhaps the only sort of "Amazonian" position allowed, is her open emulation of Thalestris in spite of Miss Glanville's concerns that Thalestris "must be a very masculine Sort of Creature" (125). Sir Charles tells Arabella that "if she had been a Man, she would have made a great Figure in Parliament, and . . . her Speeches might have come perhaps to be printed in time" (311). Arabella remarks on the androgyny of combining "perfect beauty" with "Harmony and Softness in her Looks and Person" (125), and she manfully approves of Thalestris's threatening to sever the head of her unjust lover, Orontes. Arabella delights in the opportunity to recount tales of women who command men, though Sir Charles suggests that such women could live only in kingdoms on the moon.

Actual sexual transgression, as in the case of Miss Groves, is clearly associated in the book with manliness and with gender hybridity. Arabella fails to recognize the perils of Charlotte Glanville's coquetry or of Miss Groves's unconventional life in bearing an illegitimate child. At the same time Arabella misjudges the potential for sexual assault and believes that she will be ravished by the gardener, by the foppish Mr. Selvin, and finally by men on horseback. At the conclusion of *The Female Quixote,* the deluded romantic heroine befriends a cross-dressed prostitute at Vauxhall pleasure gardens whose impersonation allows her to occupy male space as well as female.[4] Glanville, "almost mad with Vexation, endeavour'd to get *Arabella* away. Are you mad, Madam, said he in a whisper, to make all this Rout about a Prostitute? Do you see how every body stares at you? What will they think" (336). The rout about the cross-dressed prostitute suggests that uncovering her sexualized body is a radically transgressive activity. This paradigmatic moment of recognition of alignment with the prostitute leads to Arabella's "exposure" and the novel's hasty retreat from the impertinence of a woman's recognizing herself in the face and body of a whore and aligning herself with her. The nakedness of the prostitute's body, without a veil or a blush, connects these women in socially unacceptable ways and reminds the polite world of its suppressed torrid zones as romance veers perilously close to pornography. The unruly prostitute conjures up the specter of the earlier women writers Aphra Behn, Delarivier Manley, and Eliza Haywood looming over Lennox as she dallies with writing the racy sexual novels of her predecessors but accedes in the end to masculine reason and moral authority.

Arabella's exotic costuming and theatricality throughout the novel bring her dangerously close to being judged a whore herself. At Vauxhall "the Singularity of her Dress, for she was cover'd with her Veil, drew a Number of Gazers after her, who prest round her with so little Respect, that she was greatly embarrass'd, and had Thoughts of quitting the Place" (334). The incident is a sign of Arabella's absolute lunacy, a moment of bodily exposure (her veil falls off) and social exposure (she breaches decorum) as she becomes a spectacle in the public pleasure garden. Arabella's attempt to discover her sameness with the prostitute and her difference from her, to position herself clearly in relation to her, marks the height of absurdity, the limits of Glanville's patience, and the boundaries of romance. Charlotte Lennox speedily withdraws from this revisionary possibility to more predictable territory. Once "exposed" or "discovered" as one sex or the other, whores are domesticated into "women" who relegate sexual freedom to Utopia and confine their colonizing aspirations to the private empire of love. The prostitute's body, ambiguously gendered and classed, resists discovery. The embodiment of sexuality, if linked to Arabella's resistant reading and harnessed to satire, could overturn the conventions of sexual difference.

Since women know that their desires are to be hidden, even from themselves, the veiled servant or the prostitute exposes a sexuality unacceptable to the empire of love *or* adventure. Romance largely confines itself to the private empire of love, strips "discovery" of its powerful effects at home and abroad, and naturalizes it into tropes of modesty and virtue. In confronting the prostitute, attempting to bond with her, and ultimately rejecting her, the woman writer personified in Arabella rejects the incorporation of sexual hybridity into the novel.

III

The empire of love is a confined sphere "dependent upon nothing but itself" (321), and one which shines with the reflected light afforded by the *real* empire of adventure Arabella desires. At the same time romance, a female fantasy of control, arouses libidinal desire in women. Within the empire of love, women are assumed to possess extraordinary power over men, even to the point of enslaving them. Women possess more ability to arouse desire than men have to fulfill it, so that

the stronger actually depends on the weaker. Speaking of the volatile
Princess Julia, the daughter of Augustus, Arabella says, "Notwith-
standing the admirable Beauty of *Julia,* it is possible she made as many
Slaves by her light and airy Carriage, as she did by her Eyes, though
they were the fairest in the World, except the divine *Cleopatra's*" (207).
In short, women's empire of love encompasses the captives and makes
them slaves to her charms.

When her lover Glanville falls ill, it troubles Arabella that her
dominion does not extend to making him well: "Nay . . . since my
Empire over you is not so absolute as I thought; and since you think fit
to reserve to yourself the Liberty of dying, contrary to my Desire; I
think I had better resolve not to make any Treaty with you" (320).
According to romance conventions, Arabella believes that "when a
Lady has once given her Lover that Permission, she may lawfully
allow him to talk to her upon the Subject of his Passion, accept all his
Gallantries, and claim an absolute Empire over all his Actions; reserv-
ing to herself the Right of fixing the Time when she may own her
Affection" (138). Since her power rests in resistance, Arabella is in
danger of nearing the end of her adventures if she grants Glanville the
right to love her.

But romance also affords Arabella the potential to disrupt the very
world that relegates her to silence and to private self-enclosed space.
Each time Arabella speaks—and her speech is always within the frame
of romance—she both authorizes and compromises her position as
speaking subject. She disquiets those who listen and locates herself as
a silly romancer, but she also asserts her power to name reality, to
establish the conditions of comprehensibility and the terms of the
"real." Paradoxically, romance allows her to wrest a history for herself
which is not a sexual history, not a *chronique scandaleuse,* though she
eventually accepts the marriage plot which has been tugging at her
from the first chapter.

In spite of his objections, Glanville agrees "to accommodate himself, as much as possible, to her Taste" (46) and, in a radical act, to *read*
the romances that he fears will make him ill. But Glanville feigns his
reading of romances, and Arabella is freshly angered by his ruse. Just
as Glanville pretends to read the romances, he pretends to "read"
Arabella as well. Instead, he gently laughs at both her books and her
convictions, assuming his superior knowledge of her best interests. In
fact, the fate of Arabella's body becomes synonymous with the fate of
her books. Her father declares he will burn the books that represent

not only a material manifestation of her power but also her ability to withstand Glanville's entreaties and to carve out a substitute reality. Her father wishes to immolate the Arabella who defies him.

Arabella's immolation is comically averted, and rather than burn her body, she masks it with blush and veil. Arabella's body, aligned so closely with her romance books that the distinction fades, becomes something to be read and interpreted to "relate exactly every Change of my Countenance, number all my Smiles, Half-smiles, Blushes, Turnings pale, Glances, Pauses, Full-stops, Interruptions; the Rise and Falling of my Voice, every Motion of my Eyes, and every Gesture which I have used for these Ten Years past: nor omit the smallest Circumstance that relates to me" (122). Her "natural" defense through the blush both veils and reveals her desires and recalls the ambiguity of the blush satirized in Swift's "Cadenus and Vanessa":

> Where never Blush was call'd in Aid,
> That spurious Virtue in a Maid,
> A Virtue but at second-hand;
> They blush because they understand.[5]

In addition to its hiding women's intelligent perceptions, the blush is a crucial component of fashion—what the best-dressed modest woman wears—"for, without regard to that much-in-fashion virtue assurance, next to real innate modesty in ladies (which indeed never fails of giving the appearance) I think the outward blush and seeming habitude of it one of the greatest ornaments they can wear."[6] But it is after all a *seeming* modesty, a dress to be donned as an ornament like a brooch or a feather. Arabella's incessant blushing also signals her body's contradictory assertion of its masking and its availability.

My point here is that the romantic empire of love is always implicated in the empire of adventure, and that Lennox uses the blush as domestic containment and the veil as exotic fashion. Ros Ballaster has pointed out that in French romances such as Scudéry's, "the aristocratic woman reader's natural *delicatesse* and sense of propriety, signified by her blush, will determine whether a text has stayed within the bounds of convention."[7] In other words, the reader's blush or lack of it becomes a barometer of romance's propriety. Ironically, the source of Arabella's power at times is her inscrutability: "While Arabella *passed* her Time in her Closet, in the most disagreeable reflections, *Glanville* was racking his Brain to find out the Meaning of those mysterious Words she had uttered at leaving him; He examined them twenty times over, but could not possibly penetrate into their Sense" (170). Accurate reading of her language enables penetration of her body as well as her words, and the blush, like the veil, protects against full comprehension. This gives a new twist to the reason Richard Polwhele in his misogynist *The Unsex'd Females* (1798) mocks Mary Wollstonecraft for her opposition to assuming that blushing is a measure of modesty.[8] Polwhele demands that women continue to blush as an index to innocence while he accuses Wollstonecraft of wishing innocence away.

The blush is also a physiological manifestation of the dissonance between romance and satire, desire and repugnance, in *The Female Quixote*. It is a reminder of the physiological nature of sexual pleasure and of the embarrassment at having it revealed. The blush, a mark of modesty, uneasily reconciles the body's passion to the mind's anxiety, and the desire to be ravished with the desire to be deified.[9] It exposes Arabella's erotic conflicts and reveals the novel's contest over versions of the truth. Arabella's blush reveals terrible consternation as she attempts to reconcile her own version of things with reality. The world of men carefully scrutinizes Arabella: "Mr Glanville gazed on her with a passionate tenderness, Sir George with admiration, and the old Baronet with wonder and delight" (203). Arabella blushes when Glanville regards her passionately (36); she blushes with annoyance when her father orders her to entertain Glanville (43) and again when angered by Glanville's pretense that he had read romances (53). She blushes in furious recognition that Sir Charles is insulting her (66), with embarrassment when confronted with her supposed ravisher Edward at his alleged affrontery, and similarly at the mention of love in reference to Glanville. She blushes when she believes she has self-revealingly been too bold or too tender (160); she blushes with ambivalence and pleasure when commanding Mr. Glanville to serve her with "inviolable Fidelity" and refusing to agree to love him (137); and similarly, she colors when complimented, though she misconstrues the intent (145). She blushes when she believes she has enabled Glanville to speak love to her (154) with a desire which she does not acknowledge; when her uncle Sir Charles seems to seek her hand (167); and with consternation when she believes Sir George is dying of lovesickness. Men seem to blush for women rather than for themselves, as when the marquis blushes on behalf of the rude Arabella (43), when Glanville colors in anticipation of her blunders, and when Sir George blushes because she has broken convention in divulging the content of his letter to her cousins (194). Arabella's blushing is a means of displaying (false) modesty when she oversteps the bounds of appropriate speech, as when she is chiding Sir George for his infidelities (206), when Sir George teases her by calling her a divinity (215), when Glanville compliments her on a sensible speech (304), and finally, when her true feelings are revealed. When her story is told, blushes are a crucial part of her history within the empire of love. The blush is the material sign of the body's confusion: which mode of making the world intelligible will be in control?

Those who observe Arabella conjecture about the meaning of the blush. Most crucially, Sir George's dwelling on Sydimiris's blush becomes a rather transparent reading of Arabella. Sir George declares: "I interpreted *Sydimiris's* blush a Thousand different Ways: I reflected upon all the different Causes to which it might be owing, and busied myself with all those innumerable Conjectures, which, as you know, Madam, such an Incident always gives Rise to in a Lover's Imagination. At length I explained it to my own Advantage, and felt thereby a considerable Increase of my Affection" (232). Sir George's story, a hoax on Arabella, becomes a turning point for Arabella's blushing, which begins to diminish as the phenomenon of the veil substitutes for the blush in the concluding books.

The blush also represents a resolution of empire on the body of the Englishwoman in its manifestation of the modesty denied to other women of empire. The blush as a telling sign can, according to common misunderstanding, only be evidenced on a white cheek. As Ruth Yeazell remarks, "The Englishman's particular fascination with the coming and going of the blood to the cheek can never be wholly separated from a racial presumption about the visibility of the sign; and as this offhand association of a dark skin with shamelessness should remind us, the moralizing of the blush has always its potentially racist dimensions."[10] Both veil and blush disguise the body and hint at the differences among women evoked by these cultural practices. The Englishwoman's blush distinguishes her from the immodest woman at home and from the woman of color whose blush may not be seen. At midpoint in the novel the blush, indicative of domestic femininity, relinquishes its place to the veil, the sign of exotic otherness. "Symbolic mediators" for women, one of the body, the other of fashion, one the domestic, the other of women abroad, the blush and the veil obscure women's naked desires from the scrutiny of either sex.[11] In the empire of love, the blush is associated with proper English modesty, while the veil evokes the Other woman, especially the Persian and the Egyptian, the harem and the harlot. Seductively aligning Arabella with the Other woman, the veil makes her empire of love seem worldly rather than cloyingly confined.[12] While the blush is a reminder of the domestic, the veil, a sign of the larger empire, infiltrates the domestic empire of love. An unfashionable analogue, the veil evokes the Other at home and abroad, the whore and the exotic.

Though the blush implicitly calls to mind metaphors of clothing (as in Steele's calling it "that ambiguous Suffusion which is the Livery both of Guilt and Innocence"),[13] the veil is quite explicitly an element of fashion. Woefully out of fashion in eighteenth-century England, the veil represents the ancient, the mysterious, and romance itself: "The Phaenomena of the Veil, however, gave them great Disturbance. So lovely a Person seemed to promise the Owner had a Face not unworthy of it; but that was totally hid from their View: for *Arabella*, at her Entrance into the Room, had pulled the Gauze quite over her Face, following therein the custom of the ladies in *Clelia*, and the *Grand Cyrus*, who, in mixed companies, always hid their Faces with great Care" (263). (See Fig. 5, "Full Dress of a Lady of Quality in Barbary in 1700.") Arabella rules her "empire of love" through strangeness and a willingness to be ridiculous, though not of course as a conscious strategy. The veil first appears as a mourning veil upon the death of her father, but immediately serves a different purpose: "The black Gawze, which covered Part of her fair Face, was so advantageous to her Shape and complexion, that Sir Charles, who had not seen her since she grew up, was struck with an extreme surprise at her beauty" (68). When Arabella and her entourage enter the Pump-room at Bath, she again wears a veil "of black gauze, which covered almost all her face, and part of her waist, and gave her a very singular appearance" (295). Made odd to both women and men alike, she is the object of curiosity because of her peculiar dress. Again, her singularity arouses fears of scandalous contagion through which the foreign fashion for veiling might overwhelm the English custom of displaying beauty. The veil emphasizes Arabella's inappropriateness in the fashionable world to which she is introduced at Bath, a world for which she claims to have little taste. In the process, her veil paradoxically marks fashion as the site of female rebellion.[14]

In a violation of romance convention, which dictates women's scrupulous attention to dress, Arabella is distinctly *not* à la mode. The nostalgia for chivalric romance is obviously debilitating, but it also offers a strategy for resisting the hazards of encroaching mercantilism and its accompanying emphasis on fashion.[15] Taken for a foreigner, a Scotch lady, and a nun, Arabella frequently appears in disguise. The veil, like her absorption in the conventions of romance, gains her admiring attention as well as ridicule, marks her ambiguous position as a rebel, and contributes to making her the object of satire. The meanings of the veil shift according to its historical and cultural context.[16] Veiling may signal a limit to the level of intimacy a woman will tolerate, provide a mode of communication, designate her class association, or make a political statement. Perhaps because the veil enhances rather than distracts from Arabella's beauty, it also breeds antagonisms among the women who compete with her.[17] Miss Glanville, for example, finds herself eclipsed by Arabella's beauty. Jealous of the attention that Arabella attracts, she sneeringly dismisses the unfashionable veil as a country covering but she takes malicious pleasure in Arabella's exoticism. The brazen behavior of wearing a veil evokes Miss Glanville's secret envy because it attracts so much masculine attention to Arabella, albeit an ambivalent attention.

Living within romance conventions atomizes women. Though Arabella speaks of herself in the royal plural, her delusion demands an isolation that Lucy, Miss Groves, and Miss Glanville cannot penetrate. The romance books are themselves substitutes for Arabella's female companions: "Arabella not daring . . . to interpose . . . [was left] to bewail the Fate of so many illustrious Heroes and Heroines, who, by an effect of a more cruel Tyranny than any they had ever experienced before, were going to be cast into the merciless Flames; which would, doubtless, pay very little Regard to the divine Beauties of the admirable *Clelia*, or the heroic valour of the brave *Orontes*; and the rest of those great Princes and Princesses" (155). Arabella regards the seventeenth-century romance as a female tradition that links her with models arising in lone splendor from the past—Cleopatra the whore or the authoritative queen of the Amazons, Thalestris.[18] She seeks precedents for her substitute empire, a female empire, while men circumnavigate and colonize the world.

Lennox's employment of the veil toys with making all women, whether blushing innocents or seductive harlots, domestic or exotic, interchangeable. Significant to the plot, the veil confuses Sir George, who makes love to Deborah, Miss Glanville's veiled maid—who has agreed to wear Arabella's veil as a disguise—because he assumes that she is Arabella. In fact, however, Miss Glanville veils herself to impersonate Arabella because she is jealous of her ability to attract attention with the veil. As a result of the masquerade, Glanville mistakenly runs his sword through Sir George, believing that Arabella and Sir George are lovers. The ruse allows an interchange of women for women's purposes too. Miss Glanville becomes both the sexual rival to Arabella and the other woman of empire and romance. This interpretation is, however, a mistake, and the ambiguity produced by the veil is resolved in the denouement.[19] The veil—the sign of romantic delusion, the unfashionable, and the exotic Other—inspires a near-fatal misunderstanding and conveys the message that confusion and disaster occur when women misrepresent their beauty or their class identities, an ambiguity that can be tolerated only within romance. Within its frame, the alignment between women at home and the exotic, in the present and the romantic past, in possessing a sexuality unacceptable for display obscures distinctions crucial to the formation and maintenance of empire.

At the conclusion Arabella gains respect in spite of her singularity, something that she achieves only after her conversation with the countess, a model of judgment. This unveiling by the countess anticipates the final unmasking that strips Arabella of her romantic vision, her "fatal Deception" (340). But the countess's "cure" is insufficient. Arabella cannot have her man, in romance or the novel, until she reforms beyond the countess's powers. In fact, the countess unwittingly inspires the greatest threat to Arabella's freedom that the novel entertains.

Arabella's illness ensuing after her wild plunge into the Thames affords the occasion for the clergyman doctor to minister to her mind and body. Warning her that persistence in her romantic fantasies will bring sure death, the doctor tells Arabella that her only hope of recovery of a mind "at once so enlighten'd and so ridiculous" (367) is the cure of right reason.[20] Arabella insists that the earth has not changed since the days of romance, and that the same misfortunes which plagued Cleopatra, Clelia, or Candace, queen of Ethiopia, will trouble her. One crucial lesson Arabella learns in the course of *The Female Quixote* is that romance does not have universal application. Once convinced that history exists, she enters it. Counter to her belief that "the Face of the Earth is [not] alter'd since the Time of those Heroines, who experienc'd so many Changes of uncouth Captivity" (373), history has material effects: its correct interpretation alters the world. Arabella's assertion of the authority to name the romantic as real, to speak the terms of *what is*, is treated as schizophrenic madness. The doctor, extricating Arabella from romance and inserting her into the present moment of the novel, contradicts the dangerous worldview that enables Arabella's close imaginative conflation of her own "world" with that of the past and the Other.[21] Initially at a loss to find "some leading Principle," the doctor begins by suggesting that the death of romance brings the death of the empire of love. In some sense, of course, the loss of romantic illusion is no loss at all. In another, it is surrendering everything to enter into the empire of honor and adventure on its terms as a silent partner. Only by locating herself within the rational does Arabella have a chance to empower herself, and in the blended voice of the Johnsonian aether, she "recovered to the full Use of all her noble Powers of Reason" (382).

The Female Quixote distinguishes emphatically between the ideal Englishwoman (here a noblewoman of considerable property) and her Others by locating them in a rejected genre and in the past. *The Female Quixote* finally trivializes the issues of empire by confining them to an imaginative and antiquated space. Arabella's ability to maneuver within romance, such as it is, rests on this trivialization of empire as well as her transgressive insistence on the validity of reading the present through a paradigm of a "world" that is inhabited by queens of Ethiopia and Egypt whose sexual histories are irrelevant to their authority. In her recovery to reason from imagination, her search for precedents is ended, and she need live only in the historical moment of the novel. Romance carried to its extreme, according to Lennox, lifts the veil and wills away the blush to reveal romance's truth—the political power of the sexuality embodied in the body of the whorish, desiring man-woman Arabella impersonates and the transvestite mistress she exposes in Vauxhall near the conclusion.

Having regained her power of reason without the ambiguity of the blush or the veil, Arabella is restored at the end of *The Female Quixote* to her proper place, "united . . . in every Virtue and laudable Affection of the Mind" (383) to Mr. Glanville. Her imagination, as long as she does not *speak* it, remains her own as an escape from the tedium of the life without a story that faces a female heroine who desires adventure, an adventure that rests on impersonating the exotic while confined to the severely circumscribed empire of love.

IV

Like *The Female Quixote,* Johnson's *Rasselas* (1759) and Frances Sheridan's popular *History of Nourjahad* (1767) also employ the tropes surrounding Eastern women to critique romance. The oriental tale, drawing on French romance and an appeal to the imagination, had an enormous vogue in eighteenth-century England.[22] Galland's *Les mille et une nuits,* translated into English as *The Arabian Nights* in the first decade of the eighteenth century, began the vogue that extended through the final decades of the century, culminating in Beckford's *Vathek.* Johnson's library included travel narratives of Egypt and the Levant, and his descriptions of the pyramids and the catacombs are particularly indebted to eighteenth-century European narratives.[23] *Rasselas,* published in ten editions by 1798, shares *The Female Quixote*'s attention to the dangerous excess of the imagination, though Johnson finds it to be part of the human condition rather than peculiar to women. In *Rasselas* the travellers Imlac and Rasselas, Rasselas's sister Nekayah, and her maid Pekuah are welcomed in Egypt, a province of Turkey, as they search for happiness. Though ostensibly Abyssinian or Ethiopian, the national identity of the travellers is somewhat fluid, since they seem to have an "oriental" subjectivity, but at other times they are closely identified with Christianity and with European privilege.

Imlac tells Rasselas that he has earlier visited "the northern and western nations of Europe; the nations which are now in possession of all power and all knowledge; whose armies are irresistible, and whose fleets command the remotest parts of the globe. When I compared these men with the natives of our own kingdom, and those that surround us, they appeared almost another order of beings. In their countries it is difficult to wish for any thing that may not be obtained."[24] Rasselas inquires about the source of European power and the inability of other parts of the world to appropriate it: "Why, since they can so easily visit Asia and Africa for trade or conquest, cannot the Asiaticks and Africans invade their coasts, plant colonies in their ports, and give laws to their natural princes?" (47). Imlac acknowledges European superiority but takes refuge in celestial wisdom for explanation: "They are more powerful, Sir, than we . . . because they are wiser; knowledge will always predominate over ignorance, as man governs the other animals. But why their knowledge is more than

ours, I know not what reason can be given, but the unsearchable will of
the Supreme Being" (47). Knowledge, Johnson intimates, supplants
force in maintaining power, and reason is touted as the "lawful sovereign," which, like responsible government, must struggle against
"fancy, the parent of passion" (71). While the moral of *Rasselas* is that
every place within and without the Happy Valley presents the same
human situation of mortal hopes thwarted, there is a contradiction in
Imlac's acknowledgment that European power and wisdom are superior. In *Rasselas* Europeans possess greater knowledge and rationality
although their happiness is not more abundant.

The character in the moral tale most relevant to romance is Pekuah, Nekayah's maid, a bit of an afterthought for Johnson, since she
does not figure significantly until the latter half of the tale. Pekuah's
adventures occupy the portion of *Rasselas* devoted to the analysis of
public and private life conducted by Rasselas and Nekayah. Ironically,
Pekuah is captured by a band of Arabs after she stubbornly and fear-
fully refuses to enter the pyramids with her fellow travellers. Held by
"robbers and savages" in "an unfrequented and pathless country" (132),
she is granted preferential treatment over the Arab women because
of her splendid dress. In the midst of the seraglio, Pekuah's status
emerges as superior, for the "splendour of my cloaths" (133) impresses
the Arabs with her wealth and rank. Though the women surround her
admiringly, Pekuah expresses contempt for these women, who, like
innocent birds and lambs, have no energy, sprightliness, or dignity.
Pekuah's conversation and intellect contrast to the vacuity of the seraglio, into which she stalwartly resists being absorbed: "As I bore a
superiour character, I was often called to terminate their quarrels,
which I decided as equitably as I could" (139). She takes great care to
avoid exercising the empire of love over the Arab chieftain, fearing he
will never seek ransom if he becomes enamored of her. She is eventually ransomed to a convent, where she is reunited with her pining
mistress, Nekayah.

Far from being an erotic haven, the seraglio in *Rasselas,* like the
city and the country which the travellers visit, fails to provide an image
of paradise and a solution to human happiness. Arthur Weitzman
interprets the kidnapping of Pekuah as Johnson's "opportunity to destroy the hedonistic and romantic notion of the voluptuous lives led by
Moslem men, which had become a staple of Oriental fiction in the
eighteenth century."[25] These tropical zones are not torrid. Johnson
strips the seraglio of sexuality and replaces sexuality with tension and

boredom, so that it is hardly the realm of teeming passion evoked in Montesquieu's *Persian Letters*. The women of *Rasselas*'s seraglio titter and loll rather than provide sensual or intellectual pleasure to the Arab sheik. The Arab chieftain who captures Pekuah craves female companionship and intelligent conversation instead of sexual fulfillment.

In spite of being women of the East in a technical sense, both Nekayah and Pekuah take care to distinguish themselves from "savages," whether rustics or barbarians. Nekayah emerges superior because she participates in philosophical discourse with men, and Pekuah, because she understands the frivolity of the women's childish pursuits in the seraglio. When Pekuah and Nekayah make their choice of life, each chooses female friendship, one in a convent and the other in a college of learned women: "Pekuah was never so much charmed with any place as the convent of St. Anthony, where the Arab restored her to the princess, and wished only to fill it with pious maidens, and to be made prioress of the order" (175). In *Rasselas* female community substitutes for the empire of love. One could argue that, unlike Rasselas with his little kingdom, and unlike Imlac and the astronomer who are driven along the course of life, Pekuah and Nekayah learn the lesson of the inexpressible pleasure of female community, but at the expense of other women who are judged inferior to them.

V

Frances Sheridan's enormously popular *History of Nourjahad* (1767), following her well-liked *Memoirs of Miss Sidney Bidulph* (1761), reverses the terms of women's entrapment in the harem so that the male sovereign, Nourjahad, is confined to his quarters by a moralistic sultan, Schemzeddin. Intended to become the first in a series of moral tales to be dedicated to the Prince of Wales, *The History of Nourjahad* was translated into French, Russian, and Polish, as well as staged as a melodrama in 1802 and as a musical play, *Illusion*, in 1813.[26] In the novel one is tempted to compare Nourjahad's confinement to the domestic containment of Englishwomen at mid-century, for whom release was experienced through the romance of improbable trances, angels bearing enormous gifts, and wealth imagined to be buried deep in the earth: for Nourjahad, "this paradise was to be his prison."[27] Like women, he finds release from his confinement through untrammeled imagination. His confinement unmans him: "He grew lazy and effeminate" (41). Nourjahad escapes from physical entrapment through luxury, exotic drama, and the imagination, characteristics that align him

with women: "I will not waste my hours, said he, in fruitless languish-
ment for what I cannot at present attain, but make the most of the
good which now offers itself to my acceptance" (89). While Rasselas
and Nekayah stoically attempt to reconcile themselves to the limitations of a life in which much is to be endured and little enjoyed,
Nourjahad's desires send him dipping deeper into the subterranean
treasure cave of unlimited wealth granted him by a celestial visitor. As
the central character, Nourjahad is made morally ambiguous. He vir-
tuously and unflaggingly tells the truth to the doubting sultan Schemzeddin, yet lavishly indulges himself to assuage his discontent at being
physically confined. Schemzeddin, like Imlac, is a judicious and moral
counselor.

Forbidden to travel, Nourjahad experiences the world through his
seraglio, which is "adorned with a number of the most beautiful female slaves, of almost every nation, whom he purchased at a vast
expense" (39). Nourjahad is less than licentious, however, because he
unvaryingly remains faithful to one woman of the harem, Mandana:
"By Mandana he found himself equally beloved; a felicity very rare
amongst Eastern husbands; and longing to unbosom himself to one,
on whose tenderness and fidelity he could rely, to her he disclosed the
marvellous story of his destiny" (40). Nourjahad's apparently disreputable character is complicated by his nearly monogamous fidelity to
Mandana, the favored mistress who escapes domestic tyranny through
becoming a specter. As a *man* confined to the domestic, he finds his
release in the imagination.

According to Sheridan's bizarre little tale, Nourjahad supposedly
falls asleep for two years, then four, then twenty, then forty, each time
awakening to discover that his world has been transformed. His slumbers in each case occur because of some particularly egregious dem-
onstration of greed or intemperance, though in fact he has been secretly drugged, duped, and presented with masquerades by the sultan.
Among his extravagant projects to entertain himself is the creation of
a theater of virgins who impersonate the Houriis (beautiful virgins
given as a reward to true believers). Nourjahad represents Mahomet,
and Cadiga, who is his favorite mistress after Mandana's supposed
death, acts as Mahomet's wife. Nourjahad falls asleep and awakens,
fearing that his women will indulge "themselves in liberties without
that restraint to which they were accustomed in his presence" (101). In
the interim while he has slept, however, the seraglio has become "a
train of wrinkled and deformed old hags" (103). Consequently, the

self-indulgent Nourjahad reflects on human mortality and determines to fill up the seraglio anew with fresh young beauties or "I shall be at a loss how to divert the tedious hours which may yet remain of my confinement" (123). He recounts his disappointments in shopping for women in the marketplace: "One had features too large, and another's were too small; the complexion of this was not brilliant, and the air of that wanted softness; this damsel was too tall, and the next was ill proportioned" (126). Nourjahad contradictorily represents the least desirable qualities of stereotypical Eastern tyrants while he remains susceptible to traditional domestic values.

After Mandana apparently dies during one of Nourjahad's long sleeps, Cadiga's lone voice of morality counters his despotism in arguing for the laws of society and for kindness to one's fellow creatures. Nourjahad shockingly silences her by murdering her. Because the text focuses on Nourjahad's subjectivity rather than Mandana's or Cadiga's, the resulting insurrection in the seraglio is startling in its intensity. Clearly, the women's power is greater than might have been at first assumed. "Thou hadst rendered thyself so odious to thy women, that not one of them retained the smallest degree of love or fidelity towards thee," Cadiga intones. "In spite of my vigilance they made thy hated seraglio the scene of their unlawful pleasures; and at length having bribed the eunuchs who guarded them, they all in one night fled from their detested walls, taking with them the slaves who had assisted them in their purpose" (151–52). The offensive act that leads to the women's insurrection is the murder of Cadiga, a woman who dies attempting to make Nourjahad recognize his own failure of virtue. Women escape tyranny in this novel through collective action.

The beloved Mandana, it is revealed much later in the best romance tradition, has only feigned her death. Disguised and crossdressed as a youth, she becomes the agent of Nourjahad's reformation away from romance to "reality" and virtue, and then reveals herself: "The angelic youth, snatching from his head a circlet of flowers intermixed with precious stones, which encompassed his brows, and shaded a great part of his forehead; and at the same time throwing off a head of artificial hair which flowed in golden ringlets down his shoulders; a fine fall of brown hair which was concealed under it succeeded, dropping in light curls on his neck and blushing cheeks; and Nourjahad, in the person of his seraphic guide, discovered his beloved and beautiful Mandana!" (220–21).[28] All the fantastical events turn out to be a hoax, reality is restored, and Nourjahad reenters the human community invoking the moral that passion and greed should be tempered. Sheridan's romance, though apparently contributing to a virtuous woman's murder, is stripped of its deleterious effects and activates moral reform. When the veil of romance lifts in *Nourjahad,* virtue is revealed. The reader retroactively reconstitutes the way that the sultan and Mandana rather than Nourjahad actually had possessed the power to shape the story, and they reveal that the apparent romance elements are simply mundane tricks. Further, the belief that romance corrupts women's morals is thoroughly controverted, since a romance fiction effectively *cures* Nourjahad of his libidinous and licentious excesses. In *The History of Nourjahad,* dead and murdered characters resurrect themselves according to romance conventions. As in *The Female Quixote* a cross-dressed figure is the agent of crisis, but in *Nourjahad* that agent speaks and cajoles rather than simply discomfits others by her presence.

In *The Female Quixote* the cross-dressed prostitute seems to urge Arabella to confront romance with prostitution and to combine the virtuous but deluded woman with the insurrectional powers of the sexually ambiguous and transgressive. When the veil of romance is lifted in *The Female Quixote,* Arabella's alignment with the maid and the prostitute is exposed. Instead of building feminist community from that alignment, Lennox turns the encounter with the prostitute into a negative example, and Arabella relinquishes romance to yield to the preachings of the exemplary countess and doctor. The revolutionary potential of romance is thwarted. But in *Nourjahad* the cross-dressed favorite of the seraglio devolves into a virtuous, monogamous woman who is the agent of her master's deliverance. Both her sexual and cultural Otherness is erased in the body of virtue. Romance is abandoned, but only after its transformative power is realized. In Sheridan's tale the confrontation occurs between the cross-dressed Mandana and the entrapped Nourjahad rather than between women. Nourjahad marries Mandana, and the seraglio, as well as polygamy, completely slips from mind.

Like Lennox's Arabella and even Austen's Emma, Nourjahad is infuriatingly misguided. Like Arabella, who encourages suitors to pursue their adventures even until death, Nourjahad actually stabs the bearer of truth, his seraglio slave, Cadiga, when she cries, "Thou art not fit to live" (143). Just as Arabella is known as mad, yet intelligent and worthy, Nourjahad is condemned as evil and greedy but deserving of redemption because of his capacity for reform. While *The Female Quixote* is comic and satiric, *The History of Nourjahad* is fantastic and sentimental. The doctor cures Arabella of romance, Pekuah recognizes the vanity of human wishes, and the sultan and Mandana remedy Nourjahad's indulgence of luxury and cruelty. Nourjahad's dilemma is the human condition—how to be happy in an imperfect world—and his unsatisfactory solution is to luxuriate in riches. But the irony for Nourjahad is that he is held prisoner in his home by the sultan, who affects to doubt his story of celestial visitations and who controls his redemptive experience. The romance he envisions is the sultan's intentionally deceptive construction. The romance elements in *Nourjahad* prove to be the effect of the sultan's well-meant deception and Mandana's willing collusion. Nourjahad is feminized, and Mandana regains dominion over him through the empire of love. Romance is a narrative ruse which, through its ability to manipulate consciousness, does the cultural work of producing moral good.

Like Arabella, who flirts with losing her reputation by unwittingly impersonating a prostitute, Nourjahad risks his moral stature as well—but his sexual virtue is not under contest and his maintaining a seraglio is never questioned. Sheridan uses the sultan to invent a reality and hence a romance for Nourjahad but uses a woman, Mandana, to bring him to a recognition of moral duty. The potential for the real harm that romance can do—as in the supposed murder of Cadiga—is dispelled through the *deus ex machina* of the sultan's revelations of his intrigues. In both *The Female Quixote* and *The History of Nourjahad* male authority finally wins out. Benevolence and charity, sympathy and tenderness, bridge the gap between the isolation of delusion and human community; as the doctor puts it, "It is impossible to read these Tales without lessening part of that Humility, which by preserving in us a Sense of our Alliance with all human nature, keeps us awake to Tenderness and Sympathy, or without impairing that Compassion which is implanted in us as an Incentive to Acts of Kindness" (381). *Nourjahad* is a woman's vision of male power and authority employed for good ends through a woman's agency.

Romance becomes a way to disguise and absorb the historical and geographical empire into the figural empire of love. What must be veiled or blushed over is woman's "manliness" (associated with the prostitute and exotic women), her transgressive sexuality, and her potential to escape and extend the private empire of love. In Lennox and

Sheridan, women's power to produce alternative narratives about love's empire is limited to the domestic realm as a condition for the articulation of a narrative of the empire of adventure that enables the oppression of other women. The empire of love is a powerful enabling fiction, but a metaphor nevertheless, while men's imperial dominion involves actual territory and the legitimating power to colonize the world. Their imperial domain intrudes upon the domestic in spite of seeming to be distant and irrelevant. The empire of love is implicated in other kinds of empire, and the domestic is dangerously, evocatively intertwined with the exotic.

CHAPTER SIX

Feminotopias

The Seraglio, the Homoerotic,
and the Pleasures of "Deformity"

To the women's tracing a new path to honor, in which none shall walk
but such as scorn to cringe in order to rise, and who are proof both
against giving and receiving flattery! In a word, to those halcyon, or, if
you will, *Millenium* days, in which the wolf and the lamb shall feed
together, and a tyrannous domination, which nature never meant,
shall no longer render useless, if not hurtful, the industry and understandings of half mankind!

Mary Astell,
Some Reflections upon Marriage, 4th ed. (1730)

Woman was made for man, so nature meant,
And ev'ry fibre answers the intent;
Who sins against it the creation wrongs,
Must rank with beasts, nor to mankind belongs.

The Sappho-an (1749)

I

Another kind of women's empire, "feminotopia" (a term coined by
Mary Louise Pratt), describes the "idealized worlds of female autonomy, empowerment, and pleasure" often found in women's travel narratives, some of which have a "decidedly orientalist flavor." Feminotopias, "quests for self-realization and fantasies of social harmony,"[1]
contest masculine versions of experience, even though they are often
confined to the private domestic sphere. In feminotopias, women
thrive without men and find pleasure in living together without rancor
and dissent. These exclusively female spaces share the mystique of
being autonomous retreats impenetrable to masculine authority, happily sequestered from the larger patriarchal world of which they are an
inevitable part.

Eighteenth-century English women writers imagined various
idyllic communities, ranging from Mary Astell's feminist asylum for
unmarried women in *A Serious Proposal to the Ladies* (1694) to the

women's community in Sarah Scott's *Millenium Hall* (1762), which
was published one year before Lady Mary Wortley Montagu's Turkish
Embassy *Letters*. The publication of *Millenium Hall* and the Turkish
Embassy *Letters* coincided curiously with the end of the Seven Years'
War and the emergence of the second British empire in the Indian
subcontinent, Africa, and Australasia. The once large and powerful
Ottoman Empire evolved into an unacceptable model for the emerging second British empire, not only in its loss of political strength, but
also in its highly suspect religious and cultural values. In fiction and in
travel narratives, the oriental seraglio is usually depicted as an abhorrent form of domestic tyranny and slavery from which European
women are happily exempt, and as a contrast to England's more benevolent masculinity. The seraglio is, as Montesquieu pointed out in
the *Persian Letters* (1721), "like a little empire" in which patriarchal
power rests in masculine authority over wives, concubines, and servants within the women's secluded quarters.[2] But at the same time, as
we have seen in the *History of Nourjahad,* the parallel drawn between
the seraglio and the Englishwoman's predicament—closed off as she is
in the cult of domesticity, subject to the rule of her husband, and
competing with other women for his attention—makes the seraglio
seem both familiar and strange. Here I'd like to explore the orientalist
texture of female community as a way of linking its "unnatural" resistances to domesticity and maternity with empire and to give special
attention to the assumption that female communities afforded sexual
liberty to women. Englishwomen's lack of autonomy and freedom in
marriage, their sense of themselves as men's property, and their confinement to the private sphere sufficiently parallels the situation of the
women in the harem to give troubling evidence of the difficulty in
sustaining the difference.

These themes became familiar and even somewhat hackneyed to
some Europeans by mid-century. Referring to the travel literature
depicting the curiosities of the Turkish Empire, Charles Perry wrote
that "at least the more central Parts of it . . . are now become pretty
trite Subjects," and noted that "the present weak, feeble Condition of
the *Turkish* Empire" was much remarked upon.[3] Another commentator wrote: "It is lucky for Europe that the Turks are idle and ignorant;
the immense power this empire might have, were it peopled by the
industrious and ambitious, would make it the mistress of the world.
At present it only serves as a dead wall to intercept the commerce and
battles which other powers might create."[4] In spite of national bore-

dom with the subject of the East and a pervasive sense that Turkey constituted an empire gone bad, the English and the Europeans continued to consume writings about Turkey throughout the nineteenth century. The single instance in which the legendary power of the Turkish Empire remained undiminished, to the British mind, was in the seraglio. Richard Pococke, for example, wonders at the Turks' persistent patriarchal control over women: "As they have four wives, each of them has a saloon, with the apartments about it, that have no communication with the other parts of the house, except the common entrance for the servants, which is kept lock'd; and the private entrance, of which the master keeps the key."[5]

A woman's eye was required to penetrate the secrecy of the seraglio's innermost quarters, and thus, not surprisingly, the lone examples of first-person literature about Turkish women's communities were written by women. I will argue that these utopian sites, forbidden to men's view, evoke heightened libidinal desire with homoerotic overtones in the Western women who describe them. We have already noted Lady Mary Wortley Montagu's famed letters from Turkey, first published in 1763 but compiled and edited from letters written in 1717–18; a lesser-known writer was Elizabeth Craven, margravine of Anspach, whose *Journey through the Crimea to Constantinople* (1789) was addressed to a fictitious male friend.[6] Women travellers writing about the harem set up a counter-tradition to Orientalist and patriarchal versions of the Middle East, according to Billie Melman. Melman defines "harem literature" as that which takes its locus in "the separate female space of the *haremlik,* the women and children's quarters in the segregated household," which is depoliticized and cut off from the state. This literature voices, she believes, a "resistance to the essentialist *topos* of the sensual Orient and the mythically libidinous *orientale.*"[7] More than is at first evident, however, Montagu also participates in the depiction of a sensually evocative, even homoerotic Orient in which veiling paradoxically brings sexual liberty and confinement resembles paradise: "Tis very easy to see they have more Liberty than we have, no Woman of what rank so ever being permitted to go in the streets without two muslins . . . and their Shapes are wholly conceal'd. . . . This perpetual Masquerade gives them entire Liberty of following their Inclinations without danger of Discovery" (1:328). Impersonating that difference of a culture they envy and idealize, even evidencing its superiority to England, Craven and Montagu masquerade as the Other by veiling themselves. The Turkish women in their baths, seraglio, and veils create an enviable feminotopia in Montagu's eyes, and subject England's notions of its benevolent treatment of women to question.

Elizabeth Craven clearly knows Montagu's popular text, for she uses similar language in claiming that Turkish women exercise much greater liberty than Englishwomen: "According to what I hear, a Turkish husband does not care for his wife, as the object of his passion, except for a very short space of time; but as wife she enjoys all the luxury of his fortune; and I repeat it, Sir, I think no women have so much liberty, safe from apprehension, as the Turkish—and I think them, in their manner of living, capable of being the happiest creatures breathing" (305). Both Western women envy the sexual liberty that veiling brings, and it fixes their difference. Craven remarks: "All these coverings do not confound all shape or air so much, that men or women, princesses and slaves, may be concealed under them" (270). She imagines Turkey to be "an earthly Paradise" of anonymous erotic intrigue and personifies Turkey as a beautiful demonizing woman who teases her admirers into succumbing to their basest passions (284). This understanding of Turkey as an encitingly deceptive female competes with Craven's other representations of Turkey as an indolent, ignorant man; a veiled, liberated woman; and an idle, prematurely aged monster.

Both Englishwomen portray Turkish women, liberated from the constant demands of a husband, as free to indulge their sexual appetites with others in spite of apparent confinement. Craven judges these women as naive, uneducated, and self-indulgent. She expresses a popular sentiment: "The Turkish women pass most of their time in the bath or upon their dress; strange pastimes! The first spoils their persons, the last disfigures them. The frequent use of hot-baths destroys the solids, and these women at nineteen look older than I am at this moment" (296). While the general ethos of Turkey may evoke a seductive and wanton woman, Craven's orientalism alternates between locating these women as objects of envy (because of their sexual liberty) and of pitiful deformity.

Curiously, both female spectators impersonate male visitors as they gaze on the women with undisguised fascination. While Montagu yearns to possess Charles Jervas's eye and paintbrush to capture the bare beauties of the bagnio, Craven calls on Sir Joshua Reynolds to draw the draped loveliness of two Greek brides she finds in Con-

stantinople: "I would Sir Joshua had been at my elbow, his composi-
tions are fine enough to satisfy a youthful poet's imagination, but here
his pencil might not have disdained to copy two such charming origi-
nals" (306). Both women observers restore the absent male presence
through the aesthetic, express homoerotic desire by impersonating
men, and imagine that women's freedom arises from sexual liberty.
Unlike later nineteenth-century women writers, who tend to desex-
ualize the women's quarters, the upper-class eighteenth-century
women openly admire the erotic and transform it into the aesthetically
satisfying. Both Montagu and Craven aptly contest popular notions
that Turkish women completely acquiesce to the power of the sultan
and do his sexual bidding, but exoticism also has its feminine cast in
masking the European woman's desire to masquerade as the aesthet-
icized Other whom she desires.

The class-stratified nature of Montagu's feminotopia is obscured
by descriptions of the delicious nakedness of the mistresses and slaves,
who, while giving the appearance of modesty, secretly conduct sexual
intrigues, regardless of class. Montagu's prose lingers admiringly over
the naked bodies of the Turkish women in the baths at Sophia. She
attests to the impotency of a mere woman's description and affects to
yield to a man's superior ability to paint women's naked bodies, an
activity forbidden to women painters in the eighteenth century:

> The first sofas were cover'd with Cushions and rich Carpets, on
> which sat the Ladys, and on the 2nd their slaves behind 'em, but
> without any distinction of rank by their dress, all being in the state of
> nature, that is, in plain English, stark naked, without any Beauty or
> deffect conceal'd, yet there was not the least wanton smile or immod-
> est Gesture amongst 'em. They Walk'd and mov'd with the same ma-
> jestic Grace which Milton describes of our General Mother. There
> were many amongst them as exactly proportion'd as ever any Goddess
> was drawn by the pencil of Guido or Titian, and most of their skins
> shineingly white, only adorn'd by their Beautifull Hair divided into
> many tresses . . . perfectly representing the figures of the Graces. . . .
> To tell you the truth, I had wickedness enough to wish secretly that
> Mr. Gervase could have been there invisible. I fancy it would have
> very much improv'd his art to see so many fine Women naked in
> different postures, some in conversation, some working, others drink-
> ing Coffee or sherbet, and many negligently lying on their Cushions
> while their slaves . . . were employ'd in braiding their hair in several
> pritty manners. In short, tis the Women's coffee house, where all the

news of the Town is told, Scandal invented, etc. . . .I was charm'd with their Civillity and Beauty and should have been very glad to pass more time with them. . . .

   Adieu, Madam. I am sure I have now entertained you with an Account of such a sight as you never saw in your Life and what no book of travells could inform you of. 'Tis no less than Death for a Man to be found in one of these places. (313–15)

Montagu's wish to impersonate a male voyeur, I suggest, transforms the scene of utterly natural prelapsarian bathing goddesses into an erotically charged vision, in spite of her very explicit caveat that "there was not the least wanton smile or immodest Gesture amongst 'em." Her appeal to "their Civillity and Beauty" rankles incongruously against her "wickedness" in wishing that an Englishman could see and paint the forbidden women. This transvestite gazing may, I think, be interpreted as an expression of a slippery sexuality with affinities to homoerotic desire and an instance of Oriental sapphism.[8]

   Famous for her comment that there are three sexes—men, women, and Herveys—Montagu tenaciously pursued Francesco Algarotti, a man known to be bisexual, to Italy in hopes of a torrid romance during her long separation from Wortley.[9] By some accounts, Lady Mary and Lord Hervey (also bisexual) were rivals for Algarotti's love, and she funneled her letters through Hervey, who called her Sappho. Among Algarotti's papers is a verse epistle, perhaps written by Lady Mary, painting her as Sappho, who fears losing her Phaon, and Dido, who fears losing her Aeneas. In addition, Montagu certainly knew the joys of female friendship, and perhaps more than friendship. In the summer of 1721 Montagu spent considerable time with a special female friend while her husband visited Yorkshire. Though the identity of the woman is uncertain, Montagu knew Maria Skerrett (Walpole's mistress, whom he married in 1737) from 1720 on, and Skerrett stayed in Twickenham during the summer of 1725 and accompanied Lady Mary to town in the fall: "My fair companion," she reported to her sister, "puts me oft in mind of our Thoresby conversations; we read and walk together, and I am more happy in her than any thing else could make me except your conversation."[10] She also wrote an impassioned "Impromptu to a Young Lady Singing" that was perhaps addressed to Maria Skerrett:

> Sing, Gentle Maid, reform my breast,
> And soften all my Care;
> Thus I can be some moments blest,

And easy in Despair.
The power of Orpheus lives in you;
The raging Passions of my Soul subdue,
And tame the Lions and the Tygers there.[11]

Alexander Pope's favorite satiric name for Lady Mary Wortley Montagu was, not accidentally, "Sappho," and I have found that the name was clearly associated with homosexual practices *and* heterosexual promiscuity even in the eighteenth century. Pope characterized Montagu as the lewd "dirty Flavia" in his "Epistle to a Lady," and allegations of Montagu's erotic liaisons may also have been fueled by a draft of Pope's "Epistle to Lord Bathurst, Of the Use of Riches," since members of the court and the aristocracy were quick to recognize that "lewd Lesbia," paired with Phryne, referred to the friendship between Lady Mary and Maria Skerrett. In his biography of Lady Mary, Robert Halsband shies away from the homoerotic connotations of "Sappho," and he limits sapphic connotations to woman's "dangerous wit."[12]

While it would be inaccurate to say that these and other hints of Lady Mary's sapphic desires mean that she possessed a lesbian *identity* in the modern sense, since sexuality was not the locus of subjectivity in the early eighteenth century, nonetheless her sexuality was imaginatively and in reality quite fluid and multiple, and the allegations of promiscuity lodged against her relate to her unwillingness to be restricted, privately or publicly, to traditional heterosexual activities. Her languid longing for the Turkish women and her craving for their imagined freedoms indicate her belief that their sexual lives happily exceeded the contemporary English categories that confined her. Relocating female eroticism onto the Other, further distanced by viewing it through the eyes and art of male portrait painters, affords Montagu and Craven a means to celebrate and yet contain the desire for sexual freedom to the exotic; it allows them to assume that just as political tyranny breeds domestic confinement, sexual freedom (including perhaps homoerotic desire) might engender political freedom as well.

II

The Turkish bagnio (often viewed as being the same as a brothel) also conveyed homoerotic connotations to the popular mind. The best known of the bagnios was, of course, the one described in Montesquieu's *Persian Letters*, in which the slave Zelid appears to conduct lesbian relationships with Zephis and Zashi. Female homosexual practices were regarded as especially common to Turkey and appear in diverse texts, though such practices were branded as abominably sinful. In *Satan's Harvest Home; or, The Present State of Whorecraft . . . etc.* (1749) naked women delight in viewing other women's naked bodies in a passage reminiscent of Montagu entitled "Of the Game of Flatts": "But ordinarily the Women bathe by themselves, bond and free together; so that you shall many Times see young Maids, exceeding beautiful, gathered from all Parts of the World, exposed naked to the View of other Women, who thereupon fall in Love with them, as young Men do with us, at the Sight of Virgins" (61). In this ribald treatise, lesbian sexuality is directly associated with the perversity and monstrosity of the Other: "*Sappho,* as she was one of the wittiest Women that ever the World bred, so she thought with Reason, it would be expected she should make some Additions to a *Science* in which Womankind had been so successful: What does she do then? Not content with our Sex, [Sappho] begins *Amours* with her own, and teaches the Female world a new Sort of Sin, call'd the *Flats,* that was follow'd not only in *Lucian's* Time, but is practis'd frequently in *Turkey,* as well as at *Twickenham* at this Day" (18).[13] This parallel drawn between women of Twickenham and Turkey very likely alludes to Lady Mary Wortley Montagu, who lived in Twickenham after her husband purchased a house in 1722. She was, of course, associated with Pope, its most famous resident, with whom she later quarrelled.

Once we dismiss the notion that making visible women's erotic desire for women was unthinkable for the eighteenth-century Englishwoman, we can recognize, I think, the polymorphous sexualities available within the period. In the common parlance of the period, lesbian activities were unnatural acts, and lesbians by definition were associated with monsters.[14] A term that had currency throughout the eighteenth century, *lesbian* usually was applied specifically to women of the isle of Lesbos but often referred more specifically to the Greek poet Sappho, whose sexual proclivities were suspect. The word *lesbian* conveyed definite homoerotic associations when used in the case of Catherine Vizzani, a woman whose body was dissected for genital evidence of her tribadism: "Our Times," wrote the anatomy professor, "afford a Girl, who, so far from being inferior to *Sappho,* or any of the *Lesbian* Nymphs, in an Attachment for those of her own Sex, has greatly surpassed them in Fatigues, Dangers, and Distress, which terminated in a violent Death."[15] The "unnatural" brought its own punishment for Vizzani.

Sappho figures importantly in various eighteenth-century texts, sometimes as a lesbian but more frequently as a bisexual who is either unsatisfied with lesbian affections and turns to the more acceptable heterosexual impulse, or who is abandoned by seductive or rapacious men and longs for gentler female love.[16] Although Sappho was idealized as the finest female classical poet, her passion for women complicated her literary status. For Lady Mary as well as for other women writers of the period, the name of Sappho was intertwined with lesbian practices in literature and in the popular imagination. As will become obvious, I think there is convincing evidence to contest Joan DeJean's finding that "before the late nineteenth century, the two traditions—fictions of Sappho and fictions of the lesbian—were never to intersect."[17] The contemporary allusions to Sappho in reference to Montagu and others clearly connect their poetic genius to their homoerotic sexuality.

Sappho's sexual hybridity and her allegedly unnatural sexual acts were at least as threatening as her literary talent. The argument prefacing one hitherto unnoticed text, *An Epistle from Sapho to Philenis with the Discovery; or, Paradise Review'd* (London, 1728), a four-page sixpenny pamphlet, indicates the conflict that loomed between admiring her talent and questioning her sexual preferences: "Sapho was a famous Poetess, of a very amorous Disposition; who not contented with Male Lovers only, had also those of her own Sex." A bawdy imitation of John Donne's *Sapho to Philaenis* (which is in turn borrowed from Ovid's *Heroides*),[18] the anonymous eighteenth-century *Epistle from Sapho* first boldly asserts the superiority of homoerotic to heterosexual practices. Its low-comic analogy of men's semen to "manure" unwanted in nature's paradise condemns the undesirable harshness and robustness of male lovers who sexually plow women's fields. The poem shifts tone to become a high elegy to the "dear other self" (a phrase that does not occur in the Donne poem after which it was patterned). The *Epistle* prefers the refinement of homoerotic love, which avoids pain and pregnancy:

> Altho' in Worth and Lustre different, We
> Like Gems, in Silver well enchac'd, agree;
> . . . .
> Our *Skins* are white as undissolving Snow,
> Our *Wasts* are slender, and our Stature's low.
> Each Part of Me varies from those of You,
> Scarce more than they from one another do.

> Dear other self! the Likeness being such,
> Why may they not alike, and freely touch?
> None *Hand* to *Hand,* or *Lip* to *Lip* denies;
> Why shou'd thy *Breast* to *Breast*? or *Th*——*s* to *Th*——*s*?

The *Epistle* moves on to a reverie that celebrates Sappho's imaginative invocation of Philenis's presence and makes explicit that which was only hinted in the Donne poem: her connection of imagination to erotic pleasure, and touching herself to fantasize uniting with another woman while looking in the mirror:[19]

> This heightens all the Present we pursue,
> In gen'rous Bounty does the Past renew,
> And ev'n the Future opens to our View.
> Oft too this do's from small Occasions raise
> Its Force, as Sparks augment into a Blaze;
> To languish often in thy soft Embrace;
> Thro' this we oft renew our pleasing Game,
> Tremble and part, dissolve in mutual Flame,
> And jointly do —— what I forbear to Name!
> . . . .
> My Fancy so is by Resemblance caught,
> Touching my self, Thee, Thee I touch in thought.

The moment of imagined bliss dissipates as Sappho faces the reality of her lover's absence, but the poem ends with an appeal to the exquisite pleasure of Philenis's cheeks, breath, and beauty. In this poem homoerotic love is not a substitution for a more desirable heterosexual love, nor an equal alternative to it, but the rapturous preference over all other forms of romantic and sexual engagement.[20] In Donne's poem Sappho embraces and touches herself, and kisses her own hands, but in the eighteenth-century *Epistle* the caresses lead to orgasm. *An Epistle from Sapho* is extraordinary in celebrating explicitly genital lesbian lovemaking and assuming its natural occurrence while avoiding seamy language.

Still, the pornographic, satirical, and celebratory descriptions of such desire, usually written by men, most frequently leer at the unnaturalness of lesbian sexuality. Reproofs of same-sex practices certainly outnumber romantic descriptions, making *An Epistle from Sapho* the exception. One low ribald piece, *The New Epicurean; or, The Delights of Sex Facetiously and Philosophically Considered,* explicitly defines tribadism as "the love of one girl for another, which leads them mutually to gratify each others desires, by kissing and licking that salacious part of their bodies," though the narrator is at pains to indicate that such practices can only be incomplete substitutes for heterosexual intercourse.[21] *The New Epicurean* depicts explicit lesbian desire as an uncontrollable attack of one woman on another: "The Tribade saw her chance, and waited no longer; so throwing up the clothes of the young girl, she flew upon her like a panther" (30). The satirical response to Richardson's *Pamela, Pamela Censured* (London, 1741), takes the homoerotic innuendos of the original novel literally and critiques *Pamela* for inciting unnatural excesses: "There are at present, I am sorry to say it, too many who assume the characters of Women of Mrs. *Jewkes's* Cast, I mean *Lovers of their own Sex. Pamela* seems to be acquainted with this, and indeed shews so much Virtue that she has no Objection to the Male Sex as too many of her own have" (51).

These descriptions, though filtered through the male pornographic imagination, give the lie to the now defunct but tenacious belief that sexual acts between women were uncommon until after the Enlightenment.[22] Similarly, *The Adultress* (London, 1773), a satirical poem imitative of Juvenal's Sixth Satire, also disapproves of homoerotic activities in both sexes and associates lesbian women with whores:

> The Sex itself is now one common Whore,
> Mistress and Maid lewd Venery adore.
> . . . .
> Women and Men, in these unnat'ral Times,
> Are guilty equal of unnat'ral crimes:
> Woman with Woman act the Manly Part,
> And kiss, and press each other to the heart.
> Unnat'ral Crimes like these my Satire vex;
> I know a thousand *Tommies* 'mongst the Sex:
> And if they don't relinquish such a Crime,
> I'll give their Names to be the scoff of Time. (19, 26)[23]

Manly women did not need to cross-dress publicly to be judged "tommies" in their sexual performance. Another little-known text, *The Sappho-an* (1749), warns ominously that lesbians privately snag the women that men desire.[24] "Inverting nature in an horrid way" (11), same-sex love yields misery, but the satire is an excuse to detail lesbian practices, women's sexual induction of young boys, and general licentiousness. The central portion of the satire describes the homoerotic orgy of a dozen Amazonian goddesses, led by manly Juno. The lusty goddesses engage in flagellation and sex with animals, eunuchs, and dildoes, all activities that can only "imitate [the] substantial joys" of heterosexual relations (32).

Clearly, however, lesbian sexual activities were vitally alive in the popular and pornographic imagination; and I believe they were, as they are now, a relatively common if often hidden practice. As Elizabeth Harvey has pointed out, the history of lesbianism is a history of censorship, and only recently are feminist scholars increasingly recognizing what has long seemed invisible—eighteenth-century women's homoerotic writing. Harriette Andreadis finds "explicitly lesbian activity" described in Margaret Cavendish, Aphra Behn, and Anne Killigrew, and notes that Katherine Philips also employed conventions of cavalier male homoerotic friendship poetry to express female same-sex desire. Though Philips' texts are not explicitly sexual, they convey passionate feeling for women. In Delarivier Manley's utopian satiric fiction *The New Atalantis,* women of the New Cabal, "joined in an excess of amity (no word is tender enough to express their new delight) innocently embrace! . . . What irregularity can there be in this? 'Tis true some things will be strained a little too far, and that causes reflections to be cast upon the rest."[25] Recently Caroline Woodward has excavated *The Travels and Adventures of Mademoiselle de Richelieu,* which details a love story between desiring female friends.[26] The extraordinary sexual history in the newly discovered diaries of Anne Lister (1791–1840) uses veiled but unmistakable language to describe lesbian activities.[27] Acquainted with the more famous Ladies of Llangollen, Sarah Ponsonby and Eleanor Butler, Lister was taunted for her masculine appearance and often records her sexual trysts and conquests in code. The numerous examples of real women's cross-dressing include Charlotte Charke's autobiographical narrative, Hannah Snell's *The Female Soldier,* and Henry Fielding's *Female Husband,* a fictionalization of the case of the famed Mary Hamilton, who was prosecuted for her marriage to Mary Price.[28] Further, the homoerotic induction into (hetero)sexuality of women by women is a commonplace of the eighteenth-century novel, as we have seen in Richardson's *Pamela* and in Cleland's *Fanny Hill,* as well as in hackwork pornography.

It seems to me that in the eighteenth century, women themselves often perceived homosexual activities to be a seamless part of a multiplicity of sexual practices, some of which were judged "unnatural," rather than a marker of an exclusive and fixed identity, as made manifest through Romanticism's concept of "self" and Freud's later demarcation of sexuality as identity. The paradigm of two genders based on two biological sexes in the eighteenth century (with third and fourth illegitimate genders emerging) would be greatly complicated by considering the evidence of the fluid boundaries of multiple sexual practices.[29] Women in the eighteenth century did not, I think, take their identities primarily from sexual preference, since chastity was crucial to public identity. Instead, sexuality was publicly a matter of character and privately one of anatomy. If a woman's character was determined by her virtue, that woman's same-sex desires would not figure in that account unless those desires had become the topic of public scandal or unless the legitimacy of her female anatomy was called into question. In limiting lesbian activities to romantic friendships and female husbands in the period, Martha Vicinus, for example, accepts the public terms of sexual definition.[30] It seems worth stating the obvious, however: that sexual activity in the eighteenth century was increasingly a private matter conducted behind closed doors, and that legally actionable behavior (as lesbian sex was) would most likely have been described in legal documents, medical accounts, and pornography. Same-sex desire, initiation into heterosexuality through homosexuality, or bisexual activity did not *fix* sexual identity but instead influenced public opinion of a woman's character that was itself defined by the visible—that is, by cross-dressing or by publicly acceptable intimacy between women. Even more significant than public attire or behavior in judging sexual proclivity was the material body, and most explicitly, the formation of the sexual organs. Large clitorises or highly developed vulva (as in the case of Catherine Vizzani) meant that one was a hermaphroditic monster who defied the usual gender and species categories.[31] Desire moved along a spectrum that made same-sex activity an imaginable private alternative, but public exposure of such practices branded women as unnatural monsters and made them vulnerable to the law.

That spectrum of sexual practices in the eighteenth century connects homoerotics, the unnatural, and the Other in a sexual geography that involves especially the torrid zones of Asia Minor as well as Mediterranean Europe. Turkey (like the "foreign" in general, especially Italy and France)[32] resonates with homosexuality for both men and women. In *A Treatise on the Use of Flogging in Venereal Affairs* (London, 1718), John Henry Meibomius, M.D., writes that robust and lusty females satisfy each other, "to whom for the most part they can give as much Pleasure as Men do" (17). Focusing on hermaphrodites, the treatise goes on to provide details of the Italian Marguerta and the French Barbarissa, "two Females [who] were in their Statures very near equal to the largest size'd Male; they had full and rough Faces, large Shoulders, Hands, and Feet, and but slender Hips and small Breasts" (19), and another instance of Amaryllis and Theodora, who, "living in Luxury, in the prime of their Years, in a hot inciting Climate, . . . at length were naturally inclin'd to the most abominable Pollution"—dildoes (41). In *The Surprises of Love, Exemplified in the Romance of a Day* (London, 1765), Laetitia's father reports that residence in Turkey "had not helped to increase his reliance on the conduct of women left to themselves, or to strengthen his opinion of their giving, in general, a good account of the liberty allowed them by the customary courtesy of this country" (53). Here too, the sexual liberty allowed to exclusively female communities has homoerotic implications. Alexander Russell's *Natural History of Aleppo* aligns homoerotic behavior with race: "They have a few black slaves, which are commonly brought from *Aethiopia*, by way of *Cairo*; but the greater part of their slaves are white, being mostly furnished from *Georgia*, or such as are taken in war; and the beauty of a male-slave enhances the value as much as it does that of a female, occasioned by the frequency among them of a crime not to be named."[33] Every third or fourth bed in the harem was occupied by a preceptress because "abominable vices against nature reign there to excess, not only amongst the pages, but likewise amongst the girls."[34] The leisure of the women's quarters encouraged lesbian sex, the details of which the narrator of *The Present State of the Ottoman Empire* (1784) teasingly chooses to veil: "Nor is it at all astonishing that . . . girls that have nothing to do but to prepare themselves for sensual pleasures, and who think of nothing but Venus and her son, should give way to unnatural lasciviousness, for want of the proper means of gratifying their amorous inclinations."[35] He recounts tales of pairs of women lovers being bound together and tossed to their deaths into the sea as punishment for their sexual crimes.

More comic, and probably apocryphal, is Paul Rycaut's early narrative of Turkey (a text Montagu relied upon), which imagines the older women in the seraglio to be mistresses and bawds for the younger,

> employ'd in observing their actions; . . . their involuntary restraint forces them to the same unseemly actions amongst themselves, as the brutish Passions of those Young Men engages them in. . . . And this presumption has no doubt given occasion to the Fabulous Story,

which is related of their being Serv'd up with Cucumbers cut into pieces, and not intire, out of a ridiculous fear lest they should put them to undecent uses. . . . But it is not only in the Seraglio, that that abominable Vice reigns, but it is predominant also in the City of *Constantinople,* and in all the Provinces of the Empire, and the wicked Example of the Men, who, slighting the natural use of Woman-kind, are mutually inflamed with a detestable love for one another, unfortunately enclines the Women to imitate them.[36]

In the early eighteenth century, the sliced cucumbers had apparently entered the popular imagination, for Pope salaciously writes to Lady Mary Wortley Montagu (1717) before her trip to Turkey that she will soon be in "the Land of Jealousy, where the unhappy Women converse but with none but Eunuchs, and where the very Cucumbers are brought to them Cutt."[37] Lady Mary's idealization of the sexual liberty and freedom that the seraglio affords to women to move about the world anonymously must have been at least in part a response to these notions that women's sexual frustrations were being satisfied by vegetables.[38]

Eighteenth-century accounts of women's communities, of women alone together, extend the concept of women's feminotopias beyond sites of autonomy and authority to those that admit varied objects of affections. Fostering tales of sensuality and of a sexual liberty that slides easily from heterosexual to homosexual object, these accounts confirm the association of other women of empire with the "unnatural" within a specific historical context and set the parameters for women without men. Woman's desire for woman remains safely confined to a foreign practice or, in its domestic manifestation, one for which whores and monsters have a special propensity. It is precisely this notion of sexual deprivation and deformity in the harem that Montagu seeks to contest. For her these allegedly unhappy women awaiting sexual satisfaction are instead beautiful, sociable, and free to act on their sexual desires.

III

Sarah Scott's *Millenium Hall* (1762), not unrelated to the eighteenth-century fascination with the seraglio, is both a contest to male dominance over women and a testimony to its power. An epistolary novel consisting of one lengthy letter written by a gentleman (whom Scott later names as Sir George Ellison) to his bookseller friend, *Millenium*

Hall was actually written in one month and published anonymously (as were all Scott's works) in October or early November 1762. In spite of virulently negative reviews, the book saw four editions between 1762 and 1778.[39] The book parallels Scott's life in that after a brief, unhappy marriage to George Scott, she lived in a close female friendship with Lady Barbara Montagu in Bath, where they conducted the sort of charitable activities that *Millenium Hall* fictionalizes.[40]

While others have appropriately connected the novel to slavery and the West Indies via its sequel, *The History of Sir George Ellison* (1766), I would like to place *Millenium Hall* in the context of female community and its connection to homoeroticism and monstrosity.[41] Like Montagu and Craven, who as female spectators impersonated Jervas and Reynolds painting the naked Turkish and Greek women, Sarah Scott describes the accomplished and dignified women through the appreciative but colonizing vision of the male observers of her feminotopia, Sir George Ellison and Lamont. The beginning of the novel is narrated by Ellison, who is accompanied by Mr. Lamont, the young son of an old friend, and who rediscovers his relationship to a long-lost cousin, Mrs. Maynard. Returning from Jamaica to England, Ellison is so much altered by his colonial stint that Mrs. Maynard, one of the founders of the Millenium Hall community, finds him unrecognizable.

The fiction suggests that the men's visit to Millenium Hall and its surroundings restores them from the fatigue of colonial travels. The impetus for their returning to England is to recover from the effects of twenty years in "the hot and unwholesome climate of Jamaica" and from the exhausting quest for mercantile gain. Possessed by a colonizing curiosity, "one of those insatiable passions that grow by gratification" (5), Ellison and Lamont happen upon the community of Millenium Hall. The "painful suspense" (72) that it induces motivates the narrative.[42] In the idyllic woods designed by the ladies surrounding Millenium Hall, the opposite of the colonial pertains and nature is protected: "Man never appears there as a merciless destroyer; but the preserver, instead of the tyrant, of the inferior part of creation" (17). Millenium Hall represents a respite from colonialism, from the travails of being a slave owner, and an alternative to the tyrannizing curiosity and rapacity of empire. Empire and colonization are ostensibly opposed to the domestic tranquility of Millenium Hall.

The domestic enclosure of chaste, stubbornly nonsexual English gentlewomen poses the apparent antithesis to the teeming sexuality of empire and its torrid zones. The core of the "amiable family" of women who have pooled their property and economic resources includes Mrs. Maynard, Miss Selvyn, Miss Mancel, Miss Trentham, Lady Mary Jones, and Mrs. Morgan, all dressed uniformly in clean white garments without ornament. Rather than a subculture, they represent a community that organizes its resources for mutual support while differing from the norm. Like Montagu's women in the seraglio, they resemble the Graces, and their community seems Edenic in its pastoral vision of perfectly arranged flora and cattle lowing on the fields as an "asylum against every evil" (6). Their rural simplicity recalls the mythic past rather than the present moment. In contrast, the dissipated, fashionable observer Lamont rudely mocks the women's rusticity and well-regulated life.[43] The constant inquisitor, he queries the ladies' rigid routines, outmoded attitudes, and lack of concern for profit.

Technically, the women of Millenium Hall are being gazed upon by the two men, but the women attempt to control the terms of the viewing.[44] Lamont intermittently asserts himself against the female narrative, but the women triumph in *Millenium Hall* as he becomes educated to their value in the course of the novel. The men's voyeurism is motivated more from a curious, colonizing desire than from a sexual one, and the bucolic setting is a necessary preliminary to engaging the men's interest in the individual stories of the women.

Millenium Hall, recognizing the potential imprisonment of women in marriage, offers an alternative to it. This female Arcadia is remarkably sensitive to the alignment of women's oppression with slavery and physical deformity in providing a haven for the aged and the poor, the deformed and the disabled. Dwarves and giants live in a separate compound, a feature readers have found puzzling. I suggest that this is an aspect of its affinity to an Orientalized feminotopia. An English counterpart to the seraglio with its mutes, eunuchs, and slaves in a female community, it plays on the connections between domestic femininity and women's structural kinship to the perverse, the monstrous, and the deformed. For Scott, such so-called "deformity" may be both liberating and debilitating. In *Millenium Hall* the women are "deformed" in the eyes of the men, who must be persuaded to admire their eccentricity and attest to their womanhood.

In contrast to Hobbes's warlike society, Millenium Hall is a harmonious community of reason, reflection, and a freedom to speak that is unattainable outside its confines.[45] Miss Mancel launches into an argument against tyranny when Lamont wrongly assumes that the ladies keep wild beasts in an enclosed space. He asks: "What we behold is certainly an inclosure, how can that be without a confinement to those that are within it?" (19). Miss Mancel describes this community of refuge instead as one of mutual service and obligation for the poor, for dwarves, and for gentlewomen who do not wish to marry. When Lamont protests, "You seem, madam, to choose to make us all slaves to each other" (62), Miss Mancel counters that their female society is based on love and esteem rather than flattery or confinement. "What I understand by society," she says, "is a state of mutual confidence, reciprocal services, and correspondent affections; where numbers are thus united, there will be a free communication of sentiments, and we shall then find speech, that peculiar blessing given to man, a valuable gift indeed; but when we see it restrained by suspicion, or contaminated by detraction, we rather wonder that so dangerous a power was trusted with a race of beings who seldom make a proper use of it" (61). At Millenium Hall enclosure is distinguished from tyranny, and the disabled are enclosed without confinement to a benevolent servitude.

The household of six women at Millenium Hall, several times called a "family," is a feminotopia of domesticity that offers protection from unwanted marriage, pregnancy, and the disappointments and dangers of maternity. It provides daily sorority instead of isolation and a spiritual regimen to channel the women's sexual energies. The little histories of women are, in some sense, their sexual histories. Describing their rejection of marriage rather than their sexual performance constitutes an almost ritual induction into the community. Each woman first proves herself marriageable and is then freed from marital confinement. In turning to the community, the women steadfastly refuse to embrace heterosexuality while allowing that marriage is acceptable for others.

The novel redefines maternity so that it becomes something that the women generously bestow upon each other. Scott's novel declares an opposition to the more traditional women of the previous generation who wanted their daughters to imitate their coquettish, self-abnegating ways. In contrast to more traditional bourgeois domesticity, the women at Millenium Hall mother each other as well as become surrogate mothers to every fifth child among the poor families who surround their community.[46] The lack of a mother unites Miss Mancel and Mrs. Morgan (Lady Melvyn), both of whom are vulnerable to preying men and subject to the world's propensity to estrange women from women. The motherless Louisa Mancel was rescued from a dying aunt by Mr. Hintman, who agreed to adopt her. Sent to Mlle. d'Avaux's boarding school, Miss Mancel meets Miss Melvyn. Their great fondness for each other is couched in maternal terms: "Miss Melvyn . . . found great pleasure in endeavouring to instruct her; and grew to feel for her the tenderness of a mother, while Miss Mancel began to receive consolation from experiencing an affection quite maternal" (36). Though Louisa Mancel eventually discovers her lost mother in the American colonies, being motherless yokes these women together to nurture each other in a domestic economy. The various autobiographical accounts testify to the women's resistance to traditional socialization, "the little arts of behaviour which mothers too commonly inculcate with so much care":

> The first thing a girl is taught is to hide her sentiments, to contradict the thoughts of her heart, and tell all the civil lies which custom has sanctified, with as much affectation and conceit as her mother, and when she has acquired all the folly and impertinence of a riper age, and apes the woman more ungracefully than a monkey does a fine gentleman, the parents congratulate themselves with the extremest complacency in the charming education they have given their daughter. (181)

The novel supplants the scandalized renderings of lesbian relationships in female communities with an obdurate affirmation of nonsexual attachments, though an undercurrent of homoerotic bonding unsettles the narrative.[47] *Millenium Hall* actively resists the women's incorporation into conventional modes of marriage, maternity, and heterosexuality.

According to this cautionary tale, marital unions also endanger relationships among women and alienate them from each other. Miss Melvyn had been tricked into marrying the aged, unappealing Mr. Morgan to avoid being disgraced in the world. Her rank dictates her duty, and thus Miss Melvyn, like many of the other women in the autobiographical stories, is caught (in a predicament familiar to women) between two unappealing alternatives. Mr. Morgan's empire over her is complete, and she is forbidden the pleasure of female friendship with Miss Mancel, a friendship so troubling and intense that it challenges heterosexual arrangements.[48] Though the women of the community think of marriage "as absolutely necessary to the good of society," it is a "general duty" that they prefer to delegate to others. While Miss Melvyn selflessly marries an undesirable man, Miss Mancel fulfills her obligation in *refusing* to marry the man she loves, Sir Edward Lambton. Like Miss Melvyn, her alibi is rank—she deems her fortune unworthy of him. In short, the crux for women is that few may expect to find happiness with a man.

The stories of Lady Mary Jones and Miss Selvyn resemble those of the first two women in that both appear to be left motherless at a very early age, though Miss Selvyn later discovers her mother, Lady Emilia. Pregnant by Lord Peyton, whom she loved, Lady Emilia had refused to marry him because of her oddly construed sense of propriety, and the illegitimate daughter had been adopted by Selvyn. As in the case of Miss Mancel, duty dictated an unhappy choice for Lady Emilia. Of course, the shame of premarital sex seems to a modern audience a misplaced guilt, but clearly this novel insists on the eradication of public apprehension about a woman's sexuality. Miss Selvyn's discovery of her mother allows her to redefine her mother's refusal to marry as a decision based on virtue, and it connects her with the repetitive theme that duty brings unhappiness to women.

The motherless but very handsome Miss Harriot Trentham ("beloved by her grandmother and Mr. Alworth, and hated and traduced by her female cousins" [183], Miss Alworth and the Miss Denhams) also recounts a plaintive story of feminine loss and antagonisms. Harriot, who "never knew the blessing of a mother's care" (180), is the object of her female cousins' malice. In yet another testimony to the joys of asexual love, she desperately avoids marriage to Master Alworth. Contesting the notion of love as passion, the two celebrate "an affection calm and rational as theirs, totally free from that turbulency and wildness which had always appeared to them the true characteristics of love" (186), and are almost comically steady in their conviction to avoid the abhorred liaison of property and sexual intimacy that others urge them to accept. Belatedly, however, Alworth realizes he does in fact possess violent passion for Harriot (not for his coquettish wife), and she flees from his newfound erotic desire. When Harriot conveniently contracts smallpox (like her creator Sarah Scott and "the youngest Miss Tunstall" in Scott's *History of Sir George Ellison*), she "acknowledged she was not insensible to this mortification; and to avoid the observation of the envious or even of the idly curious she retired, as soon as she was able to travel, to a country house which I hired for her" (199). Rather than becoming Alworth's wife, she instead derives pleasure from avoiding marriage and acting as a surrogate parent to his daughter rather than as a birth mother.

Although the novel outlines a radical political and social scheme, Scott is not proposing overthrowing the class system or instituting female governance beyond Millenium Hall. The women's domestic economy is not put forward as a serious model for the state economy, but Millenium Hall does make it possible for women to exercise both liberty and virtue within female sorority. Precise in its plans for economic well-being, it elaborates upon a feminine fantasy of self-governance, and a woman's empire independent both of love's empire and of the masculine empire of imperial adventure. An empire without a monarch, female community and homosocial affiliation offer a feminotopia that rejects the despotic male empire of the seraglio. Millenium Hall provides an asylum for the various "deformed" who share the women's vision, and beyond that, it heretically makes possible taking genuine pleasure in that "deformity."

IV

Defining beauty as a handicap, and ugliness and deformity as agreeable, the women of Millenium Hall, like their deformed charges, are able to escape the sexual economy and its tropes. The visitors to Millenium Hall deflect their pity to admiration for the disabled because of the women's intervention: "Instead of feeling the pain one might naturally receive from seeing the human form so disgraced, we were filled with admiration of the human mind, when so nobly exalted by virtue, as it is in the patronesses of these poor creatures, who wore an air of cheerfulness" (21). The benevolent sentiment associated with philanthropic endeavors at mid-century extends here, as it had not yet in the society at large, to the handicapped.

Apparently the number of disabled people in eighteenth-century London was considerable. In Lady Mary Wortley Montagu's Turkish Embassy Letters she remarks that the streets of Rotterdam, in contrast to those of London, are free of the visual blight she believes the handicapped create: "One is not shock'd with those loathsome Cripples so common in London, nor teiz'd with the Importunitys of idle Fellows and Wenches."[49] Dwarves, giants, Siamese twins, hermaphrodites, and unusual beings with various physical deformities were regularly exhibited for profit in London in the early decades of the century. Those displayed included a Tartar with a horse's head, a man with a head growing out of his body, a man with breasts for thighs and legs, a girl without appendages, and a "midget negro" with his family at Charing Cross (see Figs. 6 and 7).[50]

Millenium Hall begins and ends with attention to deformity. Among the first group the narrator and Lamont happen upon at Millenium Hall is the colony of the disabled. The larger community includes five dwarves "just three feet high," two giants, and a prematurely old man. In addition, the housekeeper has a maimed hand, the cook is on crutches, the dairymaid is deaf, and the housemaid has only one hand. Though Susan is lame and Jane is deaf, all are engaged in the arts or in other labor. A lame youth demonstrates his accomplishment at the French horn, and a nearly blind person plays the bassoon. In fact, disability is a *recommendation* for a position at Millenium Hall. The housekeeper's deformed hand means that "what had hitherto been an impediment was a stronger recommendation than the good character I had from my last place; and I am sure I have reason to value these distorted fingers, more than ever any one did the handsomest hands that ever nature made" (120). At Millenium Hall the culture's devaluation of deformity is reversed.

The monsters, like the women saved from the marriage market, are taught to despise the profit they earned from being paraded as commodified spectacles. The community offers the deformed protection in exchange for their labor, and the women justify their seclusion at church on the grounds of protecting them from gaping onlookers. The deformed (though they include both sexes) are gendered as women, and liberty is paradoxically achieved for deformed people, as for the women, in confining themselves within "so narrow a compass" (23), in avoiding the public sphere, and in refusing marriage. The deformed are not treated as slaves but rather as servants, since they are paid a small sum for their labor. Nevertheless, when the visiting gentlemen ask Mrs. Morgan for an accounting, she has the cost of the monsters on the tip of her tongue: "The maintenance of the monsters [costs] a hundred and twenty" (205) each year. Even as those at Millenium Hall contest tyranny in favor of harmonious community, the women themselves engage in establishing domain over the disabled.

The monsters of Millenium Hall are not unlike the exotic deformed, the emasculated eunuchs of the seraglio, who, in turn, resemble the women both in their failure to engage in reproductive sex and in being sublimely agreeable, even in their deformity. Deformity is often linked with race as well as femininity, since the category of the monstrous in the eighteenth century loosely refers to the many varieties of unfamiliar beings. Black eunuchs supervised the women of the harem while white eunuchs guarded the sovereign, blackness in this case thus being associated with domestic femininity and whiteness with political authority. Deformity and racialized slavery unite at the bottom of the masculine social scale in the black eunuchs who guard the women's chastity and protect them from intruders. Deformity is commodified: "The black Eunuchs, who are brought out of *Africa*, much inferiour in point of number, are, as I said, much the dearer. The most deformed yield the greatest price, their extream ugliness being look'd on as beauty in their kind."[51] (Lady Mary Wortley Montagu remarks on the "natural deformity" of North Africans, a connection that derives in part from the belief that pygmies were believed to be apes.) Eunuchs themselves were classified as feminized monstrosities, though agreeably so, in a manner reminiscent of the dark, terrifying desirability of the sublime: "Of the many Thousands, of the Male Sex, who are there as 'twere in Prison, and have a dependance, one upon the other, none but the Prince himself has the sight of Women; for the Negro-Eunuchs, whom their deformity of body and countenance has, in a manner, transform'd into Monsters, are not to be admitted into the number of men."[52] Oriental tales such as Beckford's *Vathek* are populated with every imaginable deformity from the deaf to the humpbacked.[53] Alexander Pope too drew the connection between the East and his own agreeable deformity as Lady Mary embarked to Turkey in October 1716: "I am capable myself of following one I lov'd, not only to Constantinople, but to those parts of India, where they tell us the Women best like the Ugliest fellows, as the most admirable productions of nature, and look upon Deformities as the Signatures of divine Favour."[54] He thus aligns his deformity with the desirable exotic deformities of the East.[55]

Like Pope, William Hay, a member of the House of Commons, stood barely five feet high and was humpbacked, and he provides a kind of gloss on Sarah Scott's inclusion of the disabled within the female community. To counter the marketplace display of the deformed, Hay's seldom-discussed autobiographical pamphlet *Deformity: An Essay* (1754), on an "uncommon Subject," claims a subjectivity based on frank discussion of his very noticeable handicap, and he conceptualizes disability as an identity for the first time. Following Longinus's *Treatise on the Sublime*, Hay wishes "to write of Deformity with Beauty" (13) to reverse its association with the devil. Hay refuses the position of victim and eschews the self-pity that Burke in his

Philosophical Enquiry assumed to be part of the definition of deformity. ("So if the back be humped, the man is deformed; because his back has an unusual figure, and what carries with it the idea of some disease or misfortune.")[56] Hay also believes that his oppression resembles racism, though by his account the plight of blacks is worse than that of the disabled: his constituents, he writes, "are not like a venal Borough, of which there goes a Story; that, though they never took Exceptions to any Man's Character, who came up to their Price; yet they once rejected the best Bidder, because he was a Negroe" (13).[57] A hierarchy of oppressions is emerging.

Clubs that segregate the handicapped—even well-meaning organizations such as the *Spectator's* "Ugly Club" or the "Short Club" (members of which included Isaac Newton and Christopher Wren) mentioned in Pope's letters to the *Guardian*, Nos. 91 and 92 (June 25 and 26, 1713) —make a theatrical spectacle of deformity in Hay's opinion: "When deformed Persons appear together, it doubles the Ridicule, because of the Similitude" (14). But just as the *Spectator* recommends,[58] Hay possesses an inveterate cheerfulness about his deformity. In order to demonstrate that deformed people do not lack natural affection, Hay testifies to his own sentimentality: "If by natural Affection is here meant universal Benevolence, and Deformity necessarily implies a want of it, a deformed Person must then be a complete Monster. But however common the Case may be, my own Sensations inform me, that it is not universally true" (41–42). He traces his social uneasiness to taunts endured as a child which he has endeavored to overcome: "This Difference of Behaviour towards me hath given me the strongest Idea of the Force of Education; and taught me to set a right Value upon it" (10). Taunting persists when he enters a crowd: "When by some uncommon Accident I have been drawn into a Country Friar, Cock-pit, Bear-garden, or the like riotous Assemblies, after I have got from them, I have felt the Pleasure of one escaped from the Danger of a Wreck" (11). In spite of the taunting, Hay persistently redefines disability as advantageous. Drawing perhaps an ironic inference, Hay suggests that his treatise has in common with Hogarth's *Analysis of Beauty* that beauty "consists in Curve Lines."[59] Hay interprets the curved lines of his hunched back as the essence of beauty, and disability as "a Protection to a Man's Health and Person; which (strange as it may appear) are better defended by Feebleness than Strength" (27–28). He believes that a weak frame paradoxically encourages a man to be frugal with his energy, thus preserving it for a longer time. In giving deformity a subjectivity, Hay domesticates the exotic without sentimentalizing it, redefines deformity as beauty, and seeks transformation in societal attitudes toward the disabled.

Deformity is not the opposite of beauty but the "absence of 'the *compleat, common form,*'" according to Edmund Burke, an observation particularly relevant to our discussion of women, since the more perfect is also the more masculine.[60] Hay's essay sheds light on the confounding confluence of female subjectivity and disability because women, the disabled, and non-Europeans are defined as lacking the complete, common form. The advantages of a fragile body, the transmutation of deformity into a thing of beauty, and the propensity to become the commodified object of public spectacle make the parallels acute. Scott's novel too, playing with the association between the women and their deformed charges, emphasizes these advantages. Harriot Trentham's beauty was marred by smallpox and Lady Mary Jones's face is disfigured, but all the women at Millenium Hall are "deformed" in the larger sense that none is involved with men in reproductive sex or consanguine motherhood, and they redefine beauty as a disadvantage. Miss Mancel's uncommon beauty made her the object of spectacle before she came to Millenium Hall, yet it threatened her economic survival because it prevented her from getting a position as a maid "since her beauty was the great obstacle to its being put in execution" (86). Beauty is an impediment and deformity is meritorious in the terms of *Millenium Hall*.

A decade before *Millenium Hall* appeared, Sarah Scott had translated *La Laideur Aimable; ou Les Dangers de la Beauté* (1752), by Pierre Antoine de la Place, as *Agreeable Ugliness* (1754). Because Scott herself suffered the disfiguring effects of smallpox at seventeen, she played the ugly duckling to her beautiful sister, Elizabeth Montagu. In the translation of *Agreeable Ugliness*, the younger sister, "Shocking Monster," is morally superior to her beautiful and vain sister and ultimately finds a satisfying marriage by submitting completely to her father's will. She accepts the less interesting Dorigny, her father's favorite, to protect her from her passionate love for St. Furcy; but after Dorigny suffers a fatal wound, Shocking Monster is free to marry her original choice.[61] Like *Millenium Hall, Agreeable Ugliness* touts the perils of beauty which lead to dangerous liaisons and unsuitable marriages and connects femininity to disability.

Sarah Scott too converts deformity to advantage—literally in the case of smallpox, but more forcefully with the "deformity" of not

marrying, of refusing motherhood, and of living with and loving
women. Unlike William Hay, women cannot overcome ugliness when
competing in the marriage marketplace. Scott insists on the pleasures
of deformity that women find outside reproductive sex in creating
their own definitions and imagined alternatives. It is a crucial moment
in history when women desiring women, women who do not wish to
marry or reproduce, the deformed, and the exotic forge affinities in the
novel in the name of resistance to their commodification in a mercantilist economy. Feminotopia newly envisages the connections between
the homoerotic and the disabled in its orientalized idealization and
defines female community as an autonomous women's empire.

Montagu redefines the little empire of the Turkish women's community as a place that resists sexual slavery through uncommon sexual
license. The harem and *Millenium Hall* resemble English domesticity
but each with important differences. In each case an enclosure paradoxically brings freedom from tyranny, one through imagined sexual
liberty, the other through economic freedom and mutual protection.
Scott redefines women's secluded community as a place of rational
harmony and the failure to marry as agreeable deformity. Each contests more traditional versions of experience. Each purports to educate
male observers to the view that women's communities are not deformities but sites of beauty or self-defined sociability encompassing a
range of sexualities from female libertinism to asexuality.

Montagu, Craven, and other women are complicit in imperialist
designs. Montagu colonizes by Othering, ignores slavery in the
harem, and masquerades as the Other to free her libido. And Scott
replicates class differences and engages in the benevolence that can be
exercised only through privilege. In each case the culture's devaluation
of women is reversed, and a step is taken toward producing a collective
"Woman," offering an advance in human understanding but also participating in the more coercive aspects of the Enlightenment. As the
first empire gives way to the second more intractable empire, we can, I
think, recognize the uneven and partial resistances to gendered tyranny and traditional domesticity in Montagu and Scott without reducing our condemnation of commodification, class privilege, and
colonialism. The invention of the "Other" woman of empire enabled
the consolidation of the cult of domesticity in England and, at the
same time, the association of the sexually transgressive woman at
home—the prostitute, the lesbian, the asexual being—with the Orientalized exotic woman. In the emerging national imperative to control

women's sexuality and maternity in particular ways, these texts provide resistances to that imperative by positing alternative pleasures.

V

A measured rejection of the patriarchal dominion over women in favor of a feminotopia, *Millenium Hall* substitutes benevolent confinement for colonization and enslavement at the time of the emergence of the Second Empire. In demonstrating women's economic self-sufficiency and an imagined alternative to marriage and maternity, the novel is an implicit critique of the status of Englishwomen and an argument for the benefits of female friendship. Millenium Hall furnishes female community, seclusion, and the protection of women's chastity and virtue. Beyond that, Millenium Hall radically engenders a collective body of the oppressed that is less vulnerable than any one individual.

At some level, utopia is inherently conservative in its impulse to restrict the future to a given horizon. *Millenium Hall* may be read as an addendum to the descriptions of the seraglio by women travellers, in that it shares the exotic attractiveness of the Eastern woman's situation, imitating it even in the attachment of dwarves and eunuchs to it. In fact, the privileged women at Millenium Hall gain subjectivity and freedom in part by defining themselves as superior to the poor and to the disabled who depend on them. The aestheticization of the exotic in Montagu and Craven, like the female community's coercion of the disabled to servitude, are benevolent but colonizing acts. Further, Montagu's and Craven's idealized visions are calibrated to their class loyalties, as are those of the women in *Millenium Hall*. These feminotopias, in refusing to acknowledge other oppressions, may in fact narrow the sphere of resistance. In short, such utopias are compromised by their very conceptualization. Does feminotopia, in spite of its radical intent, sometimes participate unwittingly in ignoring history and impeding change?[62] In seeking to end patriarchal domination, exploitation, and oppression, feminism creates utopian visions. But paradoxically, implicit within its visions may be the domination of those who do not conform to its principles, as well as those who do not have the economic means or cultural sway to enter its favored inner circle.

Millenium Hall, like Montagu's powerful impression of the Turkish women, is uneven in its critique, as any representation of utopia must be. In creating a female empire, it empowers women of a certain class and nation, and it radically associates a fifth oppression—disabil-

ity—with the more familiar quartet of race, class, gender, and sexuality. It thus participates in a qualitative break with the present, what
might be called "the politics of transfiguration," emphasizing "the
emergence of qualitatively new needs, social relations, and modes of
association, which burst open the utopian potential within the old."[63]
This articulation of an alternative to the existing, in spite of its limitations, makes further change possible. Its relation to deformities—
racial, sexual, or bodily—is a problem that Western feminism in particular needs to confront as it constructs its histories. There is, of
course, a need to be alert to the dangers of empowering the privileged
to make something pleasurable, even a feminotopia, of another's vul-
nerability; but the resistance enacted through the sexual desire of
women for each other, the agreeable ugliness that allows women to
avoid marriage and its economy, and the hidden beauties of bodily
deformity may be aligned across culture and history to build newly
configured forms of feminist collectivity, new kinds of feminotopias,
that will also counteract imperial tyranny.

FIGS. 6 AND 7. London's fixation on the unusual and the deformed in the early eighteenth century: a dwarf and a giant woman, respectively. Such "oddities" were frequently displayed as human wonders at fairs and exhibitions. "A Female Dwarf" and "A Woman Seven Foot High," BL Sloane MS. 5248, *A Short History of Human Prodigies and Monstrous Births, of Dwarfs, Sleepers, Giants, Strong Men, Hermaphrodites, Numerous Births, and Extream Old Age &c.* Compiled by James Paris du Plessis (c. 1733). Reproduced by permission of The British Library.

FIG. 8. A depiction of the interior of the women's quarters. Indian women, shielded from men's gaze inside the zananah, were often treated as invisible and unmentionable. "A View of the Inside of A Zananah." From William Hodges, *Travels in India During the Years 1780, 1781, & 1783* (London 1793). Courtesy of the Division of Rare and Manuscript Collections, Cornell University Library.

FIG. 9. A woman in the seraglio smoking a pipe. Western observers regarded the sumptuously dressed feminine figure using the hooka as masculine or androgynous. From Alexander Russell, *The Natural History of Aleppo* [1756] (London 1856). Courtesy of the Division of Rare and Manuscript Collections, Cornell University Library.

FIG. 10. The funeral procession. European men believed that the spectacle of sati, the Hindu practice of immolating widows on the pyre of the deceased husband, should be concealed from European women. "Procession of a Hindoo Woman to the Funeral Pile of her Husband." From William Hodges, *Travels in India During the Years 1780, 1781, & 1783* (London 1793). Courtesy of the Division of Rare and Manuscript Collections, Cornell University Library.

CHAPTER SEVEN

"An Affectionate and Voluntary Sacrifice"

Sati, Rape, and Marriage

Nor can you imagine a sight more extraordinary, than the contrast of the Gentoo complexion with their white dresses, or the advantage I am well aware it is to us Europeans, in general, to have them about us; for who does not know the alternate and striking effects of black and white?

Phebe Gibbes,
Hartly House, Calcutta (1789)

Though the effects of black be painful originally, we must not think they always continue so. Custom reconciles us to every thing. After we have been used to the sight of black objects, the terror abates, and the smoothness and glossiness or some agreeable accident of bodies so coloured, softens in some measure the horror and sternness of their original nature; yet the nature of the original impression still continues. Black will always have something melancholy in it.

Edmund Burke,
*A Philosophical Enquiry into the Origin of our Ideas
of the Sublime and Beautiful* (1757)

I

Feminotopias offer orientalist alternatives to Englishwomen's domesticity and become the basis for feminist arguments. Yet, as we have seen in texts as diverse as *Roxana,* Montagu's Turkish Embassy *Letters, Pamela, The Female Quixote,* and *Millenium Hall,* these feminist arguments may also be erected upon the hierarchies of race, class, sexuality, and disability. In several novels and travel narratives of India written in the later eighteenth century, the putative Other women of empire often avail Englishwomen of an expedient opportunity to critique their own status while asserting racial superiority. After Robert Clive's victory at the Battle of Plassey in 1757, the public controversy aroused by the parliamentary debates leading to the defeat of Fox's East India Bill may well have sparked increased interest in the fictional representation of India. The debates about India attempted to harness the growing mercantile power of the East India Company to the British government's interests and to make the government simultaneously less oppressive and more accountable. As trade with India for her cottons and indigo, her silks and saltpeter, increased, Bengal came under the auspices of the East India Company in 1773. The eighteenth century marked the sustained intrusion of English merchants into the subcontinent as the East India Company gained a monopoly and its centralized power replaced the weakening Indian feudal structure.[1]

Opinion about the relationship of the company's capacity to be successful as both merchant and sovereign in India was divided. Edmund Burke led the movement to curb the very institution he had glorified during the 1770s but found disturbing in the 1780s as the East India Company evolved into an independent imperial power. Acting in its own self-interest, the company engaged in liquidation of Indian artisans, established free trade for itself while levying duties on Indian merchants, and interfered with the growing economic base in India. Burke's response rather naively urged Britain to continue benevolently to protect the autonomous and smoothly functioning Indian society as if the Crown's protective power did not brandish an interest that would inevitably conflict with that of the Indian government and people.[2] William Pitt the Younger's India Bill in 1784 established the East India Company as the ruling agency in India but maintained the Crown's regulation of it through the Board of Control in England.

Further, the impeachment trials of Warren Hastings (1786–94), the governor general of Bengal, fastened British public interest on the subcontinent after the loss of the American colonies and on the eve of the French Revolution. The trials, as Sara Suleri has recently shown, attempted to isolate colonial guilt and the rapacity of the East India Company in the person of Hastings.[3] England's contradictory intentions at this early stage of colonialism were to conserve India's autonomy and preserve its traditions but also to plumb its treasures and influence its trading policies. As the numbers of Englishmen increased, there emerged "a double current of increasing contact and knowledge of Indian life, and of increasing contempt of everything Indian as irrational, superstitious, barbaric, and typical of an inferior civilization."[4] Idealization of things Indian was coupled with an emergent British nationalism.

In 1784 the orientalist Sir William Jones founded the Asiatic Society of Bengal, but missionaries were not allowed in India until 1813.

The orientalist literary texts and travel narratives of the later eighteenth century are less concerned with salvation of the indigenous population than with celebrating ostensibly universal characteristics and, following the *philosophes*, seeking in the non-European world Enlightenment beliefs in the basic equality and rationality possessed by all humanity.[5] Claims to universality mask the Europeans' attitude of superiority to Indians, which is oddly combined with an adulation for Hindu spirituality and a fascination with the transmigration of the soul. These contradictions and others are apparent in a spate of novels set in India that were published in the last two decades of the eighteenth century, including *The Indian Adventurer; or, The History of Mr. Vanneck* (1780), Helenus Scott's *Adventures of a Rupee Wherein Are Interspersed Various Anecdotes Asiatic and European* (1782), *Rajah Kisna* (1786), Phebe Gibbes's *Hartly House, Calcutta* (1789), and a play, *The Widow of Malabar* (1791), based on Antoine Lemierre's *La Veuve du Malabar* (1770).[6] As women travelled to the burgeoning English community in India, the novels set in the East began to interweave the themes of sexuality and the empire of love. Colonialist accounts in the earliest stages in India reflect the conflicts of an ideology in formation.

Because India afforded a fertile place for British opportunists to become rich, free of the trading levies extracted from Indian merchants, ironically a caste-driven country enabled the English to violate their own class hierarchies by becoming nabobs. These nabobs, upon their return to England, often presented themselves as vulgarized aristocracy or rose to unaccustomed power, sometimes (like Clive) purchasing seats in Parliament.[7] Among the most interesting of the later eighteenth-century novels is *The Indian Adventurer*, which portrays the connections between masculine authority and empire in the person of a European hero who claims to protect India through rescuing Eastern women from indigenous male tyranny.[8] Curiously, the Indian adventurer of the title, Mr. Vanneck, purchases female slaves as presents for English and French ladies. The tyrannical nabob (here actually the native *nawab*), the Indian adventurer reports, captures hundreds of native girls for his seraglio, enslaves old women, and makes mothers witness the prostitution of their daughters. The adventurer presents himself as the nawab's moral superior in his releasing the women from the nawab's power and in rescuing a woman of considerable fortune from *sati*, the Hindu custom outlawed by the British in 1829 that involved a high-caste widow's throwing herself on her husband's funeral pyre.[9] When it becomes apparent that the rich widow is not sufficiently grateful to share her wealth with her Western deliverer, they part, and the adventurer's motivation for interference in Indian cultural practices becomes even more suspect.

The Indian adventurer's supposed "rescues" take on a decidedly commercial air. He joins a surgeon in the East India Company's service who keeps a seraglio himself: "In many of these excursions, he took me along with him, and it was our constant practice to pick up as many black women as we could find, whom we took home in our carriages to our lodgings" (143).[10] Later, he conducts an intrigue with "one of the most agreeable women I had ever seen in the East-Indies" (162), whom he labels as superior to Englishwomen. This woman woos him with 150 gold rupees and two diamond rings, and he gloats over this conquest and others: "I was never so happy while in the East Indies, as when in the company with the fair sex, who were always very obliging to me" (221). Remarkable because they possess inordinate wealth, the exotic Indian women are depicted as excessively sexual. The Indian adventurer excuses his sexual and economic exploitation of Indian women because of his cultural superiority, and the novel ends, predictably enough, when he becomes infatuated with a proper European lady, a Frenchwoman of English parentage.

Indian women are not granted subjectivity in this novel; instead, they are represented by others as victimized or erotic, and as greedy and vain. Claiming to save the women involved, the Western man in fact exercises gender, class, and national privilege over them. The difficulty, as Lata Mani has pointed out in another context, is that a discourse such as the Indian adventurer's, like official discourses about India, "forecloses any possibility of [Indian] women's agency, thus providing justification for 'civilizing' colonial interventions."[11] The novel exemplifies England's national policy of providing benevolent protection while extricating India's wealth through its women. Conserving its traditions in the person of the Indian woman who is silenced, the object of desire no matter what her class or caste is ultimately rejected in favor of marriage with Europeans. A retreat into a domestic union with the European woman inevitably follows colonialist men's sexual philandering in the East.

Elizabeth Hamilton, sister to the Asiatic scholar Charles Hamilton, employs the vehicle of a man's voice in *Translation of the Letters of a Hindoo Rajah; written previous to, and during the Period of his Residence in England* . . . in the person of a rajah who criticizes Englishwomen rather than the women of India.[12] The satirical travel novel, dedicated to Warren Hastings, consists of a series of letters between Zaarmilla, Rajah of Almora, and Kisheen Neeay Maandaara, Zimeendar of Cumlor. It resembles a study by Hamilton's brother, *An Historical Relation of the Origin, Progress, and Final Dissolution of the Government of the Rohilla Afghans* (1787), and follows a genre usually reserved for men. Both texts surreptitiously defend British colonial interests in India.[13] As an Oriental visiting England, the rajah remarks on the curiosities he encounters, especially the Western women who compromise their delicacy as they display their accomplishments, so that they never "shine, without exciting the alternate emotions of admiration and disgust" (1:73). A misogynist and satirist, the rajah mocks the *philosophe*'s notion of a universal humanity, especially the assumption that conspicuous women could be rational beings and free agents whose souls are equal to men's. Contrasting the uncertain fate of Hindu women after death (in spite of having sacrificed themselves on the funeral pyre of their husbands) to that of Christian women, who are granted entrance into heaven without relying on their husband's permission, he accuses Englishwomen of being ungrateful for their comparative privilege. The rajah character draws the reader's contempt because he is unconscionably unfair to all women, and the novel lodges his criticism against corrupt Christian womanhood without positing Indian women, Hinduism, or sati as sanctioned alternatives. In short, no woman, Eastern or Western, is truly the equal of man.

The point of the correspondence between the two Indian observers of the Englishwoman in *The Letters of a Hindoo Rajah* is to demonstrate, though perhaps with tongue in cheek, that current English education creates uppity learned ladies whose modesty and virtue are inferior to those of the Indian woman. Elizabeth Hamilton's *Memoirs of Modern Philosophers* (1800) had mocked the excesses of feminist philosophers such as Wollstonecraft and Mary Hays.[14] A constant theme discussed between the correspondents in *The Letters of a Hindoo Rajah* is the extraordinary vanity of European Christian women and the waste of educating them. Maandaara writes: "Allowing it possible (which I am very far from allowing) that these creatures, whose sole delight is finery, who were born to amuse, to please, and to continue the race of men, should be capable of entering the sacred porch which leads to the temple of knowledge . . . they would clothe themselves with the robes of arrogance, and rest dauntless upon the hollow reed of self-conceit" (1:50). Pointedly satirized as well is an

Englishwoman's being allowed to manage her husband's estate after his death instead of, like an Indian woman, dying with him (61). When Maandaara mocks a group of "Bibbys," or "superannuated dancing girls" (151), as loquacious and immodest, he expresses amazement to discover that they are in fact English married ladies. Similarly, the women shoppers the rajah describes display brazen "masculine" assurance as "they venture into the walks of men, their fearless eye undaunted [meeting] the glances of every beholder" (2:43).

Englishwomen abroad scandalize the Indian men, who demonstrate "moral recoil" at their forwardness in India. According to contemporary accounts, these women

> had no objection to the hookah, and occasionally smoked it themselves; they freely attended and enjoyed nautches; they adopted the fashion of the turban and carried it to London. . . . It is one of the misfortunes of the history of racial relations in India that as soon as Mussulman society began to rid itself of its traditional feelings about the unveiled woman, European society imported a fresh stock of prejudices about the veiled woman of the purdah, the joint product of the evangelical missionary and of new-born racial pride.[15]

The Indian woman, in contrast, though only vaguely present in Hamilton's novel, demurely averts her eyes, seldom ventures into public places, remains contentedly illiterate, speaks without arrogance or conceit, and accepts that her place in Paradise rests upon her husband's virtue.

The Eastern man is employed here to mock the Englishwoman rather than to admire her, but Elizabeth Hamilton's goal in conducting the cultural comparison may be both to satirize women's public display of fashion and irrationality as well as to suggest the ultimate inadequacy of the Indian woman as a substitute. *All* women are the object of satire in *The Letters of a Hindoo Rajah,* and the international observer, though extreme in his criticisms, registers complaints familiar from misogynist satire, as a convincing commentator on English femininity. This novel could be interpreted as an attempt to produce an idea of woman that transcends the boundaries of colonized and colonizer, but Hamilton's narrative berates women of both nations instead of exploring the radical potential for uniting their cause. The contradictions of desire and contempt interfere with any imagined world community of women.

A more lively and polished novel than *The Indian Adventurer* or

The Letters of a Hindoo Rajah in discerning relations between English-women and Indian women is *Hartly House, Calcutta* (1789), alleg-edly written by Sophia Goldsborne but actually the work of Phebe Gibbes.[16] Though the novel was published in 1789, its references to the coronation of George III and to Warren Hastings' departure from India on February 3, 1785, indicate that it was probably written some-what earlier.[17] A series of thirty-nine letters from Sophia Goldsborne in India to her friend Arabella in England, the novel takes some pains to insist that it does not adopt the terms of the exotic, though that intent is repeatedly compromised. Sophia professes that she travels to India in order to comfort her father, *not* to see the Orient or to marry, though soon after arriving in India she declares that her vow to avoid becoming a "nabobess" was rash. When she descends from the incom-ing ship to the barges of Calcutta, she contradictorily asserts that she is leaving the European world and becoming *"orientalised* at all points" (10), a term that comes to mean languishing in the rich, decorative strain of fashion, architecture, and colonial social life that India offers. *Hartly House* is in part a light satire against the vain Sophia, and thus an attack on the frivolity of an Englishwoman abroad. Yet her Indian adventure also inspires her with an independence that she must even-tually relinquish to the inevitable tediousness of English domesticity as she plays out her sexual hybridity against the colonized Other.

The central metaphor of the book, Hartly Mansion, evokes the sublime in its strikingly handsome and elaborately decorated building surrounded by balconies and verandas. Sophia paints India in grand and spectacular terms: "On so vast a scale, indeed, are all things in this country, both human and divine, that if any earth-born creature could be pardoned the sin of ambition, it would be the Asiatics" (47). Here, India's exquisite beauty silences the Englishwoman; its "inconceivable grandeur" renders Sophia speechless and has "a striking effect on an European beholder" (18). Although the Eastern splendor also ener-vates the European, it serves as welcome distraction from the unbear-able heat: "Too true it is, that the best pleasure of the East is, being a kind of state-prisoner, enfeebled and fettered by vertical suns, and the fatigue of veiling our distresses from vulgar optics, by gaudy trappings and the pomp of retinue" (20). Though Sophia admits to longing for St. James's Park, she mocks her own desire for England and happily succumbs to the lucre and luxury she associates with India: "I repro-bate all I have written.—My father has this instant filled my purse with gold mohrs value forty shillings, or sixteen rupees each; has purchased me a palanquin . . . and my mind is restored to the pinnacle of grandeur, from which it had so meanly fallen" (20–21). The sloth of the English in India was infamous, and Sophia is, it seems, completely corruptible as India functions as the agent of her seduction into the mercantilism, commercialism, and luxury of the nascent empire. The Englishwoman in India is constructed as a consumer, but in *Hartly House* she is also a sexualized commodity being prepared for consumption in marriage back home. The dynamics of reflection and self-consumption are at work here, as the Englishwoman becomes the cipher through which the novel both justifies and critiques colonial rapine.

Cultural differences between the occupying English and the indigenous Indians are represented as blatantly evident in *Hartly House*. The English had little social exchange with Indians as equals. In a study of the period, Percival Spear writes that the men the English merchants saw "were either agents like the dubashes of Madras or the banians and shroffs of Calcutta, servants and slaves, or superiors like an occasional Moghul governor who might visit the factory."[18] More subtle were the cultural differences between English communities at home and abroad. Even as late as 1809, there were three Englishmen for every Englishwoman in India.[19] As a consequence, rules of courtship strayed dangerously from those in the homeland, threatening the virtuous European women who were the scarce merchandise to be avidly pursued from the moment of their arrival in the torrid zone. In Gibbes's novel, men swarm to Hartly House to visit Sophia, and the courting culture allows the men to linger for the entire day. In India, unlike England, Englishwomen are less segregated and more fully interspersed among the men, some even engaging in trade: "The sexes are blended (I will not say in parts, for the men are out of all proportion to the female world) so as to aid the purposes of gallantry and good humour" (35).

Equally foreign to Sophia is the fact that marriage among the English in India does not foreclose opportunities for men's attention, since married women continue to pursue the public activities of riding, theater, and shopping in a sexually integrated colonial society: "You do not forfeit your claims to homage or adoration, on becoming a wife; whence slander is often busy" (55). In fact, the English community in India is an animated marriage market where the favorable ratio of men to women means that "we [Englishwomen] of Calcutta live only to be adored, and . . . our gentlemen ask no higher happiness than permission to pay us their unending adoration." Sophia happily occupies herself in India in the coquetry of gathering the homage bestowed on her as the loveliest of Englishwomen residing there. Her cultural authority reigns supreme from the first as she looks down on India while hoisted on the shoulders of men carrying her palanquin: "I am called by the natives, Belate Be Bee—the English lady; for, however, low rated in England, I am a sovereign princess here; and, was I so inclined, could wring the hearts of my dependents" (241). India offers Englishwomen unexpected power in the public marketplace, the *agora*, in contrast to England's more private protected retreat, and the freedom to experiment with sexual conduct forbidden to the modest woman at home.

The entire colonial world—from the admiring entourage of Englishmen to the Brahmin and the nabob—serves as a mirror enhancing the coquette's beauty. Sophia writes to her correspondent Arabella that she has no need for actual mirrors in Calcutta because "your looks are reflected in the pleasure of the beholder, and your claims to first-rate distinction confessed by all who approach you" (36). The voyage abroad justifies itself because travelling women constantly become the specular object: "It would be well worth any vain woman's while, who has a tolerable person, to make the voyage I have done, in order to enjoy unbounded homage" (10). India nurtures the Englishwoman's illegitimate display and validates it: "Flattery at Calcutta is, literally speaking, our daily bread" (71).

Though the narrator Sophia emphasizes the difference between pursuing coquetry at home and abroad, her success rests at least partially on her assumption of unspoken superiority to the indigenous women. The Englishwoman shines with a brilliance that evolves from the narcissistic reflection of the Indian woman and absorbs her light. If in England "a woman's noblest station is retreat" (the familiar line from Pope's "Epistle to a Lady" that Sophia cites) and the modest woman is forbidden to dazzle, the Englishwoman in India usurps the masculine role to become both the image itself as well as its reflection, the sun as well as the moon. Her spectacular radiance diminishes the Indian woman and deflects the gaze, the instrument of colonizing attention, from her. The Englishwoman abroad escapes the charges of prostitution that condemn characters such as the romantic Arabella in *The Female Quixote* because her behavior conforms with the British community's standards in India. Further, her presence implicitly helps prevent British officers' intermarriage with Indian women ("for the young ones . . . chuse country-born ladies for wealth") and ensures a pure national and racial line.

While national boundaries are explicitly drawn, the blurring of gender boundaries is a commonplace among English observers in eighteenth-century India. For William Hodges, among others, the entire Indian nation was gendered female. Hodges (who also accompanied Captain Cook on his voyages) describes his first impression of India upon arrival as a nation teeming with women and feminized men.[20] His *Travels in India During the Years 1780, 1781, 1782, & 1783* (London, 1793) evocatively details a sensation of a noisy femininity at the port of Madras that divides India from the West:

> Some time before the ship arrives at her anchoring ground, she is hailed by the boats of the country filled with people of business, who come in crowds on board. This is the moment in which an European feels the great distinction between Asia and his own country. The rustling of fine linen, and the general hum of unusual conversation, present to his mind for a moment the idea of an assembly of females. When he ascends upon the deck, he is struck with the long muslin dresses, and black faces adorned with very large gold ear-rings and white turbans. . . . besides this, the European is struck at first with many other objects, such as women carried on men's shoulders on pallankeens, and men riding on horseback clothed in linen dresses like women: which, united with the very different face of the country from all he had ever seen or conceived of, excite the strongest emotions of surprise! (2–4)

Hodges's pose of impartiality in figuring the Indian people's "spectacular strangeness" and his enthusiastic surprise produces an exotic surface that ignores historical or cultural complexities. What at first seems to be his judgment of the entire country as feminized becomes at second glance a reversal of gender expectations—men who appear to be dressed as women, yet who ride astride, and women who are carried on men's shoulders.[21] Robed, turbaned men seem to impersonate the secluded Indian women. Indian men are the feminized binary against which Englishwomen can experiment with unorthodox femininity.

India also affords a place for the proper Englishwoman to embody the sexual hybridity that would threaten masculinity at home, and the manners of the English ladies in Calcutta manifest outrageous contradiction. Sweetly sympathetic with strangers, they are also fearless: "A scarlet riding dress, which gives them most the appearance of the other sex, enraptures them—and, to drive a phaeton and pair with a vivacity . . . to mark their skill and unconcern, in the midst of numberless spectators, is their delight" (68–69). The phaetons are "in the high style of Eastern etiquette," an imitation of the Orient that combines the two cultures: "The phaetons are English built, and ornamented with all the taste that country can boast, and all the expence the Asiatics are forward to incur, for their exterior importance . . . and, to finish the whole, a kittesaw [a parasol] is suspended, nor unfrequently over the lady's head—which gives her the true Eastern grandeur of appearance" (69–70). The phaetons unite tasteful English construction with the ostentatious display of wealth, the gaudy mimicry of English fashion, attributed to the Asiatics. India elaborates upon and exceeds the "proper" display of wealth.

Hartly House connects *all* women's opulent adornment to the commercial trade in jewels and rich minerals that the two nations share, "for, except, in the article of mourning . . . there is little difference between the appearance of a fine lady at Bengal, and a fine lady in London—for fine ladies in London have found out the elegance of enwrapping themselves in shawls; and those treasures of the mine, and of the ocean, diamonds and pearls, are well known in England, though not in such profusion" (155). To draw the analogy between English and Indian women, whose bodies visibly display the world's wealth, disregards the unequal balance of power between the colonized and the colonizer. Commerce plays in and through women's dress and body in *Hartly House*, but because of asymmetrical relations between women, it also erases the relations of emergent imperial dominance.

Yet *Hartly House* also struggles to sustain the crucial difference between Englishwoman and Indian. Often likened to a charnel house because of its paralyzing and stultifying climate, India was assumed to be especially lethal to delicate Englishwomen.[22] Sophia succumbs briefly to the disease-producing Indian torrid zone and its hot winds. The colony also gives license for Englishwomen to be more overtly sexual in their behavior than at home; and the Indian women, both Hindu and Muslim, except for the lowest castes and the dancing "nautch-girls," are depicted as confined to the *zanannah* (the portion of the house reserved exclusively for women) or the private company of women (see Fig. 8, "A View of the Inside of a Zananah"). Sophia's quiet confidence in her national and cultural superiority ensures that Indian women provide no real competition. A contemporary visitor, Jemima Kindersley, reported in the 1770s:

The *Hindoo* women we can know little of, as none but the very lowest
are visible: they are almost in their infancy married by the care of their
parents to some of their own *cast*. Every *Hindoo* is obliged to marry
once: and polygamy is allowed, but there is generally one wife who is
held as superior to the rest. The women have no education given
them, they live retired in the *zanannahs,* and amuse themselves with
each other, smoking the hooker, bathing, and seeing their servants
dance.[23]

Kindersley's impression of the zanannah she visits is of a stratified
female community held in tedious confinement and attended by eunuchs. To retire into the zanannah is to become not only invisible but
nonexistent, for "a Mahomedan never speaks of his wives; and it is
thought a very great affront and indelicacy to enquire after them."[24]
For Sophia, however, the zanannah is mystified and romanticized, and
she imagines scandal brewing among the women, just as William
Hodges had speculated: "I cannot but here observe that, from the
close confinement of the Mahomedan women, there reigns in the
zananahs a refined spirit of intrigue unknown in Europe in the present
day" (22). She believes that women's segregation into the zanannahs
cannot be attributed to religion or to men's sexual jealousy so much as
to the cultural stigma against women's becoming a spectacle, as is
apparent in the extreme contrast between this description of the secluded zanannah and her depiction of India as a mirror for the Englishwoman's beauty.

Sophia makes an Indian woman, Miss Rolle, the object of *her*
gaze, "a *country-born* young lady" whom she finds smoking the hoo-
kah, just as Lady Mary Wortley Montagu and Elizabeth Craven acted
as voyeurs in longing to paint an aesthetically satisfying picture of
Turkish harem women (see Fig. 9). She perceives Miss Rolle's exquisite beauty coupled with an exquisite aroma as transforming the
woman's smoking into something genteel and feminine yet still inferior to English femininity: "But let me caution you against every
plebeian idea on the occasion, for that pipe was a most superb *hooka,*
the bell filled with rosewater; and instead of odious tobacco, a prepara-
tion of the betel-root, rolled up, and wetted, was placed in the bole,
which bole was beautiful china-ware, covered with a filligree silver
cap" (16). She continues, "In a word I wished to have taken her portrait on the spot, for her form is elegant, her complexion near the
European standard, and the novelty of her attitude such, as rendered
them altogether an admirable subject for the pencil" (17). Miss Rolle

transgresses recognizable gender boundaries, yet is feminized even when engaging in a traditionally masculine activity. Treating her as a European woman *manqué* and longing for her to be captured on canvas, Sophia both colonizes and regulates the Indian woman even as she admires her sexual hybridity.

Sophia's relationship with Miss Rolle is compromised by the pleasure Sophia takes in being seen to comparative advantage in public, apparently without irony, against Miss Rolle's perceived blackness. In the Calcutta theater Sophia describes Indian women as outshining the English: "Several country-born ladies figured away in the boxes, and by candle-light had absolutely the advantage of the Europeans; for their dark complexions and sparkling eyes gave them the appearance of animation and health the Europeans had no pretensions to; and their persons are genteel, and their dress magnificent" (204). But her pleasure in watching them, and in setting the women in juxtaposition to the Europeans, is spurred by her feeling that they serve as the deeply satisfying aesthetic contrast to the fair Europeans: "Nor can you imagine a sight more extraordinary, than the contrast of the Gentoo complexion with their white dresses, or the advantage I am well aware it is to us Europeans, in general, to have them about us; for who does not know the alternate and striking effects of black and white?" (196).[25] The Indian woman in these accounts is barely visible, but when glimpsed, she emerges as an aesthetic foil to the Englishwoman, as the prisoner of femininity who contrasts to the Englishwoman's bolder public presence, or as the man-woman exotic who threatens to taint the purity of the Englishwoman abroad. Through color and gender *Hartly House* plays out the contradictions of a still somewhat malleable imperial policy in its uneasy balance between the Englishwoman and the Indian woman, both imagined as consumable treasures who embody the empire's luxury, who focus its libidinal energies, and who expose its hierarchies.

II

India's commercial community furnished an open marriage market highly favorable to European women, and its system, ostensibly based on mutual affection, contrasts vividly to the limitations that arranged marriages created for Indian women. In the novel Sophia's friend and mentor Mrs. Hartly, having lived in India from an early age, blends the two cultures by believing fully in the efficacy of *arranged* marriages, though Sophia protests the power of romantic love: "I am, nevertheless, unconvinced and unconverted," for "love, I can assure you, is not so spontaneous an effect (in general) of a friendship between the sexes in India as in England; the object of admiration begins with mental charms which bid defiance to decay" (71). Rejecting suitors in India, in reality Sophia nevertheless acknowledges that she is not deeply in love with her father's ultimate choice for her husband, "the little winning Doyly" (255), whose very name is reminiscent of domestic ornament. In effect, her marriage to Edmund Doyly, an ordinary man without means who hopes that India will make his fortune, would imitate an arranged one. Sophia's prospective passionless marriage of duty aligns her with Indian women and their arranged marriages, but it also elevates her to *choose* an arranged marriage after courting the admiration of many.

When Doyly temporarily fades from the plot, Sophia flirts with a close attachment to a Brahmin who "shakes his head at the gay life I lead" (166). The Brahmin, never given a name, remains a generic representative of high-caste otherness. But because *Hartly House* defines his life as one of voluntary celibacy and withdrawal from social pleasures, he is never a serious contender for her hand. Reflecting Enlightenment free-thinking in preferring Hinduism to Christianity, she becomes enamored of the Hindu religion and its practitioners. Enchanted by the kindness and benevolence of Hindus as well as their cleanliness, and the contrast of India's ascetic life to snuff-taking England, Sophia accepts the Hindu belief in the transmigration of souls. "A convert to the Gentoo faith," she wishes for her "Bramin to instruct me *per diem*" (191). She strives to achieve the highest spiritual quality, "little inferior to the purity and the benignity of angels:—in a word, my good dispositions would be cultivated and brought forward by such an acquaintance, and my bad ones corrected; and, as celibacy is their engagement, the soul would be the only object of attachment and admiration" (89). Sophia's infatuation is a remarkable flirtation with racial alignments that become scandalized during the later, more deeply entrenched empire. In the eighteenth century the expressed need to protect Englishwomen from Indian men because of potential rape is only subtly hinted at; in the late nineteenth and twentieth centuries the rape of Englishwomen by Indians comes powerfully to stand in place of Britain's rape of empire.[26]

Sophia's affection for the exotic interferes with her attention to the dull Englishman Doyly. When the Brahmin conveniently sickens and dies, Sophia oozes sentimentality over his death. She begs a lock of his hair for a talisman and imagines erecting a pagoda to his memory in Britain: "I am plunged into the utmost concern; my amiable Bramin ... died last night. ... he was all that heaven has even condescended to make human nature—and I will raise a pagoda to his memory in my heart, that shall endure till that heart beats no more" (235–36). Instead of marrying the Brahmin, an unthinkable act, Sophia empowers herself in attaching his most desirable characteristics onto Doyly, who is described as "so pastoral and his sensibility so oriental" that he would remain monogamous even if he were to become a Muslim. Domesticity passes through colonialism in order to justify Sophia's self-abnegation in marrying Doyly. In England Doyly will impersonate the Brahmin, since she will teach him gentleness and transform him into an Indian man of sentiment à la Sterne.

In this novel India teaches the Englishwoman that by becoming convinced of her seductive power, she will learn to submit to domestic silencing at home: "Now am I convinced of the power of my charms, and shall want no farther support in my own good opinion for ever" (251). India is the site of the Englishwoman's rebellion against those strictures, of her free space in anticipation of later imprisonment in the more quiescent domesticity to which she will resign herself in England. The talisman of the Brahmin's hair inspires comically exaggerated tranquility as she anticipates a life of marital boredom: "I am content to leave Calcutta, without occasioning one scene of blood and slaughter in my name, under the spreading branches of the trees of destruction ... in contest for the honour of my hand; and am preparing myself (with my own consent) to domesticate in Britain, to the very confines of oblivion—which is carrying the virtue of humility to a most unprecedented height, in a damsel of my complexion and turn of sentiment" (259). The Brahmin's death clears Sophia's mind of exotic spiritual notions, and her loyalty to him need not compete with her relationship to Doyly in resolving the plot. In India, Sophia negotiates the terms of her approaching domestic silencing to become the invisible in England, just as she has rendered Indian women invisible in India.

Armed with new moral and spiritual authority, and a sense of sexual power unattainable at home, Sophia transports them to England. As she translates India to England, transporting the raptures of Calcutta bowers to her English garden, she descends to a more traditional femininity. In the terms of the novel, India alters her irremediably. She comes to embody the domestic woman crucial to the formation of England's national identity and its empire. An unwitting agent of imperialism, she brings India's "raw products" to be consumed at home. Rather than becoming the female individualist that some critics have seen forming among Western women at the expense of other women, Sophia retreats from feminism and independence into domesticity.

Sophia, of course, does not throw herself on the pyre of the Brahmin's grave, but she intimates that her decision to marry Doyly and to submerge herself in the private domesticity of England is not unlike sati: "And of this number are those wives who, with a degree of heroism, that, if properly directed, would do honour to the female world, make an affectionate and voluntary sacrifice of themselves upon the funeral pile of their departed husbands:—it is true, there have been instances of their shewing reluctance but those instances seldom occur" (175–76). In short, the Englishwoman's mission in India is to reconcile herself to the misery of being the domestic Mrs. Doyly in imitation of the sacrifice of the prototypical Indian woman. In fact, the comparison of sati to marriage with an uninteresting man may have been an eighteenth-century commonplace.[27] Clearly, Sophia's mission is not to rescue Indian women from their fate but to learn to respond to her own marriage with resignation and submission. The silence of the Indian woman in *Hartly House* is not so much the occasion for feminism as it is for justifying feminine sacrifice at the altar of marriage, and the power Sophia wields in India is only a very temporary sexual power that is then mobilized to enact imperialism's agenda, including her own domestic submission, in England.[28] Sophia's flirtation resembles England's pretense to an equal and harmonious union with India rather than dominance over it, an idealist hope that quickly fades as the contradictions of a nascent colonialism harden into the demands of empire.

III

In the same year that Phebe Gibbes's *Hartly House* was published, 1789, the first official discussion about colonial policy on sati ensued when M. H. Brooke, collector of the Shahabad District, interfered with an instance of widow-burning and requested an official ruling on its legality from the governor general. The response to Brooke's inquiry reasoned that preventing sati would exacerbate its occurrence: "The public prohibition of a ceremony authorized by the tenets of the religion of the Hindoos, and from the observance of which they have never yet been restricted by the ruling power would in all probability tend to increase rather than diminish their veneration for it."[29] This pronouncement began the linking of colonial policy to a purported respect for religious tradition and a policy of noninterference, though apparently the Hindu scriptures actually idealize ascetic widowhood rather than promulgate widow sacrifice. The ideological work of sati in the eighteenth century as it is manipulated by the British is not identical to its work in later periods, and historicizing the practice at its first confrontation with British attitudes helps combat a timeless notion of sati.[30]

William Hodges, the early illustrator of India, was moved to the heights of incredulity and curiosity as a spectator of sati in his *Travels*. (See Fig. 10, "Procession of a Hindoo Woman.") Hodges dwells on the incongruity presented by "the most mild and gentle of the human race," the Hindus, engaging in what he believed to be an abhorrent and unnatural practice. Introducing his own description of sati with another from J. Z. Holwell's account of India, he asserts that the original widow-sacrifice began with Brahma's wives, who were in turn enthusiastically imitated by the wives of the chief rajahs, "being unwilling to have it thought that they were deficient in fidelity and affection."[31] In this analysis sati represents an act of female competition and of women's theatrical display of piety. By recounting Holwell's narrative, Hodges ascribes religious authority to sati and, like Sophia in *Hartly House*, assumes women's willing participation in the "voluntary act of glory, piety, and fortitude" (Hodges, 81). Holwell's example from 1742–43, however, accuses a seventeen-year-old widow of ignoring the needs of her three young children by insisting on self-immolation. Portrayed as a neglectful, even narcissistic mother, the widow willfully demonstrates her determination: "She, with a calm and resolved countenance, put her finger into the fire, and held it there a considerable time; she then with one hand put fire in the palm of the other, sprinkled incense on it, and fumigated the Bramins" (Hodges, 81). Her *"voluntary sacrifice"* is made to signify her unmotherly nature and her wish to outshine other women as much to display her religiosity or devotion to her husband's memory. Holwell's account and the mythological religious history of Brahma's wives preface Hodges' witnessing an "authentic" incident of sati that demonstrates that the widow is complicit in her own death. Sati figures here as religious enthusiasm perpetrated by fanatical women who seek posthumous fame: "That the *Bramins* take unwearied pains to encourage, promote,

and confirm in the minds of the *Gentoo* wives, *this spirit of burning*, is
certain" (Holwell, pt. 2, 89). Holwell believes that sati results from
girls' early education to the conviction that burning will ennoble the
memory of the widow and enable her children to move higher in the
caste system through marriage.

In offering his own eyewitness account, Hodges aligns sati with an
upper-class theatrical display. But the incident he reports describes the
merchant class, and he puzzles over (but does not finally explain) the
occurrence of sati within that social stratum. Those Indians who as-
semble to watch are, like the young widow of Holwell's account,
unmoved by the prospect of suffering they witness, "destitute of feeling at the catastrophe that was to take place; I may even say that they
displayed the most perfect apathy and indifference" (82). Like the
gathered crowd, the widow about to engage in sati also apparently
reveals no emotion, so that the Asians' disengagement is fully distinguished from the emotion of the European observer. Hodges' description differs from Holwell's because it is narrated from the position of
the spectator, but in both cases described by British travellers, the
fearless widow (like Aphra Behn's African prince Oroonoko, who is
stoic while being mutilated) is portrayed as heroically unperturbed by
the approaching specter of pain and death:

> The procession was slow and solemn; the victim moved with a steady
> and firm step; and, apparently with a perfect composure of counte-
> nance, approached close to the body of her husband, where for some
> time they halted. She then addressed those who were near her with
> composure, and without the least trepidation of voice or change of
> countenance. She held in her left hand a cocoa nut, in which was a red
> colour mixed up, and dipping in it the fore-finger of her right hand
> she marked those near her, to whom she wished to shew the last act of
> attention. As at this time I stood close to her, she observed me atten-
> tively, and with the colour, marked me on the forehead. (Hodges, 82)

This moment of the Other woman's marking the Englishman is a
telling one, for Hodges is threatened with becoming indistinguishable
from the Indian crowd, or at least being engaged as a sympathetic
observer. The red stain, a reminder of the widow's lifeblood and a sign
of her Otherness, is a residue that threatens to incorporate him within
the Indian practice. But at this point Hodges immediately breaks off
the narrative to insult the widow's faded beauty, ascribing her willingness to die at twenty-five to her lessened value on the marriage market,

and stripping her gesture of any potential to make him complicit within it.

His European distance safely reestablished, Hodges resumes his narration at a funereal pace to pause over each visual detail—the dried branches and leaves, the taking of the body to the pile to be burned, the Brahmins' raising a prayer, and the widow's conversations with friends and relatives. Finally, she is a silent subject who willfully approaches the grave with full composure:

> This last part of the ceremony was accompanied with the shouts of the multitude, who now became numerous, and the whole seemed a mass of confused rejoicing. For my part I felt myself actuated by very different sentiments: the event that I had been witness to was such, that the minutest circumstance attending it could not be erased from my memory; and when the melancholy which had overwhelmed me was somewhat abated, I made a drawing of the subject, and from a picture since painted the annexed plate was engraved. (83)

In Hodges' version, sati is a theatrical event performed for the European spectator, who painstakingly etches the "minutest circumstance" of the horrifying event, in contrast to the confusion of the indigenous crowd. Hodges' disconsolate response contrasts to that of the jubilant, undifferentiated Indian multitude and identifies him as the rational European individual who keenly observes and records the facts of an alien and exotic practice. The minute and the specific establish the "truth," but they also arouse profound melancholy exorcised in the particular and the aesthetic rather than through the public insistence on European stoic resolve. The desire to preserve exotic traditions mystifies sati and makes the widow heroic, while the desire to extract India's treasures for export to an English audience transforms the widow for the modern reader into a metaphor for India's victimization through the English patriarchy.

Though progressive reformer Rammohun Roy argued that "*sati* functions both as the act confirming the stoicism of women and as the practice that epitomizes their weakness," eighteenth-century Englishwomen's attitudes do not validate the idea of sati as the expression of female frailty or bad mothering.[32] The British colonial government eventually abolished sati in 1829 as indicative of oppression of Indian women, but at least one eighteenth-century woman commentator argued that sati made the woman neither a victim nor a heroine, and she did not seek to abolish the custom in order to civilize or to save

Indian women. Eliza Fay accompanied her husband, a philandering advocate, to India in 1779, where she soon separated from him, even buying return passage to England for his natural son. Fay typically renders Hindu women in India as sequestered from sight, but as a woman admitted to their presence in the zanannah, she contends that their extraordinary artifice secures and maintains the attention of the men who protect them from view. Such indigenous women negotiate power in a limited way through adorning themselves. Fay, demonstrating the familiar prejudices about Indians, depicts the people as "quiet and supine . . . only half alive" and as "deluded natives" whose religion is disgusting and superstitious. Yet in her letters from India, when Fay reflects on sati in some detail, she contradicts with piercing irony Hodges' assumptions concerning the widows' motivation:

> And first for that horrible custom of widows burning themselves with the dead bodies of their husbands; the fact is indubitable, but I have never had an opportunity of witnessing the various incidental ceremonies, nor have I ever seen any European who had been present at them. I cannot suppose that the usage originated in the superior tenderness, and ardent attachment of Indian wives towards their spouses, since the same tenderness and ardour would doubtless extend to his offspring and prevent them from exposing the innocent survivors to the miseries attendant on an orphan state, and they would see clearly that to live and cherish these pledges of affection would be the most rational and natural way of shewing their regard for both husband and children. I apprehend that as personal fondness can have no part here at all, since all matches are made between the parents of the parties who are betrothed to each other at too early a period for choice to be consulted, this practice is entirely a political scheme intended to insure the care and good offices of wives to their husbands, who have not failed in most countries to invent a sufficient number of rules to render the weaker sex totally subservient to their authority. I cannot avoid smiling when I hear gentlemen bring forward the conduct of the Hindoo women, as a test of superior character, since I am well aware that so much are we the slaves of habit *every where* that were it necessary for a woman's reputation to burn herself in England, many a one who has *accepted* a husband merely for the sake of an establishment, who has lived with him without affection; perhaps thwarted his views, dissipated his fortune and rendered his life uncomfortable to its close, would yet mount the funeral pile with all imaginable decency and die with heroic fortitude. The most specious sacrifices are not always the greatest. She who wages war with a

naturally petulant temper, who practises a rigid self-denial, endures without complaining the unkindness, infidelity, extravagance, meanness or scorn, of the man to whom she has given a tender and confiding heart, and for whose happiness and well being in life all the powers of her mind are engaged;—is ten times more of a heroine than the slave of bigotry and superstition, who affects to scorn the life demanded of her by the laws of her country or at least that country's custom; and many such we have in England, and I doubt not in India likewise: so indeed we ought, have we not a religion infinitely more pure than that of India?[33]

Eliza Fay's claim to heroic endurance parallels Sophia's sentiments in *Hartly House,* and she may well have been describing her own brief but painful experience of marital endurance with an unsavory husband. Both texts finally demean sati as an irrational solution to patriarchal oppression and as less heroic than Englishwomen's self-abnegation in the face of loveless or unsatisfying marriage. In a chauvinistic claim of national and religious superiority over Indian women, they rob sati of its material reality of pain and death.[34] But crucially, at the same time, Fay's interpretation of the widow's recognition of her lack of viable alternatives to death acknowledges the complicated subjectivity of the woman who enacts sati. Widow sacrifice cannot, Fay argues, be taken simply as an indication of the superiority of Christian women's endurance over Hindu women's immolation because *both* are the result of men's invention of "a sufficient number of rules to render the weaker sex totally subservient to their authority." The Indian woman is neither heroine nor victim, neither unfeeling mother nor pious wife; rather, her self-sacrifice becomes in Fay's account a political quagmire in which the widow's feelings need to be regarded and in which their exact nature cannot be easily divined.[35] The analogy that both Phebe Gibbes and Eliza Fay draw between English marriage and sati breaks down the distinction between European and Asian on which Hodges' account is based in the interests of making alliances between English and Indian women, even as those alliances threaten to dissolve into new hierarchies of the civilized woman over the silenced exotic. Because official governmental reactions to sati were still in formation in the later eighteenth century, a feminist resistance to its patriarchal interpretations could be forged in the interstices of the contradictory accounts of European observers. On the one hand, the concept of the Indian woman as a barometer against which to judge the status of the Englishwoman takes shape in these eighteenth-century texts. Fay and Gibbes anticipate contemporary feminist debates that identify the widow as one who is "neither an archetypal victim nor a free agent."[36] Lata Mani, for example, identifies the hesitations, contradictions, and inconsistencies in the widow's own position and suggests that "voluntary" sati must be rethought; and Ania Loomba points out the bankruptcy of offering only two options: "she either wanted to die or was forced to."[37] Rather than a private act of volition engaged in by an isolated individual, sati connects community, national, and colonial interests to gender issues. The social and the psychic, as Fay recognizes and contemporary feminists reveal, "exist in a constitutive, *traumatic,* reciprocity, the violence and pathologies of one being symptomatic of the other."[38] A potent understanding of sati considers instead of victimization the vigorous struggle between the individual and her social formation—a position that Eliza Fay anticipated in her contribution to the debate.

IV

Hartly House, Calcutta concludes with two curious passages—one in which the Nawab Mubarak ud-Daula stares at Sophia enthralled, the other a truncated account of the rape of an Indian woman by an army officer. In these two passages I think we can find further disruptions to the analogy between English marriage and sati that have bearing on the solidification of emergent colonialism. In the first passage Sophia, having overcome her amorous desires for the Brahmin, nearly succumbs to the nabob's riches and sexuality, which tempt her more profoundly than did the ascetic Brahmin. Spurred by the belief that her market price exceeds the level of Doyly's fortune, Sophia imagines responding passionately to the seductive looks of the nabob: "The ambitious throbs my heart experienced, when I saw the Nabob's eyes, sparkling with admiration, fixed on my face!" (271). At this point she displaces Indian women as the object of his desire in longing for the wealth and power she imagines a nabobess would possess instead of accepting mundane English domesticity: she would be "the envy of the women and the torture of the men" (271). When the nabob stares approvingly at her, she writes, "My conquest was as evidence [*sic*] as the noon-day sun: and who could dream of a mortal female's refusing an enthroned adorer, with the wealth of the Indies at his feet?" (272). Fantasizing that the nabob is more deeply stricken in his attraction to her than the Grand Seignor was by Lady Mary Wortley Montagu, she imagines that the nabob might plot to abduct her, and the sexual speculation dissolves into colonialist tripe: "But an Englishwoman was not born to fear giant knights, or enchanted castles; and the more especially where an army would stand forth in her protection and defence. It would flatter my vanity to find them alarmed" (274). For Sophia it is not the fear of interracial rape but the fantasy of it that is compelling. She imagines that her sexual teasing will cause havoc in the colonized country and that her defense, the defense of English womanhood, could depose the allegedly self-regulating and autonomous Indian government. The passage, anticipating the later connections between rape and empire, suggests that maintaining colonial order in India is vital to defending Englishwomen.[39]

The rape incident at the conclusion of *Hartly House* allows monstrosity to intrude into the idealized Eastern world Sophia invents. The very army she expects to defend her against the nabob's abduction is, in this second disturbing passage, also the agent of sexual violence against an Indian woman. The army officer not only rapes the woman, but he also murders her father, who discovers them. The Indian woman survives to accuse the rapist. The rape precipitates and justifies Sophia's leaving India, in spite of the fact that one of her countrymen apparently perpetrated it: "I now rejoice, more than ever, that I am about to leave a country, where fiend-like acts are, I fear, much oftener perpetrated than detected" (279). The country that inspired intimations of grandeur through the course of the novel is ultimately linked, after the death of the Brahmin, to abduction by the reigning sovereign and to sexual violence against women. These two concluding passages interrupt Sophia's infatuation with India and nail her into the coffin of English domesticity. The novel concludes predictably with Sophia's marriage (and her father's) as she embarks to England.

Through the concluding description of the rape, the English men and women bond over the body of the Indian woman. Rape is indeed monstrous, but implicit in the novel is the subtext that rape is a metaphor for imperialist violence and aggression, and Sophia's ambivalence toward that colonial mainspring surfaces. For Sophia to voice that recognition would, of course, violate the terms of the novel, which require that she retreat from the political implications of her gendered oppression and acknowledge her own complicity in empire's rapacity. The colonial hierarchy of power conflicts with gender hierarchy, but rather than confront her own ambivalent erotic desires or the consequences of a soldier's rape of a native woman, Sophia retreats to England after the delicious but "harmless" sinfulness of her Indian escapade.

Hartly House was published just before Cornwallis's reforms of 1790 ended the growth of private wealth from the East India Company. Sophia's mild forays into the political world are generally sympathetic to Edmund Burke's position in Parliament that British law should not be imposed upon India.[40] But Sophia also indicates that she was fond of Warren Hastings, the governor general of Bengal, who she believes was unfairly accused of authorizing the murder and rape of Indian women. On several occasions Sophia weakly voices political opinions, as when she urges Britons to follow Hastings' example and learn the Persian language, but she soon disavows public influence because she is "getting upon political ground." The narrator is also critical of the East India Company's interference in Indian affairs and conducting "wars with the Marattas, and Prince Hyder Ally" (Letter V), a fact which leads A. L. Basham to conclude that the novel was written by a man because eighteenth-century women were purportedly uninterested in politics.[41] In addition, Sophia dares to express reservations about the activities of the East India Company, asserting that "their Governors should interfere as little as possible in the domestic or national quarrels of the country powers; peace and tranquility best promoting their commercial interests. The wars with the Maratas, and Prince Hyderally, indeed prove that these maxims have not always been properly adhered to" (31). But she then retreats by saying that she is not really a politician.

Through Sophia's silencing, the commercialism and rapacity of the British venture in India is erased, and the potential for cultural parity dissolves into exporting the Gentoo's qualities for absorption by Englishmen returning after they have made their fortune. Fears of miscegenation are laid to rest, for the British army would come to the defense of an Englishwoman if she were seduced by a nabob. Heterosexual union between Englishwoman and Englishman passes through Indian men—the Brahmin and the nabob—to consolidate the empire and educate Englishwomen to their proper domesticity. Domesticity also traverses the rape of the Indian woman by the English officer of the East India Company and justifies a hasty retreat from the monstrous, seductive Orient to the womb of the mother country. When confronted with the dark sublime of India, having finally represented it as uncatalogable and unclassifiable, Sophia domesticates and simplifies race, class, and gender relations.

A number of postcolonial critics have contended that the stories of native women and Englishwomen cannot coalesce because feminism, particularly feminist individualism, is complicit with imperialism.[42] The eighteenth century certainly provided the historical situation for the production of "us" and "them," but "worlding" feminism, even in its earliest stages, makes interrupting this production possible by imagining links among women's multiple subjectivities that acknowledge their stake in each other's social and political fates. Such moments of shared mutual concern under patriarchy do exist, in my opinion, and the task of global feminism is to construct and produce them in the current moment rather than assuming that they exist as a reality waiting to be retrieved. While the stories of the Indian woman and the Englishwoman may not be coequal or possess an identity, they are complexly bound together within systems of oppression. Just as the forms of patriarchy are historically contingent, varying across time as economic and social arrangements shift, gendered power relations are culturally various. A global feminist collectivity takes care to avoid mistaking mutual goals for identity, especially by recognizing difference without dominance over other women, regardless of class interests and sexual preferences.

Eliza Fay's feminism need not, then, simply be dismissed as an emergent feminist individualism complicit with imperialism. Her visionary call to resist men's "rules to render the weaker sex totally subservient to their authority," whether those rules legislate gender relations in England or in India, may be taken as a premise for a new historically located global feminism without reducing the condemnation of colonialism or the commitment to its demise. Eliza Fay and the character "Sophia" can only speak *alongside* and *with* the widow, who is most powerful when she dips her finger in the red color of the coconut and is able to implicate Hodges, the representative of the colonizing Englishman, in her practice of sati. Indigenous and colonizing patriarchies take disparate forms, and in order to rewrite the history of feminism, Fay's account, Sophia's fiction, and the widow's actions will need to be woven together, not in marriage or self-abnegation, but in a collective struggle that acknowledges the formation of subjectivities in the context of thinking anew about the history of women's differences, their representation, and their material effects across the globe, in order to forge feminist solidarity.

Whose
Enlightenment
Is It?

Enlightenment is man's emergence from his self-imposed nonage. Nonage is the inability to use one's own understanding without another's guidance. . . . *Dare to know!* "Have the courage to use your own understanding," is therefore the motto of the enlightenment.

Immanuel Kant,
"What Is Enlightenment?" (1784)

There is a certain sort of understanding that the hero of this scenario, of this narrative [of the knowing subject], has been in fact Western man.

Gayatri Chakravorty Spivak,
The Post-Colonial Critic:
Interviews, Strategies, Dialogues (1990)

I

Mary Wollstonecraft's *A Vindication of the Rights of Woman* (1792) forwards an Enlightenment feminism closely tied to liberty, equality, and a belief in women's capability to reason. Though Wollstonecraft had insisted that reason had no sex, her desire for an inclusive concept of reason is complicated by the masculine limitations embedded in the concept of the "universal."[1] She appeals to women to acquire physical and mental stamina while acknowledging that such strength is deemed masculine rather than applicable to both sexes:

> I am aware of an obvious inference: From every quarter have I heard exclamations against masculine women, but where are they to be found? If by this appellation men mean to inveigh against their ardour in hunting, shooting, and gaming, I shall most cordially join in the cry; but if it be against the imitation of manly virtues, or, more properly speaking, the attainment of those talents and virtues, the exercise of which ennobles the human character, and which raises

females in the scale of animal being, when they are comprehensively termed mankind, all those who view them with a philosophic eye must, I should think, wish with me, that they may every day grow more and more masculine.[2]

Wollstonecraft recognizes that the reason, civic virtue, and individual autonomy that the Enlightenment assumed would follow naturally from a discourse of rights are defined as masculine.[3] Excluded from attempts to reconstruct the narrative of the rational knowing subject is, however, an acknowledgment of feminism's pervasively Western bias. In fact, *A Vindication* launches its argument by defining "Mahometanism" as the enemy that treats women "as a kind of subordinate being, and not part of the human species, when improvable reason is allowed to be the dignified distinction which raises men above the brute creation, and puts a natural sceptre in a feeble hand" (80). According to Wollstonecraft's narrative, the Egyptian slavemaster and the Muhammadan treat women most viciously, and she adopts the popular notion that Muhammadans (whom she compares to Milton in his construction of Eve) deprive women of souls. Further, the seraglio is held to be a threat that the worst women actually deserve, and current education for Englishwomen is "worse than Egyptian bondage." Eastern women, she believes, exemplify indolent and languid femininity, their seductive weakness a characteristic that the woman who seeks equality should eschew in favor of conjugal friendship and maternal tenderness aimed at promoting virtue. In *A Vindication* the middle-class Englishwoman seems to climb to liberty, closely associated with civilization, on the backs of the Egyptian, the Turk, the African slave, and the servant. As we have seen throughout this book, in the eighteenth century the domestic woman is defined by the exotic and the "savage." For the European woman to attain the individual autonomy associated with Enlightenment emergence from nonage, she must engage in a civilizing process and promote a revolution in manners that distinguishes her from other women elsewhere and confirms her superiority. Clearly, feminism at its roots is intertwined with a racist and imperialist agenda, but recognizing the limits of the Enlightenment's narratives, its exclusions, and its silences can point toward a recognition of what it cannot do.

Positing a "ground" of the Enlightenment has enabled postmodernists, including postmodern feminists, to assume a foundation against which some versions of contemporary theory draw their arguments in order to produce counter-representations. In these narratives

"Enlightenment" in its various formulations is the location of unmediated truth, an empiricism that postmodernism must overturn, and the site of all-encompassing universals that paralyze rather than energize human subjects. This version of Enlightenment essentialism that postmodernism's heterogeneity can help us to escape also taunts us with the failed promise of emancipation. From this positing of a stable ground of truth, postmodernism's arguments for contingent meaning are then launched and the organizing principles of the Enlightenment contested. In this way, many versions of postmodernism have often caricatured the Enlightenment. Defenders of these brands of postmodernism may look for the historical past through their own "pop images" about that past and, rather than seeking a referent in the world, content themselves with mere reflections of it.[4] In addition, casual references to the Enlightenment often obscure postmodernism's virtual abandonment of history, what Fredric Jameson has described as "the disappearance of a sense of history, the way in which our entire contemporary social system has little by little begun to lose its capacity to retain its own past, has begun to live in a perpetual present and in a perpetual change that obliterates traditions of the kind which all earlier social formations have had in one way or another to preserve."[5]

One difficulty with such an artificial divide between Enlightenment and postmodernism is that it blocks historical understanding and conceptual progress. My aims here are multiple: first, to displace assumptions about an easily codified Enlightenment and consider instead a richly historicized and contextualized Enlightenment in the hope that it may release us, as Foucault urges, from the "intellectual blackmail" of being "for or against the Enlightenment";[6] second, to question the strategies of those postmodernists who ignore historical subtleties or take refuge in undecidability as a counter to Enlightenment certainties; and finally to advance a postcolonial global feminism that takes as its task interweaving the situated histories of feminism and empire while critiquing its own terra firma. If we explore the purposes of recuperating the "Enlightenment" to this or that effect, or on the other hand, of disavowing association with it, we may begin to rethink our links to the apparent "foundation" of postmodern thought.

In its most familiar form, the Enlightenment represented an epistemological break with an oppressive past in order to allow individuals to think independently and develop sufficient self-mastery to become emancipated from intellectual and political tyranny. Postmodernism also represents itself as a rupture from the past, but as a divergence from Enlightenment certainties about the nature of reality. The Enlightenment was the source of grand narratives, of historical metanarratives of progress, reason, and liberty that postmodernism overturns.[7] These universal theories are the contestatory ground that postmodernity's relativism, fragmentation, and discontinuity resist. Many proponents of postmodernism self-consciously distance themselves from the totalizing interests they find represented in the Enlightenment and, like Horkheimer and Adorno, find its "false clarity" pernicious.[8] According to these understandings, the Enlightenment paradoxically produced its own prisons. The optimism aroused by these narratives polluted itself by turning freedom's hope into dominance and oppression while insisting on the Enlightenment's liberating value. Its failed hopes, according to Foucault, made the Enlightenment a "victim of its own excesses," ruled by a rationality which brought terror instead of clarity, and a brand of reason which was deployed "to control and dominate rather than to emancipate."[9] In short, the Enlightenment was complicit with myth rather than distanced from it and reduced diversity to an illusion of unity—but formulating the Enlightenment into an apparent unity paradoxically affords antifoundationalist postmodernisms a narrative foundation that they may contest.

In sum, for some postmodernists, the Enlightenment was a set of encoded principles from which humanity needs to be released in order to achieve rationality and freedom. Nancy Hartsock, for example, believes that the Enlightenment was the location for "totalizing and universalistic theories," and her concern is that both metanarratives *and* postmodernism deny voice to the margins.[10] For both counter-Enlightenment postmodernists who reject Enlightenment metanarratives, and for revisionary postmodernists, many of whom follow Habermas in seeking to extend and complete its progressive aspects,[11] the "Enlightenment" has become a shorthand code for the optimism, progress, and faith in reason promulgated by the *philosophes*, and for those totalizing theories and philosophies which the more local interests of postmodernism challenge, as well as a historical marker that announces the modern age.

There is, of course, considerable contest concerning the term *postmodernism,* itself a knotty cluster of discursive and material practices. Is postmodernism a political moment that characterizes all history after the American and French Revolutions? Is it a historical turning point, or is it a recurring event with various manifestations in time and space? Alternatively, does postmodernism indicate an ineradicable disjunction between one version of capital in the West and other versions in the Second, Third, and Fourth World arenas? Does postmodernism collude with the mode of production, especially late capitalism, to reflect and reproduce it rather than to counter the asymmetrical relationships between the empowered and disempowered? To what extent does postmodernism rely on a reification of prior understandings of language, the subject, history, and disciplinarity in order to establish its positions? Some theorists emphasize postmodernism's deconstructive power, its ludic critique of metanarrative that keeps language in perpetual play and staves off meaning and commitment.[12] On the contrary, this book has sought to engage a transformative postmodernism that contests hierarchies premised upon difference to critique the epistemological uncertainty in postmodernism's less political versions.

Both the Enlightenment and postmodernism are most often construed as something fixed which one must be for or against. In seeming to echo, perhaps consciously, Foucault's similar observation about Enlightenment mentioned earlier, Michèle Barrett writes that "postmodernism is not something that you can be for or against. . . . For it is a cultural climate as well as an intellectual position, a political reality as well as an academic fashion."[13] Yet Barrett also implicitly acknowledges that the pluralism of postmodernism produces an equivalence among its versions. Because postmodernism's valuations of "Enlightenment" itself are multiple as it shifts meanings in various contexts and historical moments, in the process of distinguishing one postmodernism from another, one Enlightenment from another, there is, of course, a danger that the new narratives we elaborate will be as simplified as the old and that we will remain dogmatic in inserting the *right* history in its place. Another course of action, however, rather than providing a new "master" discourse, is to create a flexible but systematic, historically situated and materially based approach to Enlightenment's analytic and practices, with an eye to recognizing contradiction and contingency but without being paralyzed by them. This approach analyzes what is at stake in this or that interpretation of Enlightenment in order to avoid the trap of essentialism and universalism on the one hand, or of indeterminacy on the other. Proposing understandings of the postmodern and the Enlightenment that escape the binary of affirmative or negative responses will avoid postmodern caricatures of Enlightenment and at the same time—beyond Foucault's or Barrett's formulation—freshly critique its Eurocentrist emphasis on knowledge that freely circulates among independent reasoning minds to focus on the way those minds are empowered because of class, gender, racial and national privilege.

II

Foucault's essay "What Is Enlightenment?" (1984), written near the end of his life, grapples with concepts expressed in Kant's essay by the same name written two hundred years before. Usually taken as the most fundamental expression of modernity's newfound confidence in individual reason ("*Dare to know!* [*Sapere aude!*]"), Kant's essay urges that the motto of this new self-conscious historical moment should be, "Have the courage to use your own understanding."[14] Freed from the shackles of external authority through the process of independent reasoning, informed individuals will evolve a system of universally applicable principles to govern themselves. In this context Enlightenment involves relinquishing a defunct mode of operation in history and substituting a modernity that emboldens the individual's pursuit of his own understanding.

In Kant the onus is of course on individual autonomy. Courage and decisiveness, once developed, enable individuals to risk taking the hazardous step toward maturity (defined as "the ability to use one's own understanding without another's guidance") which will displace the false guardians who perpetuate the notion that such a step is fraught with danger. Among the principles relevant to exercising individual autonomy is the freedom to engage in the public use of one's reason at all times.[15] Public rational debate enables citizens to connect to others engaged in free reasoning within the larger sphere and without the strictures of sovereign or despotic authority. Real progress toward full maturity, and thus the age of enlightenment, is most fully enacted by the scholar who engages with a worldwide audience (though the "world" is conceived to be the European world alone) and aims to conform to universal reason. Individual voices of public reason raised in the interests of freedom and autonomy are responsive to the evolving standards of reason and justice shared by the enlightened.

In Foucault's essay based on Kant and bearing the same title, he too finds the achievement of Enlightenment to rest in a move into modernity (which he does not distinguish here from postmodernity) and into maturity through reasoned critique. While Kant believed that the advance toward maturity would establish new general princi-

ples, Foucault interprets "Enlightenment" as enabling a critical stance
within history: "It is not the legacy of Enlightenment which it is our
business to conserve, but rather the very question of this event and its
meaning, the question of the historicity of the thought of the universal, which ought to be kept present and retained in mind as that which
has to be thought."[16] Both Kant and Foucault emphasize the distinction between an individual's independent reasoning and his obedience
to military, political, and religious authority. For both, public reason
enables connection to others engaged in free reasoning within the
public sphere and outside the restraints of despotic authority in the
private realm.

Foucault finds that Kant's seminal essay marks an originary moment because of its consciousness of "today," its reflection on the
historical situation, and its difference from the past, all of which he
calls "the attitude of modernity" ("What Is Enlightenment?" 39).
Foucault contends that "the thread that may connect us with the
Enlightenment is not faithfulness to doctrinal elements, but rather the
permanent reactivation of an attitude . . . a permanent critique of our
historical era" (42). In interpreting the Enlightenment as posing a
permanent question about the relation between truth and liberty, Foucault offers a valuable strategy for infusing postmodernity in a particular historical moment. In Foucault's interpretation, Kant's move into
maturity and modernity allows us, as his interpreters Hubert Dreyfus
and Paul Rabinow have indicated, "heroically and lucidly to face up to
the breakdown of the old order" in the present moment.[17] For Foucault, then, Enlightenment is an attitudinal "ironic stance" loosened
from history and shaken from its moorings, in the sense that its philosophical conjuncture can occur at any time and does not rest on the
validity of universal structures. Modernity is not a one-time event, as
it would seem to be for Kant, but "an event, or a set of events and
complex historical processes, that is located at a certain point in the
development of European societies."[18] At the same time, however,
Foucault insists that Kant's particular moment at the end of the eighteenth century provides crucial historical conditions enabling that attitude of critique.

At the crux, Kant's Enlightenment exudes the confidence of pure
identity and essence, while Foucault's characterization of the Enlightenment evokes uncertainty and questioning. Foucault takes from the
ironic yet heroic Enlightenment posture the imperative for perpetual
examination and reshaping of our "selves." He maintains, of course,

that the terms which Kant employs are utterly inadequate in their reliance on general structures and universals, yet because they are also steeped in an analytic of truth, they offer an unfulfilled promise. In that sense, Foucault is among those postmodernists who do not wish to reject Enlightenment altogether, however it may be defined, but who wish to extend it. Beyond Kant he encourages producing "an interpretive analytic of our current situation" and creating "an ontology of the present, an ontology of ourselves" rather than regrounding our present in a set of universal truths or understandings. Foucault's essay substitutes a dynamic, continuing, self-reflexive critique of fixed principles for a rejection of Enlightenment. Though he believes that Enlightenment failed in its goal to make us mature adults, we may extract from Kant's Enlightenment "an attitude, an ethos, a philosophical life in which the critique of what we are is at one and the same time the historical analysis of the limits that are imposed on us and an experiment with the possibility of going beyond them" (50). Crucially, however, Foucault does not critique Enlightenment for its gender and racial omissions, and his attitude of perpetual critique means that it is difficult to locate a place to stand in order to act. In addition, the desire to avoid universals means that analysis may be limited principally to the local and the anecdotal rather than extended to the systemic analysis that more politically committed avenues of postmodernism undertake. Foucault's axes of discipline and power need not exclude, but also do not necessarily bring to the foreground, issues of gender and race. Foucault, then, is not so much a counter-Enlightenment postmodernist as one who entertains the idea that the Enlightenment project, while flawed, deserves to be engaged and interrogated; it remains for those more committed to social change to augment this version of postmodernism.

Habermas more than Foucault argues for an elaboration of the Enlightenment project. The question, as he puts it, is "should we try to hold on to the *intentions* of the Enlightenment, feeble as they may be, or should we declare the entire project of modernity a lost cause?" He continues, "I think that instead of giving up modernity and its project as a lost cause, we should learn from the mistakes of those extravagant programs which have tried to negate modernity."[19] Habermas places continuing hope in "communicative rationality" or consensus about valid claims of truth and appropriateness.

In *The Structural Transformation of the Public Sphere* Habermas argues that a consensual bourgeois public sphere—the Kantian moment of detachment from despotic authority—developed at the point of separation between the sovereign and the sacred.[20] With the loss of faith in European monarchies also came the development of a public consensual space or reasoned consensus, allowing rational discussion among common people and aiding in the formation of the middle class. The power of this public opinion manifested itself in cafes and newspapers, in coffeehouses and periodicals, where taste was arbitrated and matters of state debated so that the authority of this consensual group usurped the authority that previously had belonged to the state. Habermas, as Thomas McCarthy has pointed out, "agrees with the radical critics of enlightenment that the paradigm of consciousness is exhausted. Like them, he views reason as inescapably situated, as concretized in history, society, body, and language. Unlike them, however, Habermas holds that the defects of the Enlightenment can only be made good by further enlightenment."[21]

For Habermas and those who follow him, reason must be trumped with even greater rationality, so that the Enlightenment project may be expanded even as we recognize that its metaphysical ground is lost. Rational agreement will be attained through "unforced intersubjectivity" in ideal speech communities, but the question of whose subjectivity will be taken into account and how those with less cultural cachet will be heard remains unaddressed. As Terry Eagleton wittily mocks the polemical split within leftist political theory, it is between Habermasian rationalism "with his 'ideal speech communities' of universal abstractly equal subjects from whom all inclination has been drained, and the anarchic particularism of the poststructuralists, with their heady celebrations of delirium, pure difference, the fragment, flashes of libidinal intensity, against a rational totality now denounced as brutally totalitarian."[22] Habermas's rational idealism is inadequate to the project because it offers no remedy for the inequalities among individual speakers or within their communities. But neither is the euphoric celebration of the pleasures of difference an effective use of postmodernism, which ought instead to be employed to contest both Habermas's rational idealism and postmodernism's "anarchic particularism."

Among those who also pursue the "unfulfilled project of modernity" are Chantal Mouffe and Ernesto LaClau, who "believe that there is no longer a role to be played in this project by the epistemological perspective of the Enlightenment."[23] Enlightenment as Mouffe envisions it is essentialist rather than cognizant of its own historical limitations: "an obstacle in the path of understanding those new forms of politics, characteristic of our societies today, which demand to be approached from a nonessentialist perspective" (33). Proceeding along two levels of analysis, Mouffe believes that the Enlightenment project may be divided between an epistemological one, which she rejects as a project of self-foundation, and a democratic project, which she defends. This project extracts the ideas of liberty and freedom from traditional democracy while abandoning individualism to enable an ongoing critique of Western versions of democracy through a post-modern subjectivity, not an autonomous self. Yet Mouffe, while rejecting Habermas's universalist liberalism, follows his thought in remaining committed to a consensual pluralism rather than a more contestatory collectivity. Pluralism emphasizes the ability of the unitary self to act and the equivalence of various truth claims, while collectivity engages in critique within the solidarity of common convictions, acknowledging difference but without employing it as a basis for hierarchies. "Genuine collectivities," writes Seyla Benhabib, "are formed out of struggle, not out of the logic of substitution that preempts the experience of one social group with categories derived from the language of another."[24]

If the Enlightenment is constituted as individual subjects involved in open and public consensual discussion from which commonsensical reason derives, the public opinion resulting from such a rational exchange is bound to conserve and consolidate the hegemonic class and race. In addition, as Nancy Fraser has pointed out, an "unthematized gender subtext" undergirds Habermas's theory; and in failing to analyze the connections between the public bourgeois sphere and the family, his theory "defends an institutional arrangement which is widely held to be one, if not the linchpin of modern women's subordination."[25] Woman is the possessed rather than the possessor, the natural rather than the rational, dispossessed and ravished. The Enlightenment does not seem to be woman's, nor does her place within it seem to be one of liberty; maturity means that "man" assumes responsibility for his own critical reasoning.[26] As Gayatri Spivak puts it, "There is a certain sort of understanding that the hero of this scenario, of this narrative [of the knowing subject], has been in fact Western man."[27]

The debate over the Enlightenment's legacy to contemporary feminism has been especially fraught, since, as Nancy Hartsock has written, "At their worst, postmodernist theories merely recapitulate the effects of Enlightenment theories—theories that deny marginalized people the right to participate in defining the terms of interaction with people in the mainstream."[28] A recent instance of postmodern feminism's categorical use of the eighteenth century appears in Jane Flax's summary of the Enlightenment into eight succinct but highly simplified principles in her recent book *Thinking Fragments: Psychoanalysis, Feminism, and Postmodernism in the Contemporary West*, in which she argues that a postmodernism that eschews the Enlightenment and is contestatory to it is most productive for feminist theory. Flax's Enlightenment categories include a stable, coherent self; reason as an objective foundation for knowledge; the possibility of true understanding as it derives from reason; science as the paradigm for real knowledge; the transparency of language; and so on. She believes that feminist notions of the self, knowledge, and truth are too contradictory to those of the Enlightenment to be contained within its categories.[29] Flax thus constructs a philosophically unified eighteenth century in order to identify the present moment as distinct from it and to urge that we perceive reality as decentered and unstable.

In her work on feminism and postmodernism, Sandra Harding is another among contemporary theorists who seeks to rewrite a narrative of Enlightenment rather than assume that it is the ground to be contested.[30] Indebted to Habermas, Harding wishes to complete the modernist Enlightenment project, which she construes as a ground on which to build, rather than rejecting it through postmodernism. Harding does not distinguish between those versions of postmodernism that are simply engaged in ongoing critique and those with more explicit political goals. Yet she also argues that feminism needs the opposite poles of both Enlightenment and the postmodern agenda in spite of the inadequacies of each. Harding bifurcates feminism into "scientific" and "postmodern" branches. The scientific project is an emancipatory one that seeks to continue Enlightenment (and modernist) projects in order to achieve feminist epistemologies. The other, postmodern project is less hopeful about the establishment of truth and more inclined to abandon the Enlightenment. Her version of feminist postmodernism addresses the failure of past efforts to bring progressive change, and it seeks to continue Enlightenment (and thus modernist) hopes in order to "produce less partial and perverse representations" (100). Harding finds the postmodern project only limitedly productive in establishing science or theory, but the standpoint theory she offers in its place makes truth claims based on women's

superior "experience" and rationality that are compromised by in-
attention to racial and class differences. Harding largely subsumes
these problems within the interests of a strategic "principled ambivalence" (86).

Harding's project usefully diminishes the distinctions between
Enlightenment and postmodernism in order to unify the feminist
project, maintain its resistance politics, and claim a systematic critique
of patriarchal structures. She avoids abandoning "Enlightenment" because of its alignments with feminism's history, but her strategic ambivalence in ignoring the ways the binaries of Enlightenment feminism and postmodern feminism *cannot* be reconciled clouds rather
than clarifies, melds without precise definition, and produces a feminist pluralism rather than a collectivity of competing claims. Thus,
Harding's project neither rewrites the narratives of Enlightenment
nor advances to the markedly new theoretical territory that a recognition of the Eurocentric limitations of Enlightenment feminism would
provide. The current challenge is to reconfigure global feminism as an
incommensurable, but renderable, collectivity that takes account of
racial and other hierarchies.

III

Just as the individual's rational capacity in the Enlightenment was
differentially calibrated according to gender, it was also measured according to racialized standards. In an essay on the history of the
concept of "race" that parallels Richard Popkin's earlier work arguing that Enlightenment theories may be interpreted to be nonracist,
Henry Louis Gates, Jr., seeks to rewrite a narrative of the Enlightenment and to demonstrate the way its terms of debate are still our terms
rather than proposing that it is the ground to be contested.[31] Gates
reasserts hope in the liberating force of the Enlightenment, though he
is also engaged in constructing its genealogy differently. His focus is
on the way the Enlightenment identifies color as the distinguishing
feature among human beings. He begins by citing Sprat's *History of the
Royal Society* (1667) as characteristic of Enlightenment methods of
inquiry, "its metaphysics of continuity and hierarchy," "the will to
classify" (319), and the passion for order exemplified in the chain of
being. He locates in Linnaeus's and Blumenbach's classifications the
tendency to codify but also the avoidance of hierarchies and the promise of an escape from a racist essentialism. In other words, rather than
finding in Enlightenment biology and anthropology the foundations

of nineteenth-century scientific racism, Gates revises the terms of Enlightenment history to make them available as a philosophical basis for antiracism. Racial divisions, he asserts, are best read as arbitrary, even in the eighteenth century.

Gates's reevaluation of Enlightenment's terms is an ambitious attempt to escape the binary of being for or against the Enlightenment and contribute to its revision. For Gates, the Enlightenment itself is benign and neutral, but it was transformed into the basis for a racist ideology. Most crucial to his argument is the claim that Locke's dividing, classifying, and distinguishing among human beings by color is for nominal purposes only, and is unconnected to their real essences. Buffon too believed that classifications were not natural but nominal, not nature's but man's. Gates's thesis is that "what we have inherited from the Enlightenment . . . is a conceptual grammar of antiracism" (323).

This thesis, startling in its validation of Enlightenment categories while turning them to an antiracist end, nevertheless presents difficulties. Though we cannot gain access to the "real essence" of human beings, do real racial differences exist in some idealist way according to these early scientists and biologists? Is it not possible that the "real" essence, even though it cannot be known, is figured in some of these accounts as racist in the extreme? Kant himself, for example, wrote that "the Negroes of Africa have by nature no feeling that rises above the trifling," and he used Hume's famous racist footnote as a philosophical justification for his views.[32] Gates's project opposes postmodernism as a "paradigm of dismantlement" (325) which he resists in part because it would seem to destroy human agency and the possibility of socially transformative action. Gates worries that "the imperative to historicize will, at the limit, be equally incapacitating" (327). If "race" is only a nominal category, then crucial aspects of existence may be denied in the process.

These are the increasingly familiar arguments of a strategic essentialism, or here, of a "nominal essence." But what is fresh and useful in Gates's argument is his attempt to transform our understandings of the Enlightenment, not as a fixed thing about which the "real" meaning can be known and upon which premises later theories are based, but as a set of events and discourses constructed into fluid narratives which may be woven into alternative paradigms that contest racism. Gates's is a muted though forceful political agenda of rereading history to extract its possibilities for antiracism.

In the eighteenth century Soame Jenyns categorized the hierarchy of rational capacity as progressing from a generic "Hottentot" to the individual European philosopher when he wrote, "From this lowest degree in the brutal Hottentot, reason, with the assistance of learning and science, advances, through the various stages of human under-standing, which rise above each other, till in a Bacon or a Newton it attains the summit."[33] Two theories of racial origin dominated—the polygenetic argument of multiple origins, which created distinctly different human natures, and the degenerative or racial superiority argument, which insisted on the biological inferiority of those who were not white European or Christian.[34] The polygenetic theory claimed, in contradiction to biblical accounts, that pre-Adamic people were a separate and savage race created before Adam. This theory evolved into a highly racialized argument that only Adam's descendants, sometimes limited to Jews, were the superior peoples. While the degeneracy theories could sometimes be used to argue against essentialism and in behalf of change, the polygenetic theories were consistently deployed to justify a belief in different *races*, not just differences in behavior, appearance, or cultures.[35] Though it may certainly be turned to racist ends, the polygenetic argument in some of its versions may also be read in a neutral way. By this interpretation, it is simply an explanation for the origins of obvious differences rather than a justification for inferiority, and some accounts suggest that movement out of degeneracy is possible.

While Linnaeus contended that climatic differences influence color and character, he clearly established a hierarchy in which the European is "fair, sanguine, brawny," his personality "gentle, acute, inventive," and his society "*governed* by laws"—while the African is "black, phlegmatic, relaxed," his habits "crafty, indolent, negligent," and his community "governed by caprice."[36] Climate was believed to influence color and personality, but as the distance between countries was compressed and trade increased travel, the human race seemed categorized by something less easily defined. As Popkin pointed out, some of the degeneracy theorists, such as Blumenbach and anthropologist James Prichard, believed in climatic determinism, even among those populations who were assumed to be inferior to the European.

Degeneracy theory became increasingly significant in the later eighteenth century, and it led directly to nineteenth-century scientific racism. For Thomas Hodgkin, the idea of the noble savage, the "Rousseauian picture of an African golden age of perfect liberty, equality and fraternity," rankles dissonantly against the representation of pre-European Africa as a blank space of savagery, "in which there was no account of Time; no Arts, no Letters, no Society; and which is worst of all, continued fear, and danger of violent death."[37] Further, he writes, the Enlightenment provided the technical definitions of savagery through its scientific discourse.

This formulation, like that of Gates, offers new theoretical potential by refusing to fit either into counter-Enlightenment postmodernism or with those who would extend and complete the Enlightenment. Rather, it demonstrates the contradiction inherent within "Enlightenment." Gates insists that those who reject the Enlightenment project have little to offer a racially liberatory project, but he also revises the "Enlightenment" by retrieving and rethinking its debates. In spite of the shortcomings of his essay, he usefully encourages retrieving the exclusions of the Enlightenment, in particular by arguing the counterhegemonic philosophical assumption that racial difference is merely nominal. His purpose is to fault what he calls "Theory" for its failure to offer analytic terms for human agency and cultural identity. This argument fails, however, to recognize the way postcolonial feminist theorists, especially African-American feminists and other women of color, have already engaged in extensive critical controversies over identity and difference, essentialism and constructionism, agency and subjectivity—and they have theorized precisely those issues that Gates would like to address in his rereading of the Enlightenment. This leads to another unhappy exclusion, this time one in the current moment.

IV

For many feminists the problem with Enlightenment is so closely bound to racism that it must be rejected as the originary point for anything of significance. This rejection is not intended to favor Enlightenment's universals rather than postmodernism's playful particularism but to contest a notion of history which assumes Enlightenment's vital significance to non-Western people and especially to women of color. Kumari Jayawardena, for example, recognizes the limitations of Enlightenment's universal knowing subject in terms of Eurocentricism, gender, and the class alignments: "The bourgeois males of these countries were faced with the usual liberal dilemma: the democratic rights championed by followers of the Enlightenment in Europe, though ostensibly 'universal,' were intended for bourgeois males to the exclusion of the workers, colonial peoples and women."[38] In another example of the assumption that Western feminism grounds its project in an essentialized Enlightenment, Aihwa Ong writes: "As an oppositional subculture reproduced within the Western knowledge of the non-Western world, [feminism] is a field defined by historicism. This post-Enlightenment view [feminism] holds that the world is a complex but unified unity culminating in the West. . . . With common roots in the Enlightenment, masculinist and feminist perspectives share the notion that enlightened reason has been a crucial force in social emancipation."[39]

Ong is surely right in noting the primarily Western history of feminism and its tendency to weave a narrative of the power of reason. In reconceiving feminism's "origins," Ong, Jayawardena, Spivak, and other Third World feminists and women of color are engaged in decentering its Eurocentricism and transforming its history beyond the binaries of postmodernism and Enlightenment. As Jayawardena explains, "In the West, too, there is a Eurocentric view that the movement for women's liberation is not indigenous to Asia and Africa, but has been a purely West European and North American phenomenon, and that where movements for women's emancipation or feminist struggles have arisen in the Third World, they have been merely imitative of Western models."[40] The Enlightenment, though often the defining moment for European and North American feminism, may not be the defining moment or the origin for Third World women and other women of color who may seek alternative paradigms.

Third World feminists critique the position of Western Anglo-feminism and entertain the possibility of an altogether different imaginary that would displace the centrality, whether interpreted as a positive or negative force, of the Enlightenment and situate the terms of the Enlightenment/postmodernism debate on very different terrain. Wahneema Lubiano, for example, notes that African-American voices have not generally been raised in postmodern debates. The political African-American postmodernist project in which she participates is one that is "able to see when color hangs us all as well as when gender or sexuality adds weight to the tree limb."[41] Lubiano negotiates between her belief in the efficacy of metanarratives of freedom and the necessity to "translate" or situate them as they are applied to local instances. If postmodernism allows for thinking about difference, the emphasis she prefers is on "*how* difference operates" rather than what difference is, and she questions the relevance of Enlightenment at all:

three hundred and fifty years ago some of us were already in
to be both cynical about the Enlightenment and less than
tic about modernism." According to this account, the philosophies, practices, and institutions of European Enlightenment clearly
emerge as part of a logic of Western expansion and colonization.[42]

Lubiano is among the practitioners of feminist cultural studies
who are transforming the model of feminism and thus imagining
possibilities for a new problematic of feminism, postmodernism, and
Enlightenment that confronts the triad's blindnesses and exclusions.
Postmodernist appeals to Enlightenment as a point of reference may
reduce it to discontinuity and fragmentation against a past that knew
only universals and unity. In addition, such postmodern appeals paradoxically assume the definitiveness of Enlightenment as a point of
origin. That unity may be disrupted if we investigate instead the way
the Enlightenment encoded asymmetries in race, gender, class, and
sexualities and recognize that a postmodernism without commitment
to resistance is an insufficient answer to its metanarrative. Working
within the logic of operations of Enlightenment thought may lead to
complicity with its shortcomings. Chandra Mohanty, like Lubiano,
questions the significance of the Enlightenment and considers the
year 1492 as a date more momentous than the European eighteenth
century to the histories of women. Mohanty argues that "black, white,
and other third world women have very different histories with respect to the particular inheritance of post-fifteenth-century Euro-
American hegemony: the inheritance of slavery, enforced migration,
plantation and indentured labor, colonialism, imperial conquest, and
genocide."[43] And when Chela Sandoval asserts that "US Third World
feminism" presents "a new condition of possibility" that exceeds the
potential of hegemonic feminism, we might extend the Enlighten-
ment/postmodernism debate beyond the now bankrupt binary of determining whether the failure of "Enlightenment" can be remedied
only by the playful contention of postmodernism or, alternatively, by
elaborating upon its original premises.[44] In short, "worlding" feminist
literary history means considering alternatives to consensual reason,
limited in its association with the masculine but also with European
feminism, and with its connotations of colonialist dominance and
violence, as in Trinh T. Minh-ha's query, "What do I want wanting to
know you or me?" Rationality and liberty are heavily entwined in the
colonialist project, she argues: "The idealized quest for knowledge and

power makes it often difficult to admit that enlightenment (as ex-emplified by the West) often brings about endarkment."[45]

In critiquing the terms by which we understand Enlightenment and its problematic, we will need to exert considerable effort to avoid simply multiplying the various histories of the Enlightenment, mixing them together, and construing a new "ground" for future theorists. Alternative inquiries might ask at what moments the commitments of the revisionist literary historian, the feminist materialist, the postcolo-nialist critic, and the oppositional postmodernist theorist are con-gruent. Which stories, which partial and contestatory narratives of the eighteenth-century world, might be drawn into conjunction in order to transform our understandings of the Enlightenment rather than to augment or extend them? These transformations involve establishing a perpetual critique of Enlightenment to avoid reifying it, as well as seeking other definitive historical conjunctures viable for feminist analysis for social, economic, and political change. A postcolonial global feminist collectivity addresses the hierarchies and oppressions women exert on each other, in addition to the usual feminist agenda of examining patriarchal structures, in order to avoid allowing women's antagonisms to be a covert means of working out men's issues with women, sexuality, or the empire. These issues contaminate women's relationships with each other across generations (mother and daugh-ter), races, and classes.

This book has linked the exotic and the domestic in the figural as well as the actual to show that metaphor gestating in human con-sciousness may produce and reflect material consequences at home and abroad. I have yoked the apparently heterogeneous in struggle together to recover reciprocal cultural meanings of maternity and sex-uality in the eighteenth century: the domestic Pamela with polyg-amous Africa, the life of Richard Savage with "savage" mothers at home and abroad, the cross-dressing or sexually transgressive woman with Turkish homoeroticism, a community of unmarried learned ladies and their disabled charges to a seraglio and the exotic deformed, the blush on the body of the Englishwoman with the veiling of the Other, domestic prostitution and pornography to the interests of em-pire, and Englishwomen's self-interested comparisons of unhappy marriage to sati. It should be clear that I am not arguing that the "savage" Other is simply equivalent to the English prostitute, that the homoerotics of the seraglio are identical to the unmarried ladies of

Millenium Hall, or that Pamela's fear of being Mr. B's other woman is the same as African polygamy. These various instances of maternity and sexuality in the larger eighteenth century reflect a systemic *whole* rather than a unity or an identity among them. As we have seen in various novels and travel narratives, the Englishwoman's investment in the imputed Other woman and her impersonation, whether veiled or costumed, is often designed to extend her own unfettered independence and to construct a more coherent subjectivity at the expense of various women of empire. Yet women everywhere confront and challenge the effects of patriarchy.

I have attempted to make the ideological workings of empire and of Englishwomen's complicity within it more legible, in part through recovering hints of agency and of the struggle between the individual subjectivity and the social in the native woman's snatching of her child from the slave trader's arms in Snelgrave's account, in Savanna's courageous feminist retort to her abusive employer, in the ironic songs of the African women in Mungo Park's description, in Queen Clara's resistance to wearing European dress in Anna Falconbridge's travel narrative, in the complex subjectivity of a widow approaching sati, and in separating libidinal freedom from political liberty in Lady Mary's Turkish women, Defoe's Roxana, and the Amazonian prostitute. These resistances of women around the globe contravene Enlightenment's Eurocentricism, and the articulation of them here is an attempt to contribute to feminism's embryonic multiracial and international history. The Enlightenment belongs to those who revise and reclaim it, but the very relevancy of Enlightenment to a "worlding" of the eighteenth century remains to be charted as a postcolonial global feminism animates a mode of inquiry that is flexible and capacious enough to encompass the narratives of maternity and sexuality, not just of Europe or the West, but of the world.

NOTES

Introduction

1. James Boswell, *Life of Johnson*, ed. George Birkbeck Hill, rev. L. F. Powell, 6 vols. (Oxford: Clarendon, 1934–64), 4:308.

2. Ann L. Stoler, "Carnal Knowledge and Imperial Power: Gender, Race, and Morality in Colonial Asia," in *Gender at the Crossroads of Knowledge: Feminist Anthropology in the Postmodern Era*, ed. Micaela di Leonardo (Berkeley and Los Angeles: University of California Press, 1991), 55.

3. Kimberle Crenshaw, "Demarginalizing the Intersection of Race and Sex: A Black Feminist Critique of Antidiscrimination Doctrine, Feminist Theory, and Antiracist Politics," *University of Chicago Legal Forum* 4 (1989): 139.

4. Nupur Chaudhuri and Margaret Strobel, eds., *Western Women and Imperialism: Complicity and Resistance* (Bloomington: Indiana University Press, 1992), 3. Ronald Hyam, "Empire and Sexual Opportunity," *Journal of Imperial and Commonwealth History* 14, no. 2 (1986): 34–89, is chief among those who have developed a sexual theory of British imperialism: "The driving force behind empire building was . . . the export of surplus emotional or sexual energy." But see Mark T. Berger, "Imperialism and Sexual Exploitation: A Response to Ronald Hyam's 'Empire and Sexual Opportunity,'" *Journal of Imperial and Commonwealth History* 17, no. 1 (1988): 83–89.

5. The Orient is most famously described in its invention as Other and as woman by Edward W. Said, *Orientalism* (London: Penguin, 1978).

6. For example, in her book *Ends of Empire: Women and Ideology in Early Eighteenth-Century English Literature* (Ithaca: Cornell University Press, 1993), Laura Brown argues that the female figure negotiates the ideological tensions between the satisfactions of commodification and trade, and the disharmonies wrought by violence and difference. "Woman" in *Ends of Empire* signifies primarily "Englishwoman," and as a consequence, the differences between and among women, especially those of class and color, are somewhat blurred in the interests of making a powerful unified argument about the uses of the female figure for imperial goals.

7. Hazel V. Carby, "White Woman Listen! Black Feminism and the Boundaries of Sisterhood," in *The Empire Strikes Back: Race and Racism in 70s Britain* (London: Hutchinson, with the Center for Contemporary Cultural Studies, University of Birmingham, 1982), 232.

8. Chandra Talpade Mohanty, "Under Western Eyes: Feminist Scholarship and Colonial Discourses," in *Third World Women and the Politics of Feminism*, ed. Chandra Talpade Mohanty, Ann Russo, and Lourdes Torres (Bloomington: Indiana University Press, 1991), 73.

9. Arlene Elowe MacLeod cautions, "The dichotomization in the literature on Middle Eastern women between women-of-the-harem victimization

and behind-the-scenes-but truly-powerful agency tends to produce arguments which flatten out the subtleties of women's subjectivities under power." MacLeod, "Hegemonic Relations and Gender Resistance: The New Veiling as Accommodating Protest in Cairo," *Signs: Journal of Women in Culture and Society* 17 (Spring 1992): 535.

10. Audre Lorde, "An Open Letter to Mary Daly," in *This Bridge Called My Back: Writings by Radical Women of Color,* ed. Cherríe Moraga and Gloria Anzaldúa (Watertown, Mass.: Persephone Press, 1981), 96.

11. For an example of this occlusion, see Lisa Lowe, "Rereadings in Orientalism: Oriental Inventions and Inventions of the Orient in Montesquieu's *Lettres persanes," Cultural Critique* 15 (Spring 1990): 115–43, who emphasizes the play of differences within Orientalism: "The view that a dominant discourse produces and manages Others, univocally appropriating and containing all dissenting positions within it, underestimates the tensions and contradictions within a discourse, the continual play of resistance, dissent, and accommodation by different positions" (142). In emphasizing the heterogeneity of these discourses, Lowe obscures the systemic nature of imperialism and its economic and political consequences.

12. Linda Alcoff, "The Problem of Speaking for Others," *Cultural Critique* 20 (Winter 1991–92): 24.

13. The terms come from Trinh T. Minh-ha, *Woman, Native, Other: Writing Postcoloniality and Feminism* (Bloomington: Indiana University Press, 1989), 101.

14. See, for example, Rey Chow, *Woman and Chinese Modernity: The Politics of Reading between West and East* (Minneapolis: University of Minnesota Press, 1991).

15. Lata Mani, "Cultural Theory, Colonial Texts: Reading Eyewitness Accounts of Widow Burning," in *Cultural Studies,* ed. Lawrence Grossberg, Cary Nelson, and Paula A. Triechler (New York: Routledge, 1992), 392–408.

16. Gayatri Chakravorty Spivak uses this term in "Can the Subaltern Speak?" in *Marxism and the Interpretation of Culture,* ed. Cary Nelson and Lawrence Grossberg (Urbana: University of Illinois Press, 1988), 297.

17. Chela Sandoval, "US Third World Feminism: The Theory and Method of Oppositional Consciousness in the Postmodern World," *Genders* 10 (Spring 1991): 1.

18. Inderpal Grewal and Caren Kaplan, eds., "Introduction: Transnational Feminist Practices and Questions of Postmodernity," in *Scattered Hegemonies: Postmodernity and Transnational Feminist Practices* (Minneapolis: University of Minnesota Press, 1994), 17.

19. See, for example, Gyan Prakash, "Postcolonial Criticism and Indian Historiography," *Social Text* 31/32, 10.2 and 10.3 (1992): 8–19.

20. See Frederick Cooper and Ann L. Stoler, "Introduction: Tensions of

Empire: Colonial Control and Visions of Rule," *American Ethnologist* 16 (November 1989): 609.

21. Oliver Goldsmith, *An History of the Earth and Animated Nature*, 8 vols. (1774), 2:212. Differences in climate were mitigated by property relations for John Millar in *The Origin of the Distinction of Ranks; or, An Inquiry into the Circumstances which give rise to the Influences and Authority in the Different Members of Society* (1771), 3rd ed. (London, 1781). See Paul Bowles, "John Millar, the Four-Stages Theory, and Women's Position in Society," *History of Political Economy* 16, no. 4 (1984): 619–38.

22. Adam Ferguson, LL.D., *An Essay on the History of Civil Society* (1767), ed. Duncan Forbes (Edinburgh: University of Edinburgh Press, 1966), 27.

23. Millar, *Origin of the Distinction of Ranks*, 8.

24. Especially relevant to the climate debates are John Brown, *Estimate of the Manners and Principles of the Times* (London, 1758); John Arbuthnot, *Essay on the Effects of Air* (London, 1733); and James Dunbar, *Essays on the History of Mankind* (London, 1780). See also F. T. H. Fletcher, *Montesquieu and English Politics, 1750–1800* (Philadelphia: Porcupine Press, 1939), 93–103.

25. Sylvana Tomaselli, "The Enlightenment Debate on Women," *History Workshop* 20 (Autumn 1985): 101–24. Tomaselli is to be commended for locating women's agency in the production of culture, though she seems to confine woman's achievement to infusing civilization with manners. Unfortunately, the terms of the debate in her otherwise pioneering article are simply reversed in her rendering, so that woman is defined as culture, man as nature.

26. As Lynn Hunt points out in the volume she edited, "Sexual enlightenment was consequently a part of the Enlightenment itself." *The Invention of Pornography: Obscenity and the Origins of Modernity, 1500–1800* (New York: Zone Books, 1993), 34. The way women's supposed sexual enlightenment worked itself out differently from men's is, however, the subject of the chapters that follow here.

27. "Like her predecessors in Enlightenment sociology, Wollstonecraft aligned her view of progress with her wish for a reformation of manners." G. J. Barker-Benfield, *The Culture of Sensibility: Sex and Society in Eighteenth-Century Britain* (Chicago: University of Chicago Press, 1992), xxix. See also G.J. Barker-Benfield, "Mary Wollstonecraft: Eighteeenth-Century Commonwealthwoman," *Journal of the History of Ideas* 50 (1989): 95–115.

28. William Alexander, *The History of Women from the Earliest Antiquity, to the Present Time; giving some Account of almost every interesting Particular concerning that Sex, among all Nations, Ancient and Modern*, 2 vols., 3rd ed. (London, 1782).

29. Rousseau, *De l'inégalité*, in *Du contrat social et autres oeuvres politiques*, ed. J. Ehrard (Paris, 1975), 61–62. Diderot finds the civilized woman to be much happier than the savage Indian woman living on the banks of the

Oroonoko. See Denis Diderot, "Sur les femmes," in *Oeuvres complètes*, ed. Roger Lewinter (Paris, 1971), 10:28–53.

30. See S. N. Mukherjee, *Sir William Jones: A Study in Eighteenth-Century British Attitudes to India*, 2nd ed. (Hyderabad: Orient Longman, 1987), 13.

31. Millar, *Origin of the Distinction of Ranks*, 28.

32. Alexander, *History of Women from the Earliest Antiquity*, 1:254.

33. Moira Ferguson argues that antislavery arguments waged by English women authors contributed to feminist debates but in that process they also distorted the meaning of slavery. In her comprehensive book, *Subject to Others: British Women Writers and Colonial Slavery, 1670–1834* (New York: Routledge, 1992), Ferguson treats slavery as an institution, but is less interested in distinguishing slave women from slave men.

34. Bernard Semmel, *The Liberal Ideal and the Demons of Empire: Theories of Imperialism from Adam Smith to Lenin* (Baltimore: Johns Hopkins University Press, 1993), 1–38.

35. While directed specifically to the modern moment, the introduction to Nira Yuval-Davis and Floya Anthias's edited volume, *Woman-Nation-State* (New York: St. Martin's Press, 1989), is still a relevant caution: "The 'myth of the one British nation' has postulated that women are its members essentially in and through their relations with men, as dependents, particularly in their capacity as wives and mothers" (12).

36. Urs Bitterli, *Cultures in Conflict: Encounters between European and Non-European Cultures, 1492–1800,* trans. Ritchie Robertson (Stanford: Stanford University Press, 1989), 36–37, notes that over 50 percent of the slave trade of 10 million slaves took place during the eighteenth century. Since 10–20 percent died, the total numbers may have been as much as 15.5 million.

37. D. K. Fieldhouse, *The Colonial Empires: A Comparative Survey from the Eighteenth Century* (New York: Delacorte Press, 1965), 144.

38. Ibid. See also Robert A. Huttenback, *The British Imperial Experience* (New York: Harper and Row, 1966).

39. Elias Habesci, *The Present State of the Ottoman Empire . . . translated from the French Manuscript* (London, 1784), 309.

40. Major John Taylor, *Travels from England to India, in the Year 1789 . . .*, 2 vols. (London, 1799), 1:21–22.

41. Though associated with sensuality and lassitude, Turkey does not literally lie within the geographical area bordered by the Tropics of Cancer and Capricorn. On the other hand, the seraglio was placed imaginatively within the torrid zones.

42. Judith Drake, *An Essay in Defence of the Female Sex*, reprinted in *The Other Eighteenth Century: English Women of Letters, 1660–1800*, ed. Robert W. Uphaus and Gretchen M. Foster (East Lansing, Mich.: Colleagues Press, 1991), 31.

Chapter 1: Torrid Mothers

1. Henrietta Moore, *Feminism and Anthropology* (Minneapolis: University of Minnesota Press, 1988), 23. Recent feminist discussions of motherhood from varying perspectives include Elisabeth Badinter, *The Myth of Motherhood: An Historical View of the Maternal Instinct* (New York: Macmillan, 1981); Nancy Chodorow, *The Reproduction of Mothering: Psychoanalysis and the Sociology of Gender* (Berkeley and Los Angeles: University of California Press, 1978); Ann Ferguson, *Blood at the Root: Motherhood, Sexuality, and Male Dominance* (London: Pandora, 1989); Hortense J. Spillers, "Mama's Baby, Papa's Maybe: An American Grammar Book," *diacritics* 17 (Summer 1987): 65–81, and "'The Permanent Obliquity of an In[pha]llibly Straight': In the Time of Daughters and Fathers," in *Daughters and Fathers*, ed. Lynda E. Boose and Betty S. Flowers (Baltimore: Johns Hopkins University Press, 1989), 157–76; and Sara Ruddick, "Maternal Thinking," *Feminist Studies* 6 (Summer 1980): 343–67.

2. See Domna Stanton, "Difference on Trial: A Critique of the Maternal Metaphor in Cixous, Irigaray, and Kristeva," in *The Poetics of Gender*, ed. Nancy K. Miller (New York: Columbia University Press, 1986), 177.

3. "By lifting the argument about sex differences out of the realm of 'pure' science and placing it within its social context," Londa Schiebinger writes, "this strand of the biological debate has relieved feminists of the task of minimizing sex differences." Schiebinger, "The History and Philosophy of Women in Science: A Review Essay," in *Sex and Scientific Inquiry*, ed. Sandra Harding and Jean F. O'Barr (Chicago: University of Chicago Press, 1987), 29. Among the revisionary historians of science are Ann Fausto-Sterling, *Myths of Gender: Biological Theories about Women and Men* (New York: Basic Books, 1985); Sandra Harding, *The Science Question in Feminism* (Ithaca: Cornell University Press, 1986); Ruth Hubbard, *The Politics of Women's Biology* (New Brunswick: Rutgers University Press, 1990); and Nancy Leys Stepan, "Race and Gender: The Role of Analogy in Science," *Isis* 77 (June 1986): 261–77.

4. Donna Haraway, "A Manifesto for Cyborgs: Science, Technology, and Socialist Feminism in the 1980s," *Socialist Review* 15 (March–April 1985): 99–100.

5. See especially John Sitter's important article, "Mother, Memory, Muse, and Poetry after Pope," *ELH* 44 (Summer 1977): 312–36, and Jill Campbell's "'The Exact Picture of His Mother': Recognizing Joseph Andrews," *ELH* 55 (Fall 1988): 643–64. Campbell points out that Joseph's strawberry mark, the mark that he misses in Wilson's story because he slumbers unaware, "links him specifically to his mother rather than his father."

6. Susan Staves, "Douglas's Mother," in *Brandeis Essays in Literature*, ed. John Hazel Smith (Waltham, Mass.: Brandeis University, 1983), 51–67, argues

that the popularity of Home's tragedy *Douglas* arose from its spectacles of maternal sentiment.

7. G. J. Barker-Benfield, *The Culture of Sensibility: Sex and Society in Eighteenth-Century Britain* (Chicago: University of Chicago Press, 1992), 160. See also E. A. Wrigley, "Marriage, Fertility, and Population Growth in Eighteenth-Century England," in *Marriage and Society: Studies in the Social History of Marriage*, ed. R. B. Outhwaite (London: Europa Publications, 1981), 137–85.

8. Ros Ballaster, *Seductive Forms: Women's Amatory Fiction from 1684 to 1740* (Oxford: Clarendon, 1992), 203 n. 15, argues that "mothers play a remarkably small part in earlier amatory fiction in contrast with later domestic fiction," though in the later fiction—such as *Sir Charles Grandison, Amelia,* and *Camilla*—she sees maternity as "the activitating principle." It may be rather misleading to generalize from amatory fiction in the earlier period, however, for maternity is a crucial consideration in *Moll Flanders, Roxana, Pamela,* and several of Haywood's novels.

9. Nancy Armstrong, *Desire and Domestic Fiction: A Political History of the Novel* (New York: Oxford University Press, 1987), and Irene Q. Brown, "Domesticity, Feminism, and Friendship: Female Aristocratic Culture and Marriage in England, 1660–1760," *Journal of Family History* 7 (1982): 406–24.

10. For the possibility of resistance to prevailing views of maternity, see my *Autobiographical Subject: Gender and Ideology in Eighteenth-Century England* (Baltimore: Johns Hopkins University Press, 1989), 201–24.

11. Londa Schiebinger, "Why Mammals Are Called Mammals: Gender Politics in Eighteenth-Century Natural History" (paper delivered at the Center for Seventeenth and Eighteenth Century Studies, Clark Library, October 1992).

12. Ruth Perry, "Colonizing the Breast: Sexuality and Maternity in Eighteenth-Century England," *Studies in the Eighteenth Century 8* in *Eighteenth-Century Life* 16, n.s. 1 (February 1992): 185–213. Barbara Gelpi, *Shelley's Goddess: Maternity, Language, Subjectivity* (New York: Oxford University Press, 1992), on the other hand, composes a narrative that suggests that the maternal is increasingly eroticized in the 1790s, and that the seminude breast is linked with both nursing and sexuality. The bared breast is also a symbol of republican liberty in the French Revolution, and Mary Sheriff finds that the lover in Fragonard's paintings may function as both lover and child, though the impact on the viewer remains opaque; see "Fragonard's Erotic Mothers and the Politics of Reproduction," in *Eroticism and the Body Politic,* ed. Lynn Hunt (Baltimore: Johns Hopkins University Press, 1991), 14–40.

13. Belinda Meteyard, "Illegitimacy and Marriage in Eighteenth-Century England," *Journal of Interdisciplinary History* 10 (Winter 1980): 479–89, emphasizes shifts in England's economic conditions that increased illegitimacy, including the fact that younger sons postponed marriage to build a trade or

profession, and the Marriage Act enacted in 1754, which changed the relationship of sex to marriage. Meteyard does not draw the connection to empire-building, though clearly, younger sons often traveled abroad to seek their fortune. Feminist literary historians have recently called attention to the connections between motherhood and "the new political and economic imperatives of an expanding English empire" (Perry, "Colonizing the Breast," 185).

14. M. Dorothy George, *London Life in the Eighteenth Century* (New York: Capricorn, 1965), 22.

15. Alan Macfarlane, *Marriage and Love in England: Modes of Reproduction, 1300–1840* (New York: Basil Blackwell, 1986), 20.

16. See R. K. McClure, *Coram's Children: The London Foundling Hospital in the Eighteenth Century* (New Haven: Yale University Press, 1981), and James S. Taylor, "Philanthropy and Empire: Jonas Hanway and the Infant Poor of London," *Eighteenth-Century Studies* 12 (1979): 285–305.

17. Thomas Man, *The Benefit of Procreation Together with Some Few Hints towards the better support of Whores and Bastards* (London 1739), 26, 18.

18. I am grateful to the Thomas Coram Foundation for Children for permission to examine and publish selections from these papers, which are deposited with the Corporation of London, Greater London Record Office.

19. Gayatri Chakravorty Spivak, "Theory in the Margin: Coetzee's *Foe*—Reading Defoe's *Crusoe/Roxana*," in *Consequences of Theory: Selected Papers from the English Institute, 1987–88,* n.s. no. 14, ed. Jonathan Arac and Barbara Johnson (Baltimore: Johns Hopkins University Press, 1991), 165.

20. Laura Brown, *Ends of Empire: Women and Ideology in Early Eighteenth-Century English Literature* (Ithaca: Cornell University Press, 1993), argues convincingly that the Englishwoman, dressed in the spoils of empire, is associated with consumption and trade, so that mercantile capitalism is itself figured as feminine.

21. See Spivak, "Theory in the Margin," 164.

22. Daniel Defoe, *Roxana: The Fortunate Mistress; or, A History of the Life and Vast Variety of Fortunes of Mademoiselle de Beleau, afterwards called the Countess de Wintselsheim in Germany Being the Person known by the Name of the Lady Roxana in the time of Charles II,* ed. Jane Jack (Oxford: Oxford University Press, 1988), 104, 126. All subsequent references are to this edition.

23. In Elizabeth Inchbald's novel *Nature and Art* (2 vols. [London, 1796]), Hannah, the mother of an illegitimate child, considers committing infanticide with the umbilical cord. The impulse makes another character say, "I always heard that you were brought up in a savage country" (2:33). Once she suckles the child, Hannah finds herself unable to kill it and abandons it instead, but her desire to keep the child is associated with her class position. When asked, "Do not most of our first women of quality part with their children?" she answers, "Women of quality have other things to love—I have nothing else" (2:39).

24. David Blewett, "The Double Time-Scheme of *Roxana:* Further Evidence," in *Studies in Eighteenth-Century Culture,* vol. 13, ed. O. M. Brack, Jr. (Madison: University of Wisconsin Press, 1984), 19–28. Roxana has historical roots in both the period of Charles II and of George I, according to Maximillian E. Novak, *Realism, Myth, and History in Defoe's Fiction* (Lincoln: University of Nebraska Press, 1983), 115–17.

25. Rachel Weil, "Sometimes a Scepter Is Only a Scepter: Pornography and Politics in Restoration England," in *The Invention of Pornography: Obscenity and the Origins of Modernity, 1500–1800,* ed. Lynn Hunt (New York: Zone Books, 1993), 125–53.

26. Rachel Weil cites this passage in "Sometimes a Scepter," 149.

27. For the connections between homoeroticism and Turkey in the eighteenth century, see Chapter 6 below.

28. According to Alev Lytle Croutier, "The excessive interference of the harem women in state politics was instrumental in the decline and fall of the [Turkish] empire. Ironically, such meddling began during the reign of Suleyman the Magnificent, the most powerful period in the empire's history (1520–66). It was then that the women moved with Roxalena from the Old Palace, built by Mehmed the Conqueror, to the Seraglio harem (1541), and approached the seat of power. This marked the beginning of the Sultanate, or the Reign of Women, which lasted a century and a half, until the end of the struggle between Kösem and Turhan sultanas (1687)." Croutier, *Harem: The World behind the Veil* (New York: Abbeville Press, 1989), 105.

29. Katie Trumpener, "Rewriting Roxane: Orientalism and Intertextuality in Montesquieu's *Lettres persanes* and Defoe's *The Fortunate Mistress,*" *Stanford French Review* 11 (1987): 178.

30. Mary Wollstonecraft writes, "Necessity never makes prostitution the business of men's lives; though numberless are the women who are thus rendered systematically vicious." *Vindication of the Rights of Woman,* in *The Works of Mary Wollstonecraft,* ed. Janet Todd and Marilyn Butler (Washington Square, N.Y.: New York University, 1989), 5:140.

31. Major John Taylor, *Travels from England to India, in the Year 1789,* 2 vols. (London, 1799), 1:209.

32. In *The Natural History of Aleppo,* for example, a Turkish woman is represented as "sitting carelessly on a divan, smoking a pipe, and her servant presenting a dish of coffee in the usual manner." Alexander Russell, *The Natural History of Aleppo and Parts Adjacent* (1756; London: A. Millar, 1856), 101.

33. Laura Brown aptly notes that Roxana's Turkish dress allows her to market herself and "evokes the spoils of an expansionist culture" (*Ends of Empire,* 147). In addition, the Turkish dress represents "the outfitting of the English female body in the complete and gorgeous costume of an exotic and exploited other" (148). Here it is useful to note, however, that the exploitation

rests on slavery, a slavery practiced by the Turks as well as Western Europe, and that it was based on class, race, and gender as much as imperial desires.

34. Georgian women were highly prized as "the handsomest people, not only in the east, but . . . in the whole world. . . . Nature has given most of the women such graces as are no where else to be seen; and it is impossible to behold, without loving them." *The World displayed; or, A Curious Collection of Voyages and Travels,* 20 vols., 4th ed. (London, 1774–78), 15:156.

35. Maternity and sexuality were actually interestingly aligned in the harem. Leslie P. Peirce, *The Imperial Harem: Women and Sovereignty in the Ottoman Empire* (New York: Oxford University Press, 1993), 119–25, indicates that European visitors failed to recognize that the Queen Mother, the mother of the sultan, held power in the harem rivaled only by the favorite concubine.

36. Gail Paster, *The Body Embarrassed: Drama and the Disciplines of Shame in Early Modern England* (Ithaca: Cornell University Press, 1993), suggests that "egregious bodily openness associated with the prostitute meant that her womb rarely closed tightly enough to retain seed and made her deliveries suspiciously easy" (189). Popular wisdom held that prostitutes were less likely to conceive. Painless births were, of course, also associated with primitive women.

37. Curiously, Amy had mentioned the Rachel/Jacob story before there was any question of Roxana's fertility. For a different but related discussion of Amy and Roxana, see Terry Castle, "'Amy, Who Knew My Disease': A Psychosexual Pattern in Defoe's *Roxana,*" *ELH* 46 (1979): 81–96. Castle sees Amy as the mother to the child Roxana, who is watching the sexual adventure of her parents in the "doubling" of mistress and maid.

38. See Terry Castle, *The Apparitional Lesbian: Female Homosexuality and Modern Culture* (New York: Columbia University Press, 1993) on lesbian specters: "What better way to exorcize the threat of female homosexuality than by treating it as ghostly?" (34).

39. William E. Ober, "Infanticide in Eighteenth-Century England: William Hunter's Contribution to the Forensic Problem," *Pathology Annual* 21 (1986): 311–19, provides statistics.

40. Man, *The Benefit of Procreation,* 9. Child murder was apparently rampant in the mother country. Burning, drowning, suffocation, and poisoning were the most common methods of parental negligence and child homicide, according to Thomas R. Forbes, "Deadly Parents: Child Homicide in Eighteenth- and Nineteenth-Century England," *Journal of the History of Medicine* 41 (April 1986): 175–99, and Peter C. Hoffer and N. E. H. Hull, *Murdering Mothers: Infanticide in England and New England, 1558–1803* (New York: New York University Press, 1981).

41. James R. Sutherland, *Daniel Defoe: A Critical Study* (Cambridge: Harvard University Press, 1971), writes that "it is hard to resist the assumption that *Roxana* got out of hand, and that Defoe didn't know how to finish his

own story; or, alternatively, that he knew what must be done but couldn't bring himself to do it" (201). I am suggesting that cultural forces were at work in making the resolution of the novel difficult to achieve.

42. Amelia Opie, *Adeline Mowbray: The Mother and Daughter* (London: Pandora Press, 1986), 41. All subsequent references are to this edition.

43. Mary Wollstonecraft writes: "No employment of the mind is a sufficient excuse for neglecting domestic duties, and I cannot conceive that they are incompatible. A woman may fit herself to be the companion and friend of a man of sense, and yet know how to take care of his family." *Thoughts on the Education of Daughters: with Reflections on Female Conduct, in the More Important Duties of Life* (London, 1787), in *Works*, ed. Todd and Butler, 4:21.

44. The foods of the West Indian islands are delicacies that make sick people well, as the ideal domestic economist of the eighteenth century is supposed to know. Adeline is seeking a pineapple for Glenmurray when she rescues Savanna's husband from debtor's prison; she prepares delicacies for Berrendale, and in the concluding scene, Savanna comments on the importance of money to provide good food to make people well. The empire serves to cure England's illnesses.

45. The tawny boy's loyalty to Editha also proves crucial in preserving her "life and beauty" from smallpox. Deformity, femininity, and empire are closely aligned in this friendship.

Chapter 2: "Savage" Mothers

1. A partial explanation for the mid-century focus on the mother might be found in the failed Jacobite rebellion of 1745, which became an unhappy reminder of the lost hope for restoring a Stuart patriarchy to the throne. Issues of monarchical legitimacy called into question the authority women possessed in recognizing their own progeny. The scandal concerning Mary Modena's birthing of James Edward Stuart, son of James II, and his legitimacy are discussed in papers by Toni-Lynn [O'Shaughnessy] Bowers, "Maternity, Legitimacy, and Political Authority: Queen Anne and the Myth of Maternal Power" (paper presented at the American Society for Eighteenth-Century Studies, Minneapolis, 1990), and Rachel Weil, "The Politics of Legitimacy: Women and the Warming Pan Scandal," in *The Revolution of 1688–89: Changing Perspectives*, ed. Lois Schwoerer (Cambridge: Cambridge University Press, 1992).

2. For discussions of the vital interest in motherhood and domesticity at mid-century, see Susan Staves, "Douglas's Mother," in *Brandeis Essays in Literature*, ed. John Hazel Smith (Waltham, Mass.: Brandeis University, 1983), 51–67; Mitzi Myers, "Impeccable Governesses, Rational Dames, and Moral Mothers: Mary Wollstonecraft and the Female Tradition in Georgian Children's Books," *Children's Literature* 14 (1986): 31–59; and Ruth Perry, "Colonizing the Breast: Sexuality and Maternity in Eighteenth-Century En-

gland," *Studies in the Eighteenth Century 8* in *Eighteenth-Century Life* 16, n.s. 1 (February 1992): 185–213.

3. For a discussion of republican motherhood, see Linda Kerber, *Women of the Republic: Intellect and Ideology in Revolutionary America* (Chapel Hill: University of North Carolina Press, 1980), and Jane Rendall, *The Origins of Modern Feminism: Women in Britain, France, and the United States, 1780–1860* (New York: Schocken, 1984). Jay Fliegelman, *Prodigals and Pilgrims: The American Revolution against Patriarchal Authority, 1750–1800* (Cambridge: Cambridge University Press, 1983), draws an analogy between American independence and rebellion against parental authority and the law of nature, although his emphasis is on the rejection of the father.

4. Both Londa Schiebinger, *The Mind Has No Sex? Women in the Origins of Modern Science* (Cambridge: Harvard University Press, 1989), 189–213, and Thomas Laqueur, *Making Sex: Body and Gender from the Greeks to Freud* (Cambridge: Harvard University Press, 1990), discuss the complexities of reproductive biology in the eighteenth century.

5. Ludmilla Jordanova, "Naturalizing the Family: Literature and the Bio-Medical Sciences in the Eighteenth Century," in *Languages of Nature: Critical Essays on Science and Literature,* ed. Jordanova (London: Free Association Books, 1986).

6. Thomas Hobbes, "Of dominion Paternal and Despotical," in *Leviathan; or, The Matter, Forme, and Power of A Commonwealth Ecclesiasticall and Civil* (1651), ed. Michael Oakeshott (New York: Collier, 1966), 152. According to Hobbes, if the mother exposes the child, the person who nurtures it should be granted dominion. In Locke's *Second Treatise of Civil Government* (1690), paternal authority is equally distributed between mother and father, but maternal power is implicitly restricted to the domestic domain.

7. Thomas McKeown and R. G. Brown, "Medical Evidence Related to English Population Changes in the Eighteenth Century," *Population Studies* 9 (November 1955): 119–41, find that 51.5 percent of baptized infants in London from 1770 to 1789 were dead before the age of five. Opinion is divided as to whether an increase in the birthrate may have contributed to the lowered rate of infant mortality at the end of the century. M. W. Beaver, "Population, Infant Mortality, and Milk," *Population Studies* 28 (July 1973): 243–54, believes that increased consumption of milk contributed to the decrease in mortality. (Beaver's specific figures for London's infant mortality rates are as follows: 1730–49, 74.5 percent mortality rate; 1750–59, 63 percent; 1770–89, 51 percent; 1790–1809, 41.3 percent; and 1810–29, 31.8 percent.)

8. "This Woman was carried from *Angola* in *Africa,* amongst other Slaves, to *America,* from whence she was brought to *Bristol.* She is about six and twenty Years old, has no Beard on her chin, nor any Thing masculine in her Countenance; her Arms above the Elbow are thick and fleshy, as many Womens are, but soft; her Breasts are small, her Voice effeminate in the

common Tone of speaking, and it was reported she has often been lain with by Men." James Parson, *A Mechanical and Critical Enquiry into the Nature of Hermaphrodites* (London, 1741), 134–35. The drawings that Parsons includes depict the "monstrous" genitals of this Angolan female slave. On European hermaphroditism, see especially Julia Epstein's groundbreaking article, "Either/Or—Neither/Both: Sexual Ambiguity and the Ideology of Gender," *Genders* 7 (Spring 1990): 99–142.

9. Oliver Goldsmith, *An History of the Earth and Animated Nature*, 8 vols. (London, 1774): 2:224.

10. Simon Ockley, *An Account of South (or West) Barbary* (London, 1713), 34; Denis Diderot, "Sur les femmes," in *Oeuvres de Diderot*, ed. André Billy (Paris: Bibliothèque de la Pléiade, 1962); James Adair, *The History of the American Indian* (London, 1775), 5. Diderot wrote in response to Antoine-Léonard Thomas's *Essay on the Character, Morals, and Mind of Women in Different Centuries* (Paris, 1772). See also Sylvana Tomaselli, "The Enlightenment Debate on Women," *History Workshop Journal* 20 (Autumn 1985): 101–24.

11. Mary Poovey, *Uneven Developments: The Ideological Work of Gender in Mid-Victorian England* (Chicago: University of Chicago Press, 1988), 18.

12. John Locke, *An Essay Concerning Human Understanding*, ed. Peter H. Nidditch (Oxford: Clarendon, 1975), 1:4. Mary Wollstonecraft gives equal weight to nature and nurture in *Thoughts on the Education of Daughters: with Reflections on Female Conduct, in the More Important Duties of Life* (London, 1787), remarking that "maternal tenderness arises quite as much from habit as instinct" (7).

13. Bernard de Mandeville, *The Fable of the Bees; or, Private Vices, Publick Benefits* (1728), ed. Phillip Harth (New York: Penguin, 1989), 68. But later in *The Fable,* Mandeville writes, "All Mothers naturally love their Children; but as this is a Passion, and all Passions center in Self-Love, so it may be subdued by an Superiour Passion, to sooth that same Self-Love, which if nothing had interven'd, would have bid her fondle her Offspring" (108).

14. Johnson tells Boswell, " '[Savages] have no affection, Sir.' BOSWELL. 'I believe natural affection of which we hear so much, is very small.' JOHNSON. 'Sir, natural affection is nothing: but affection from principle and established duty is sometimes wonderfully strong.' " James Boswell, *Life of Johnson*, ed. George Birkbeck Hill, rev. L. F. Powell, 6 vols. (Oxford: Clarendon, 1934–64), 4:210.

15. Robert Norris, *Memoirs of the Reign of Bossa Ahadee, King Of Dahomy* (London, 1789), 89.

16. William Alexander, *The History of Women from the Earliest Antiquity, to the Present Time*, 3rd ed., 2 vols. (London, 1782), 1:263, believes primitive women commit infanticide because social conditions overrule maternal feelings: "Yet, to such a degree is the ill-usage of the sex carried in some savage

countries, that it even obliterates this [maternal] feeling, and induces them to destroy the female children of their own body, that they may thereby save them from the wretchedness to which they themselves are subject."

17. Johnson's views on imperialism are not easily characterized. The introduction to *The World displayed; or, A Curious Collection of Voyages and Travels, selected from the Writers of all Nations*, 20 vols. (London, 1774), apparently written by Johnson, launches a critique: "The *Europeans* have scarcely visited any coast, but to gratify avarice, and extend corruption; to arrogate dominion without right, and practice cruelty without incentive" (1:xvi).

18. William Snelgrave, *A New Account of Some Parts of [the African Coast] of Guinea and the Slave Trade* (London, 1734), introduction. A second edition appeared in 1745, and the 1734 edition was reprinted in 1754 with a new title page. Hortense Spillers acutely describes the way the dominant culture "*misnames* the [maternal] power of the [African-American] female regarding the enslaved community" in "Mama's Baby, Papa's Maybe: An American Grammar Book," *diacritics* 17 (Summer 1987): 65–81.

19. Hortense Spillers, "'The Permanent Obliquity of an In[pha]llibly Straight': In the Time of Daughters and Fathers," in *Daughters and Fathers*, ed. Lynda E. Boose and Betty S. Flowers (Baltimore: Johns Hopkins University Press, 1989), 175.

20. Samuel Johnson, *Life of Savage*, ed. Clarence Tracy (Oxford: Clarendon, 1971), hereafter cited by page number in the text. Boswell argues with Johnson on May 15, 1768: "'As you expelled Lady Macclesfield from society, why not so bury Wilkes, Kenrick, Campbell, &c.? [If you succeeded] you would have done real service.' JOHNSON. 'Sir, I don't know but I've been wrong.'" *Boswell in Search of a Wife, 1766–1769*, ed. Frank Brady and Frederick Pottle (New York: McGraw-Hill, 1956), 168. The context is a discussion of English liberty and Baretti's belief that it was an "unjust and barbarous thing to turn away your king."

21. See especially the introduction to the Tracy edition of the *Life of Savage* for a summary of the arguments for and against Savage's claim to his birthright. George Irwin, *Samuel Johnson: A Personality in Conflict* (Auckland: Auckland University Press; Oxford: Oxford University Press, 1971), and Walter Jackson Bate, *Samuel Johnson* (New York: Harcourt Brace Jovanovich, 1975), pursue Johnson's psychological entanglements with his mother.

22. Savage eventually gained a pension from the queen in spite of his support for the Opposition, especially Bolingbroke, against George II and Walpole. Apparently he wrote five poems supporting the Jacobite uprising in 1715. See *The Poetical Works of Richard Savage*, ed. Clarence Tracy (Cambridge: Cambridge University Press, 1962), 15–26.

23. Alured Clarke, *An Essay Towards the Character of her late Majesty*, 2nd ed. (London, 1738), 20.

24. The description appears in *The London Magazine*, September 21, 1738.

An Essay Toward the Character of the Late Chimpanzee Who Died Feb. 23, 1738–9, remarks, "'Tis much to be lamented she was not married, as we have the greatest Reason in the World to believe she wou'd have made a most excellent Figure in the different Characters of a Wife, a Mother, Mistress, and a Friend" (23). For details, see G. S. Rousseau, "Madame Chimpanzee," parts 1 and 2, *The Clark Newsletter,* no. 10 (Spring 1986): 1–4; no. 12 (Spring 1987): 4–7. Donna Haraway calls attention to that endlessly mystified state, "primate motherhood," in *Primate Visions: Gender, Race, and Nature in the World of Modern Science* (New York: Routledge, 1989), 304.

25. Johnson misdates the poem, which antedates the quarrel with Lord Tyrconnel by seven years. It is published in Savage's *Poetical Works,* 88–92.

26. The title continues: "upon his Majesty's most gracious Pardon granted to Mr. Richard Savage, Son of the Late Earl Rivers." The poem was published as a brief sixpenny pamphlet. The pun on Richard Savage's name and "savage" (which I take to be a deferral of political meaning) is perpetuated in the Savage Clubs of London and Melbourne still in existence. According to the brochure for Melbourne Club, "The name of the London Club is attributed to the minor eighteenth-century poet, Richard Savage, as well as being a wry double-entendre on the spirited nature of its founding members." The club "is spacious, restful, and presents a civilized place of meeting, conversation and relaxation against a background of superb furnishings and appointments." These furnishings include "native artifacts," shrunken heads, racial caricatures, and "aboriginal murder shoes."

27. Johnson cites this poem in the *Life of Savage,* 93. The full text appears in Savage's *Poetical Works,* 219–33. John Sitter suggests in regard to mid-century poetry, "Again and again the feminine image is used as a focus of withdrawal, a symbol of retreat from the harsh world of traditionally male history, 'ambition,' greed, London, politics, social strife." John Sitter, "Mother, Memory, Muse, and Poetry after Pope," *ELH* 44 (Summer 1977): 319.

28. Mungo Park, *Travel in the Interior Districts of Africa: Performed Under the Direction and Patronage of the African Association, in the Years 1795, 1796, and 1797,* 2nd ed. (London, 1799). Three editions of Park's travels were printed in 1799 alone. The popular travels were reprinted throughout the nineteenth century, beginning with a fifth edition appearing in 1807. Park sought to improve on the "science of Geography" on behalf of the African Association, and he equivocates concerning his views on slavery. Kenneth Lupton, *Mungo Park, the African Traveler* (Oxford: Oxford University Press, 1979), provides biographical details about Park.

29. Wylie Sypher, *Guinea's Captive Kings: British Anti-Slavery Literature of the Eighteenth Century* (Chapel Hill: University of North Carolina Press, 1942), includes the duchess's song (pp. 225–26), and James Montgomery cites another version in *The West Indies* (1807).

30. Michele Wallace, *Invisibility Blues: From Pop to Theory* (London: Verso, 1990), 254.

31. William Epstein, *Recognizing Biography* (Philadelphia: University of Pennsylvania Press, 1987), 56.

Chapter 3: Polygamy, *Pamela*, and the Prerogative of Empire

1. Michele Wallace uses this phrase in reference to all black women in *Invisibility Blues: From Pop to Theory* (London: Verso, 1990).

2. Homi K. Bhabha, "The Other Question: Difference, Discrimination, and the Discourse of Colonialism," in *Literature, Politics, and Theory: Papers from the Essex Conference, 1976–84*, ed. Francis Barker et al. (London: Methuen, 1986), 156. For the concept of "consolidating the imperialist self," see especially Gayatri Spivak, "Three Women's Texts and a Critique of Imperialism," in *Race, Writing, and Difference*, ed. Henry Louis Gates, Jr. (Chicago: University of Chicago Press, 1986), 262–80, and Aihwa Ong, "Colonialism and Modernity: Feminist Representations of Women in Non-Western Societies," *Inscriptions* 3/4 (1988): 79–93.

3. For representations of Africa in the period, see V. Y. Mudimbe, *The Invention of Africa: Gnosis, Philosophy, and the Order of Knowledge* (Bloomington: Indiana University Press, 1988).

4. *Horace Walpole's Correspondence with Sir Horace Mann*, ed. W. S. Lewis, Warren Hunting Smith, and George L. Lam (New Haven: Yale University Press, 1967), 24:21.

5. Mungo Park, *Travels in the Interior Districts of Africa: Performed under the Direction and Patronage of the African Association, in the Years 1795, 1796, and 1797*, 2nd ed. (London, 1799). For a publication history, see Kenneth Lupton, *Mungo Park the African Traveler* (Oxford: Oxford University Press, 1979), esp. 109.

6. Robin Hallett, Introduction to *Records of the African Association, 1788–1831*, ed. Robin Hallett for the Royal Geographical Society (London: Thomas Nelson, 1964), 10. The African Association, a group of wealthy aristocratic men, grew to 109 members by 1791.

7. Hallett, *Records of the African Association*, 31.

8. Preface to William Smith, *A New Voyage to Guinea: Describing the Customs . . . Appointed by the Royal African Company to survey their settlements, etc.* (London, 1744), iii. The preface to this volume was apparently not written by Smith.

9. Willem Bosman, *A New and Accurate Description of the Coast of Guinea, Divided into the Gold, the Slave, and the Ivory Coasts*, trans. from the Dutch (London, 1705), preface.

10. Captain Philip Beaver, *African Memoranda: Relative to an Attempt to Establish a British Settlement . . . on the Western Coast of Africa, in the Year 1792*

(London, 1805), 395, writes that "slaves are the money, the circulating medium, with which great African commerce is carried on; they have no other." For a discussion of the parallel commodification of the novel, see Terry Lovell, *Consuming Fiction* (London: Verso, 1987).

11. Jean Baptiste Labat, *Voyages and Travels along the West Coast of Africa, from Cape Blanco to Sierra Leone* (1731), vol. 2 of *A New General Collection of Voyages and Travels; Consisting of the most Esteemed Relations, which have been hitherto published in any Language: comprehending every thing remarkable in its Kind in Europe, Asia, Africa, and America . . .* , [compiled by John Green?], 4 vols. (London, 1745–47); and Francis Moore and Captain B. Stibbs, *Travels into the Inland Parts of Africa: Containing a Description of the Several Nations . . .* (London, 1738). See also Hallett, *Records of the African Association*, 25.

12. Ignatius Sancho, *Letters of the Late Ignatius Sancho, an African to which are prefixed Memoirs of his Life*, 2 vols. (London, 1782), 2:4–5.

13. William Alexander, *The History of Women from the Earliest Antiquity to the Present Time*, 3rd ed., 2 vols. (London, 1782), 1:158.

14. Caleb Fleming, *Oeconomy of the Sexes; or, The Doctrine of Divorce, the Plurality of Wives, and the Vow of Celibacy Freely examined* (London, 1751), 32.

15. A. Owen Aldridge's articles "Polygamy and Deism," *JEGP* 48 (1949): 343–60, and "Polygamy in Early Fiction: Henry Neville and Denis Veiras," *JEGP* 65 (1950): 464–72, remain the definitive studies. Defoe comically opposes polygamy in *Conjugal Lewdness: A Treatise Concerning the Use and Abuse of the Marriage Bed* (London, 1727), stating that if polygamy had been destined, God would have made Adam's rib into six wives (23).

16. P. Dubliniensis, *Reflections upon Polygamy, and the Encouragement given to that Practice in the Scriptures of the Old Testament* (London, 1737), 1. This treatise also argues that in polygamous relationships, women are deprived of their natural right, sufficient sexual gratification. This defense of women's sexuality as a natural right appears in the writings of several of Madan's antagonists, including T. Hawkes, *A Scriptural Refutation of the Argument for Polygamy Advanced in a Treatise entitled Thelyphthora* (London, [1781]), 101. Bigamy was apparently common practice. According to Lawrence Stone, *The Road to Divorce: England, 1530–1987* (Oxford: Oxford University Press, 1990), 191, "The most common reason in the late seventeenth and early eighteenth centuries for declaring a marriage intrinsically void was bigamy arising from a previous marriage. . . . The [Marriage] Act followed custom in exempting persons whose spouses had been overseas or absent without news for seven years or more." Famous cases include *Tipping v. Roberts*, 1704–33; Teresa Constantia Phillips's many bigamous marriages (described in Lawrence Stone, *Uncertain Unions: Marriage in England, 1660–1753* [Oxford: Oxford University Press, 1992], 232–74); and the duchess of Kingston, who was accused of bigamy while in Rome in 1776. Legal cases of multiple marriage, often involving a wife from another country or religion, debated the

status of such marriages under English law. In *Warrender v. Warrender* (1835) the ruling stated: "Marriage is one and the same thing substantially all the Christian world over. Our whole law of marriage assumes this: and it is important to observe that we regard it as a wholly different thing . . . from Turkish or other marriages among infidel nations, because clearly we never should recognize the plurality of wives, and consequent validity of second marriages . . . which . . . the laws of those countries authorise and validate." J. H. C. Morris, *The Recognition of Polygamous Marriages in English Law* (Tübingen: J. C. B. Mohr, 1952), 291.

17. [Sophia Watson], *Memoirs of the Seraglio of the Bashaw of Merryland* (London, 1768), 2.

18. For these references to polygamy, see Olaudah Equiano, *The Interesting Narrative of the Life of Olaudah Equiano or Gustavus Vassa, the African,* in *The Classic Slave Narratives,* ed. Henry Louis Gates, Jr. (New York: New American Library, 1987), 13; Jerom Merolla da Sorrento, *A Voyage to the Congo and Several other Countries* (1682), in *A General Collection of the Best and Most Interesting Voyages and Travels in all Parts of the World,* ed. John Pinkerton, 17 vols. (London, 1814), 16:213; Moore and Stibbs, *Travels into the Inland Parts of Africa,* 133; John Barbot, *A Description of the Coasts of North and South Guinea, and of Ethiopia Inferior, Vulgarly Angola* (1732), in Awnsham and John Churchill, *A Collection of Voyages,* 6 vols. (London, 1732), 5:240; J. Grazilhier, *Voyages and Travels to Guinea and Benin* (1699), in *New General Collection,* comp. John Green (London: Frank Cass & Co., 1968), 3:113; and Smith, *A New Voyage to Guinea,* 26, 102.

19. John Millar, *The Origins of the Distinctions of Ranks; or, An Inquiry into the Circumstances which give rise to the Influence and Authority in the Different Members of Society,* 3rd ed. (London, 1781), 124.

20. Paul Lovejoy, "Concubinage in the Sohoto Caliphate, 1804–1903," *Slavery and Abolition* 11, no. 2 (1990): 180. He adds, "Concubinage is virtually ignored in the literature on slavery, yet it was the central mechanism for the sexual exploitation of women in Islamic societies" (159). Alexander Falconbridge, *An Account of the Slave Trade on the Coast of Africa* (London, 1788), 12, maintains that women slaves seldom exceeded a third of those transported. Claire Robertson, "The Perils of Autonomy," *Gender and History* 3 (Spring 1991): 91–96, convincingly argues that transporting more males than females was due to African "desire to retain women slaves, *not* to European's preference for male labor. Women slaves were kept primarily because of their agricultural labor value and secondarily due to their reproductive capabilities that were useful for expanding African lineages" (95).

21. Harriet Jacobs, *Incidents in the Life of a Slave Girl: Mrs. Harriet Brent Jacobs, Written by Herself* (1861) (New York: AMS Press, 1973), 57. The narrative by "Linda Brent" was edited and framed by white women.

22. *Some Historical Account of Guinea, Its Situation, Produce, and the Gen-*

eral Disposition of its Inhabitants with an Inquiry into the Rise and Progress of the Slave Trade (London, 1788), 76.

23. Henry Neville, *The Isle of Pines; or, A Late Discovery of a fourth Island near Terra Australis, Incognita by Henry Cornelius Van Sloetten* (London 1668), 12.

24. Martin Madan, *Thelyphthora; or, A Treatise on Female Ruin in its causes, effects, consequences, prevention, and remedy; considered on the basis of the Divine Law,* 2 vols. (London, 1780). One of Madan's most unusual arguments is that polygamy is justified because Christ was born of a polygamous relationship. See John Towers, *Polygamy Unscriptural; or, Two Dialogues Between Philalethes and Monogamus* (London, 1780), 8.

25. Richard Hill, *The Blessings of Polygamy Displayed, in an Affectionate Address to the Rev. Martin Madan occasioned by his late Work, entitled Thelyphthora, or A Treatise of Female Ruin* (London, 1781), 39.

26. Saunders Welch, *A Proposal to Render Effectual a Plan to Remove the Nuisance of Common Prostitutes from the Streets of the Metropolis* (London, 1758), 7.

27. Martin Madan, Letter 4 to Rev. Mr. G (April 14, 1781), *Letters on Thelyphthora: with an Occasional Prologue and Epilogue by the Author* (London, 1782).

28. John Matthews, *A Voyage to the River Sierra-Leone, on the Coast of Africa* (London, 1788), 99.

29. David Hume, "Of Polygamy and Divorces" (1742), reprinted in *Essays Moral, Political, and Literary* (Oxford: Oxford University Press, 1963), 185–95. Hume believed that blacks were "naturally inferior to the Whites. There scarcely ever was a civilised nation of that complexion. . . . Such a uniform and constant difference could not happen, in so many countries and ages, if nature had not made an original distinction betweeen these breeds of men." Hume, "Of National Characters," ibid., 213 n.1. Hume, in charge of the British Colonial Office from 1766, added this note to the 1753–54 edition of this essay, and it was later used as a basis for scientific racism. See Richard H. Popkin, *The High Road to Pyrrhonism* (San Diego: Austin Hill Press, 1980), 251–66.

30. According to Francis Moore and Captain Stibbs, *Travels,* 40, Mumbo Jumbo was a cant language spoken exclusively by men. Mumbo Jumbo, as a folkloric invention dressed in a long coat and a tuft of straw on top, kept women in awe of masculine authority. Women fled when Mumbo Jumbo arrived.

31. T. C. Duncan Eaves and Ben D. Kimpel, *Samuel Richardson: A Biography* (Oxford: Clarendon, 1971), 135.

32. Terry Castle, *Masquerade and Civilization: The Carnivalesque in Eighteenth-Century English Culture and Fiction* (Stanford: Stanford University Press, 1986), 132. Though she does not mention polygamy, Castle richly de-

scribes the way the sequel to *Pamela* must "be different, but also *exactly the same.*"

33. *Pamela; or, Virtue Rewarded,* in *The Works of Samuel Richardson,* ed. Leslie Stephen (London: Henry Southeran, 1893), 3:53. For a subtle analysis of Pamela's double jeopardy as wife and mother, see Ruth Perry, "Colonizing the Breast: Sexuality and Maternity in Eighteenth-Century England," *Studies in the Eighteenth Century 8,* in *Eighteenth-Century Life* 16, n.s. 1 (February 1992): 185–213.

34. It seems possible that breast disfigurement was associated with the milky lower class. See Gail Paster, *The Body Embarrassed: Drama and the Disciplines of Shame in Early Modern England* (Ithaca: Cornell University Press, 1993), 163–280.

35. Fatna A. Sabbah, *Woman in the Muslim Unconscious,* trans. Mary Jo Lakeland (New York: Pergamon Press, 1984), 25, discusses the way that Muslim women's visible physical attributes are openly interpreted as indicators of veiled sexual organs.

36. The classic statement of this view is, of course, Friedrich Engels, *The Origin of the Family, Private Property, and the State* (New York: Penguin, 1985).

37. A[nna] M. Falconbridge, *Narrative of Two Voyages to the River Sierra Leone during the Years 1791–2–3,* 2nd ed. (London, 1802), 122. Falconbridge depised colonial policies but equivocated about abolishing the slave trade.

38. These revised and elaborated letters were published later as *Letters of the Right Honourable Lady M——y W——y M——e: Written during her Travels in Europe, Asia, and Africa,* 2 vols. (London, 1763). I have cited the modern edition, *The Complete Letters of Lady Mary Wortley Montagu,* ed. Robert Halsband, 2 vols. (Oxford: Clarendon, 1965). See also Joseph W. Lew, "Lady Mary's Portable Seraglio," *ECS* 24 (Summer 1991): 432–50. Lew believes that Lady Mary "subverts both Orientalist discourse and eighteenth-century patriarchy itself."

39. Leslie P. Peirce, *The Imperial Harem: Women and Sovereignty in the Ottoman Empire* (New York: Oxford University Press, 1993), believes that "in the absence of indigenous descriptions of the workings of the harem institution, we must turn to accounts written by European observers of the Ottomans, our only contemporary sources" (114).

40. Billie Melman, *Women's Orients: English Women and the Middle East, 1718–1918: Sexuality, Religion, and Work* (Ann Arbor: University of Michigan Press, 1992), 72.

41. On tattoos, see Harriet Guest, "Curiously Masked: Tattooing, Masculinity, and Nationality in Late-Eighteenth-Century British Perceptions of the South Pacific," in *Painting and the Politics of Culture,* ed. John Barrell (Oxford: Oxford University Press, 1992).

42. Mary Wollstonecraft, *A Vindication of the Rights of Woman*, ed. Miriam Kramnick (Harmondsworth: Penguin, 1975), ch. 4. Wollstonecraft compares the weakest and most frivolous Englishwomen to women in a seraglio. Muhammadanism is defined as woman's brutish enemy.

43. John Reinold Forster, *Observations Made During a Voyage Round the World on Physical Geography, Natural History and Ethic Philosophy* (London, 1788), 425–26.

44. Alexander, *The History of Women from the Earliest Antiquity*, 1:313.

45. Trinh T. Minh-ha, "Not You/Like You: Post-Colonial Women and the Interlocking Question of Identity and Difference," *Inscriptions* 3/4 (1988): 73. For a discussion of the use of the veil in protest against the shah of Iran, see Nayereh Tohidi, "Gender and Islamic Fundamentalism," in *Third World Women and the Politics of Feminism*, ed. Chandra Talpade Mohanty, Ann Russo, and Lourdes Torres (Bloomington: Indiana University Press, 1991), 251–67.

Chapter 4: Prostitution, Body Parts, and Sexual Geography

1. In "North and South," *Eighteenth-Century Life* 12, n.s. 2 (May 1988): 101, Pat Rogers writes: "Real geographical and climatic differences depend upon the latitude, rather than the longitude; seasons relate to the one as they do not to the other. The equator is more than a metaphysical entity, whereas the degree zero of modern cartography had been drawn at an arbitrary point on the globe." Terry Castle discusses the invention of scientific instruments to measure gendered bodily heat in "The Female Thermometer," *Representations* 17 (Winter 1987): 1–27.

2. Lyndal Roper, "Will and Honor: Sex, Words, and Power in Augsburg Criminal Trials," *Radical History Review* 43 (1989): 45–71.

3. Francis Foster, *Thoughts on the Times, But Chiefly on the Profligacy of our Women, and It's Causes* (London, 1779), 11. On prostitution in the period, see Vern L. Bullough, *Prostitution: An Illustrated Social History* (New York: Crown, 1978); Stanley Nash, "Prostitution and Charity: The Magdalen Hospital, A Case Study," *Journal of Social History* 17 (Summer 1987): 617–28; and Vern L. Bullough, "Prostitution and Reform in Eighteenth-Century England," in *Unauthorized Sexual Behavior during the Enlightenment*, ed. Robert P. Maccubbin, *Eighteenth-Century Life* 9, n.s. 3 (May 1985): 61–74.

4. The definitive study remains David Foxon, *Libertine Literature in England, 1660–1745* (New Hyde Park: University Books, 1965). See also Peter Wagner, *Eros Revived: Erotica of the Enlightenment in England and America* (London: Secker and Warburg, 1988).

5. James Turner traces associations between women's increasing economic power and allegations of promiscuity in his unpublished paper, "'News from the New Exchange': Commodity, Erotic Fantasy, and the Female Entrepreneur" (William Andrews Clark Library Lecture, April 1991).

6. Stephen Marcus, *The Other Victorians: A Study of Sexuality and Pornography in Mid-Nineteenth-Century England* (New York: Basic Books, 1964), 266–86, defines such a "no place" as "pornotopia."

7. Roy Roussel, *The Conversation of the Sexes: Seduction and Equality in Selected Seventeenth- and Eighteenth-Century Texts* (New York: Oxford University Press, 1986), defines pornography rather restrictively as that which incites masturbation.

8. Robert Dingley, *Proposals for Establishing a Public Place of Reception for Penitent Prostitutes* (London, 1758), and John Fielding, *An Account of the Origin and Effects of a Police Set on Foot . . . to which is added a Plan for Preserving those deserted Girls in this Town, who Become Prostitutes from Necessity* (London, 1758).

9. Dingley, *Proposals*, 3.

10. Saunders Welch, *A Proposal to Render Effectual a Plan to Remove the Nuisance of Common Prostitutes from the Streets of the Metropolis* (London, 1758). Prostitution increased elsewhere too: Linda Mahood, *The Magdalenes: Prostitution in the Nineteenth Century* (London: Routledge, 1990), finds that in Edinburgh the number of brothels increased from five or six at the beginning of the century to twenty at its end.

11. E. J. Burford, *Wits, Wenchers, and Wantons: London's Low Life: Covent Garden in the Eighteenth Century* (London: Robert Hale, 1986).

12. Hilary Evans, *Harlots, Whores, and Hookers: A History of Prostitution* (New York: Taplinger Publishing Co., 1979).

13. Welch, *Proposal*, 19. See also Randolph Trumbach, "Sex, Gender, and Sexual Identity in Modern Culture: Male Sodomy and Female Prostitution in Enlightenment London," *Journal of the History of Sexuality* 2 (October 1991): 186–203.

14. Welch, *Proposal*, 7.

15. M. D'Archenholz, *A Picture of England*, 2 vols. (London, 1789), 2:95.

16. *Satan's Harvest Home; or, The Present State of Whorecraft, Adultery, Fornication, Procuring . . .* (London, 1749), 35.

17. Barbara Littlewood and Linda Mahood, "Prostitutes, Magdalenes, and Wayward Girls: Dangerous Sexualities of Working Class Women in Victorian Scotland," *Gender and History* 3 (Summer 1991): 163.

18. A "Man-Woman" is not necessarily the same as an Amazon who possesses a woman's body *sans* one breast and engages in warlike activities, and a "Man-Woman" also need not be identical to a multiply sexualized body. For one treatment of subtle and not always distinct differences among hermaphrodites, tribades, and men-women, see Julia Epstein, "Either/Or—Neither/Both: Sexual Ambiguity and the Ideology of Gender," *Genders* 7 (Spring 1990): 99–142.

19. Thomas Man, *The Benefit of Procreation Together with Some Few Hints towards the better support of Whores and Bastards* (London, 1739), writes that

the name "whore" should be "applied only to those jaded, tough, callous Prostitutes who are incapable of Procreation" (4).

20. William Dodd, Preface to "A Sermon Preached before the . . . Governors of the Magdalen-House," in *An Account of the Rise, Progress, and Present State of the Magdalen Hospital, for the Reception of Penitent Prostitutes. Together with Dr. Dodd's Sermons* (London, 1767), 197.

21. [Bernard Mandeville], *A Modest Defence of Publick Stews* (1724), intro. Richard I. Cook, Augustan Reprint Society no. 162 (Los Angeles: William Andrews Clark Memorial Library, 1973), 31.

22. M. D. T. Bienville, *Nymphomania; or, A Dissertation Concerning the Furor Uterinus* (London, 1775), 146.

23. Speaking of the current historical moment, Eve Sedgwick in *Epistemology of the Closet* (Berkeley and Los Angeles: University of California Press, 1991), articulates the ways that the axes of gender and sexuality may be different, and she turns our focus to the ways that categories work, rather than what they essentially *mean*. The sex/gender distinction is "a problematic *space* rather than a crisp distinction" (29).

24. For a history of the clitoris, see Thomas Laqueur, *Making Sex: Body and Gender from the Greeks to Freud* (Cambridge: Harvard University Press, 1990).

25. See *Philosophical Transactions*, no. 32 (1745): 117.

26. William Ten Rhyne, Native of Deventry, Physician in Ordinary and a Member of the Council of Justice, to the Dutch East India Co. . . . , *An Account of the Cape of Good Hope and the Hottentotes, the Natives of that Country*, in John Churchill, *A Collection of Voyages and Travels*, 6 vols. (London, 1732), 4:774. M. LeVaillant, *Travels into the Interior Parts of Africa*, 2 vols. (London, 1790), 2:353, provides a similar description.

27. In *The New Epicurean; or, The Delights of Sex Facetiously and Philosophically Considered* (London, 1740; repr. 1875), female ejaculation seems to be suggested during sexual relations, as in "She was spending, and her shift was quite wet" (21); "I sent a spirting shower over her tongue, while her virgin dew drenched her own" (47); or there was "a gush of spending from Mrs. J" (63).

28. Edmund Burke, *The Complete Works of the Right Honourable Edmund Burke*, rev. ed. (Boston: Little, Brown, 1866), 2:462. Cleland's stint just preceded the great expansion of the British naval presence in India following the Anglo-French wars of the 1740s. Most British stationed in India may have remained ghettoized on ships and in military barracks, because before 1756 there were insufficient numbers among foreigners to form the discrete communities so prevalent in the nineteenth century. See P. J. Marshall, "Taming the Exotic: The British and India in the Seventeenth and Eighteenth Centuries," in *Exoticism in the Enlightenment*, ed. G. S. Rousseau and Roy Porter (Manchester: Manchester University Press, 1990), 48. According to Percival Spear, *The Nabobs: A Study of the Social Life of the English in Eighteenth-*

Century India, 2nd ed. (London: Curzon, 1963), 78, "In 1720 the list of 'free merchants, seafaring men, etc. at Bombay' including women, totalled fifty-nine; in 1750 it was fifty-two."

29. *Early Records of British India* (London, 1878), 91–92. See also William H. Epstein, *John Cleland: Images of a Life* (New York: Columbia University Press, 1974), 38, who cites this passage.

30. John Cleland, *Memoirs of a Woman of Pleasure,* ed. Peter Sabor (Oxford: Oxford University Press, 1985). All subsequent references are to this edition. Among the most pertinent essays on the novel are Robert Markley, "Language, Power, and Sexuality in Cleland's *Fanny Hill,*" *Philological Quarterly* 63 (Summer 1984): 343–56; and Randolph Trumbach, "Modern Prostitution and Gender in *Fanny Hill:* Libertine and Domesticated Fantasy," in *Sexual Underworlds of the Enlightenment,* ed. Roy Porter and G. S. Rousseau (Chapel Hill: University of North Carolina Press, 1988), 69–85.

31. Randolph Trumbach, "Erotic Fantasy and Male Libertinism in Enlightenment England," in *The Invention of Pornography: Obscenity and the Origins of Modernity, 1500–1800,* ed. Lynn Hunt (New York: Zone, 1993), 253–82, maintains on very slight evidence that Cleland believes that the clitoris is located inside the vagina. My differences with Trumbach's formulation of categories of sexual identity are suggested here and in Chapter 6.

32. Nancy K. Miller, "The 'I's' in Drag: The Sex of Recollection," *The Eighteenth Century: Theory and Interpretation* 22 (1981): 47–57; Julia Epstein, "Fanny's Fanny: Epistolarity, Eroticism, and the Transsexual Text," in *Writing the Female Voice: Essays on Epistolary Literature,* ed. Elizabeth C. Goldsmith (Boston: Northeastern University Press, 1989), 135–53.

33. Judith Butler, "Imitation and Gender Insubordination," in *Inside/Out: Lesbian Theories, Gay Theories,* ed. Diana Fuss (New York: Routledge, 1991), articulates this concept: "Drag is not the putting on of a gender that belongs properly to some other group . . . [but] constitutes the mundane way in which genders are appropriated, theatricalized, worn, and done; it implies that all gendering is a kind of impersonation and approximation. If this is true, it seems there is no original or primary gender that drag imitates, but *gender is a kind of imitation for which there is not an original;* in fact, it is a kind of imitation that produces the very notion of the original as an *effect* and consequence of imitation itself" (24; emphasis in original). For recent work on "drag" in the eighteenth century, see Madeleine Kahn, *Narrative Transvestism: Rhetoric and Gender in the Eighteenth-Century Novel* (Ithaca: Cornell University Press, 1991), and Kristina Straub, *Sexual Suspects: Eighteenth-Century Players* (Princeton: Princeton University Press, 1992).

34. Rebecca Weller catalogues these and other "firsts" in her unpublished paper, "Reclining Women/Declining Men: An Examination of John Cleland's *Memoirs of a Woman of Pleasure.*" I am grateful for her permission to

refer to this essay and also to the Stanford University graduate students in my Winter 1992 seminar for their discussions of the novel.

35. Whores and lesbians have been connected throughout history as the site of the erotic and the taboo. Whores are not necessarily the sign of hetero-sexuality but may also engage in same-sex practices. In *Genuine Memoirs of the Celebrated Maria Brown*, 2 vols. (London, 1766), Maria recounts her ulti-mately unsatisfying lovemaking with a Miss P. And of course, historically, prostitutes are frequently initiated into prostitution through homoerotic ac-tivities. Joan Nestle, *A Restricted Country* (Ithaca: Firebrand Books, 1987), points out that both whores and lesbians have been called a third sex and thus are aligned in redefining the concept of woman and her erotic boundaries. Learning the pleasures of the body, she suggests, often involves female bond-ing over erotic experiences. She begins an investigation of the way "lesbians and prostitutes have always been connected, not just in the male imagination but in their actual histories" (158).

36. Similarly, when fellow prostitute Harriet recounts her tale of being raped after swooning from the heat (102), her narrative may be doubly inter-preted as a male-male encounter.

37. Lee Edelman, "Seeing Things: Representation, the Scene of Sur-veillance, and the Spectacle of Gay Male Sex," in Fuss, *Inside/Out*, 105.

38. The prostitute and the racial Other are explicitly compared in the religious discourse of the period to the detriment of the Other. The prostitute is judged to be more malleable than the Ethiopian, who cannot be washed white. See Fig. 4, William Hogarth's "Discovery," for an example of the conflation of the two. The quotation from Ovid is translated, "What once was white is now its opposite." The idiot is also a kind of parodic inversion of the black eunuch who guards the harem, commonly compared to the brothel.

39. Significantly, this passage was cut in the expurgated version.

40. In *The Body Embarrassed: Drama and the Disciplines of Shame in Early Modern England* (Ithaca: Cornell University Press, 1993), Gail Kern Paster writes that the "egregious bodily openness associated with the prostitute meant that her womb rarely closed tightly enough to retain seed and made her deliveries suspiciously easy" (189). Deflecting erotic attention away from the increasingly maternal breast to the genitalia puts heightened erotic charge on the lower part of women's bodies. When Cleland expurgated *Memoirs of a Woman of Pleasure* (1748–49) to publish a less offensive *Memoirs of Fanny Hill* (1750), he excluded the mention of thighs but retained discussions of breasts.

41. Catherine Gallagher, "Who Was That Masked Woman? The Pros-titute and the Playwright in the Comedies of Aphra Behn," *Women's Studies* 15 (1988): 23–42, is especially helpful on the connections between writer and whore.

42. Henry Merritt finds that Cleland was accused of sodomy in "Bio-graphical Notes," *Notes and Queries* 28 (1981): 305–6.

Chapter 5: The Empire of Love

1. Ann Snitow makes the analogy in her classic text: "How different is the pornography for women, in which sex is bathed in romance, diffused, always implied rather than enacted at all." Snitow, "Mass Market Romance: Pornography for Women Is Different," in *Powers of Desire: The Politics of Sexuality*, ed. Ann Snitow, Christine Stansell, and Sharon Thompson (New York: Monthly Review Press, 1983), 257.

2. Charlotte Lennox, *The Female Quixote; or, The Adventures of Arabella*, edited by Margaret Dalziel with an introduction by Margaret Anne Doody (Oxford: Oxford University Press, 1991). All quotations are from this edition. Jane Austen was also among its admirers. See Miriam R. Small, *Charlotte Ramsay Lennox: An Eighteenth-Century Lady of Letters*, Yale Studies in English, No. 85 (New Haven: Yale University Press, 1935), 84 and 87.

3. Laurie Langbauer, *Women and Romance: The Consolations of Gender in the English Novel* (Ithaca: Cornell University Press, 1990), suggests that in *The Female Quixote* women and romance are so closely associated that Arabella must cease being a woman to escape from romance (81). But of course to escape from conventional femininity is also precisely what she attempts to do. See also Deborah Ross, "Mirror, Mirror: The Didactic Dilemma of *The Female Quixote*," *SEL* 27, no. 3 (1987): 455–73.

4. Susan Staves, "*Evelina;* or, Female Difficulties," *Modern Philology* 73 (May 1976): 368–81, remarks on Evelina's confrontation with whores in Marybone: "Contact between the pure maiden and fallen woman is, in fact, nearly an obligatory scene in certain kinds of eighteenth-century novels." Staves does not speculate about the effect of this paradigmatic moment. Evelina, unlike Arabella, fears being identified with whores.

5. *The Poems of Jonathan Swift*, ed. Harold Williams, 3 vols. (Oxford: Clarendon, 1937), 2:691–92, lines 168–71.

6. Delarivier Manley, *The New Atalantis*, ed. Rosalind Ballaster (London: Penguin, 1991),235.

7. Ros Ballaster, *Seductive Forms: Women's Amatory Fiction from 1684 to 1740* (Oxford: Clarendon, 1992), 46.

8. Ruth Bernard Yeazell includes this example in *Fictions of Modesty: Women and Courtship in the English Novel* (Chicago: University of Chicago Press, 1991), 65–66.

9. John Mullan, "Hypochondria and Hysteria: Sensibility and the Physicians," *The Eighteenth Century: Theory and Interpretation* 25 (Spring 1984): 160, notes, "The distinction between the flush of an improper excitement and the virtuous blush of an entranced sensibility is a difficult and shifting one."

10. Yeazell, *Fictions of Modesty*, 72. She also cites Charles Darwin, *The Expression of the Emotions in Man and Animals* (1872), 236: "No doubt a slight blush adds to the beauty of a maiden's face . . . and the Circassian women who

are capable of blushing, invariably fetch a higher price in the seraglio of the Sultan than less susceptible women."

11. I take the term "symbolic mediator" from Arlene Elowe MacLeod, "Hegemonic Relations and Gender Resistance: The New Veiling as Accommodating Protest in Cairo," *Signs: Journal of Women in Culture and Society* 17 (Spring 1992): 550. MacLeod writes, "Through the veil these women express their distress with their double bind; they want to reinstate their position as valued centers of the family but without losing their new ability to leave the home." She adds, "Veiling involves a struggle over women's identity and role in society, a negotiation of symbolic meaning that women initiate."

12. The extensive literature on the political meanings of the veil include Nesta Ramazani, "The Veil—Piety or Protest?" *Journal of South Asian and Middle Eastern Studies* 7 (Winter 1983): 20–36; Alene Elowe MacLeod, *Accommodating Protest: Working Women, the New Veiling, and Change in Cairo* (New York: Columbia University Press, 1991); and Lila Abu-Lughod, *Veiled Sentiments: Honor and Poetry in a Bedouin Society* (Berkeley and Los Angeles: University of California Press, 1986). The veil need not encourage antagonisms among women, but it is remarkable that such antagonism is one of its effects in *The Female Quixote*.

13. Richard Steele, *The Spectator* no. 390 (May 28, 1712), cited in Yeazell, *Fictions of Modesty*, 67.

14. Farzaneh Milani, *Veils and Words: The Emerging Voices of Iranian Women Writers* (Syracuse: Syracuse University Press, 1992), 19, writes, "An emblem now of progress, then of backwardness, a badge now of nationalism, then of domination, a symbol of purity, then of corruption, the veil has accommodated itself to a puzzling diversity of personal and political ideologies."

15. For an exemplary essay on the connections between romance and empire, see Laura Brown's "The Romance of Empire: *Oroonoko* and the Trade in Slaves," in *The Ends of Empire: Women and Ideology in Early Eighteenth-Century English Literature* (Ithaca: Cornell University Press, 1993), 23–63. Brown connects the nostalgic impulses of romance to distancing the contemporaneous Other from the present both historically and geographically, and thus from its current urgent predicament.

16. In the context of modern history, for instance, Chandra Talpade Mohanty notes that Iranian women of the middle class allied themselves with working-class women during the 1979 revolution by joining them in veiling, while current Iranian laws insist that all women wear veils: "In the first case, wearing the veil is both an oppositional and a revolutionary gesture on the part of Iranian middle-class women; in the second case, it is a coercive, institutional mandate." Mohanty, "Under Western Eyes: Feminist Scholarship and Colonial Discourses," in *Third World Women and the Politics of Feminism*, ed. Chandra Talpade Mohanty, Ann Russo, and Lourdes Torres

(Bloomington: Indiana University Press, 1991), 67. In an essay in the same volume, "Gender and Islamic Fundamentalism: Feminist Politics in Iran," 251–67, Nayereh Tohidi remarks on the way the policing of the veil under Reza Shah (1935) made it politically charged: "Not to wear it became associated with identifying with the West, and the abusive and brutal politics of the Pahlavi regime. This partially explains why the adoption of the veil became a symbolic protest against the Shah" (266 n. 3).

17. Though Charlotte Lennox was deeply admired by Samuel Johnson, Fielding, and Richardson, Fanny Burney reported that while Lennox's books "are generally approved, nobody likes her," and she was estranged from the Bluestockings. See Miriam R. Small, *Charlotte Ramsay Lennox* (New Haven: Yale University Press, 1935), 49 and 228.

18. Of course, in the early anthropological accounts such as John Millar's *Origin of the Distinction of Ranks; or, An Inquiry into the Circumstances which give rise to the Influence and Authority in the Different Members of Society* (3rd ed. 1781), women of the Hottentot, Formosan and Marian islanders, and North American tribes were thought to be akin to Amazons in indulging their sexual appetites and exercising military authority: "So extraordinary a spectacle as that of a military enterprise conducted by women, and where the men acted in a subordinate capacity, must have filled the enemy with wonder and astonishment, and might easily give rise to those fictions of a *female republic*, and of other circumstances equally marvellous, which we meet with in ancient writers" (68).

19. The use of the veil in this passage is reminiscent of Lady Mary Wortley Montagu's remark on Turkish women being able to remain in disguise by veiling themselves in the streets; see *The Complete Letters of Lady Mary Wortley Montagu*, ed. Robert Halsband, 3 vols. (Oxford: Clarendon, 1965), 1:328.

20. Samuel Johnson may have penned the moralizing chapter "Being, in the Author's Opinion, the best Chapter in this History." Patricia Meyer Spacks, *Desire and Truth: Functions of Plot in Eighteenth-Century English Novels* (Chicago: University of Chicago Press, 1990), 20, draws parallels between Johnson's view of desire as both energizing imagination and misdirecting it to *The Female Quixote*.

21. B. G. MacCarthy, *The Female Pen: Women Writers and Novelists* (New York: Cork University Press, 1994), 300, points out in discussing the difficulties for a female satirist that "Cervantes' knight could wander where he would in search of adventure: Arabella was forced to find her adventures wherever she happened to be and, although the scene changes, her immediate circumstances do not, because the conventions require that she should be accompanied everywhere by an entourage of her nearest relatives. Don Quixote could initiate romantic empires as the spirit moved him. Arabella could merely give romantic interpretations to the actions of others (the one exception being when, to escape imaginary ravishers, she jumps into the river—an

incident which seriously jars one's ideas of probability)." Fielding wrote a favorable review in the *Covent Garden Journal,* March 24, 1752, and Johnson may be the author of another in *Gentleman's Magazine,* 22 (March 1752), 146.

22. See M. P. Conant, *The Oriental Tale in England in the Eighteenth Century* (New York: Columbia University Press, 1908).

23. Arthur J. Weitzman, "More Light on *Rasselas:* The Background of the Egyptian Episodes," *Philological Quarterly* 48 (January 1969): 42–58, is especially helpful. See also Weitzman's unpublished dissertation, "The Influence of the Middle East on English Prose Fiction, 1600–1725" (New York University, 1963).

24. Samuel Johnson, *Rasselas and Other Tales,* ed. Gwin J. Kolb, *The Yale Edition of the Works of Samuel Johnson,* vol. 16 (New Haven: Yale University Press, 1990), 46. All subsequent references are to this edition.

25. Weitzman, "More Light on *Rasselas,*" 50.

26. See McCarthy, *The Later Women Novelists,* 21. Other oriental tales include Ellis Cornelia Knight's *Dinarbas* (1790) and Maria Edgeworth's *Murad the Unlucky* (1804). Sheridan's novel was published posthumously; she died in 1766. See the entry on Sheridan in *A Dictionary of British and American Women Writers, 1660–1800,* ed. Janet Todd (Totawa, N.J.: Rowman and Allanheld, 1985).

27. Frances Sheridan, *The History of Nourjahad* (London: Carpenter and Sons, 1818), 92. All subsequent references are to this edition.

28. Margaret Anne Doody, "Frances Sheridan: Morality and Annihilated Time," in *Fetter'd or Free: British Women Novelists, 1670–1815,* ed. Mary Anne Schofield and Cecilia Macheski (Athens, Ohio: Ohio University Press, 1986), 353, believes, on the contrary, that "*Nourjahad* is consistent in maintaining a masculine point of view" and that "women have only a subordinate walk-on part to play in the narrative."

Chapter 6: Feminotopias

First epigraph: Mary Astell, Appendix to *Some Reflections upon Marriage,* 4th ed. (1730), reprinted in *The "Other" Eighteenth Century: English Women of Letters, 1660–1800,* ed. Robert W. Uphaus and Gretchen M. Foster (East Lansing, Mich.: Colleagues Press, 1991), 49. A reference to the biblical passage appears in Sarah Scott, *A Description of Millenium Hall and the Country Adjacent Together with the Characters of the Inhabitants . . . ,* intro. Jane Spencer (New York: Virago, 1986), 17: "The wolf shall dwell with the lamb, and the leopard shall lie down with the kid; and the calf, and the young lion, and the fatling together, and a young child shall lead them. The wilderness and the solitary place shall be glad for them, and the desert shall rejoice, and blossom as the rose." All subsequent quotations of Scott's novel are from this edition.

1. Pratt cites Latin American examples such as Flora Tristan's utopian vision of the women in Peru, and Maria Graham's description of women in

Brazil and Chile, in *Imperial Eyes: Travel Writing and Transculturation* (London: Routledge, 1992), 155–71.

2. Montesquieu, *Persian Letters,* trans. C. J. Betts (London: Penguin, 1973). Though the harem is technically the women's quarters within the seraglio or the sultan's domain, I follow common eighteenth-century parlance in using the terms interchangeably. One eighteenth-century source, Elizabeth Craven, *A Journey through the Crimea to Constantinople* (New York: Arno Press and The New York Times, 1970), is more precise: "Serail, or Seraglio, is generally understood as the habitation, or rather the confinement of women; here it is the Sultan's residence; it cannot be called his palace, for the kiosks, gardens, courts, walls, stables, are so mixed, that it is many houses in many gardens" (269).

3. Charles Perry, M.D., *A View of the Levant, Particularly of Constantinople, Syria, Egypt, and Greece in 4 Parts* (London, 1743), preface and 9.

4. Craven, *A Journey through the Crimea to Constantinople,* 272.

5. Richard Pococke, LL.D., *A Description of the East, and Some Other Countries,* 2 vols. (London, 1743), 1:37.

6. See *The Complete Letters of Lady Mary Wortley Montagu,* ed. Robert Halsband, 3 vols. (Oxford: Clarendon, 1965): 1:xiv–xvi. All subsequent citations of Montagu's letters are to this edition. For Craven, the edition cited is that indicated in n. 4, above.

7. Billie Melman, *Women's Orients: English Women and the Middle East, 1718–1918. Sexuality, Religion, and Work* (Ann Arbor: University of Michigan Press, 1992), 16–17. Leslie Peirce, *The Imperial Harem: Women and Sovereignty in the Ottoman Empire* (New York: Oxford University Press, 1993), argues that men and women were not rigidly separated in the Ottoman Empire and that women participated in its political life because "the household was the fundamental unit of Ottoman political organization" (149).

8. Terry Castle, *The Apparitional Lesbian: Female Homosexuality and Modern Culture* (New York: Columbia University Press, 1993), asserts that "the homosexually inclined woman will inevitably be attracted to the next best thing: to images of *men* desiring women" (104).

9. See Robert Halsband, *The Life of Lady Mary Wortley Montagu* (Oxford: Clarendon, 1956), 159 n. 1.

10. Ibid., 106.

11. Lady Mary Wortley Montagu, *Essays and Poems and "Simplicity: A Comedy,"* ed. Robert Halsband and Isobel Grundy (Oxford: Clarendon, 1977), 286.

12. Halsband, *The Life of Lady Mary Wortley Montagu,* 140–42. Jill Campbell has discussed Lady Mary's desire for husband Edward Wortley's sister, Anne, in an unpublished paper, "'Practical or Speculative Anatomy': Lady Mary and Erotic Desire," delivered at the 1993 Modern Language Association meeting in Toronto.

13. Eric Partridge, *A Dictionary of Slang and Unconventional English*, 8th ed. (New York: Macmillan, 1984), 404, defines "flat-fuck" as "simulated copulation by a pair of women: lesbian colloquially." The definition is cited in George Haggerty, "'Romantic Friendship' and Patriarchal Narrative in Sarah Scott's *Millenium Hall*," *Genders* 13 (Spring 1992): 108–22. A woman is also a "flat-cock." The "flats," then, is like "rubbing," another term current in the century.

14. Harriette Andreadis, "The Sapphic-Platonics of Katherine Philips, 1632–1664," *Signs* 15, no. 1 (1989): 56, remarks that "lesbian activities, as the twentieth century understands them, had been publicly articulated by women by the late 1660s and were regarded as scandalous infractions of the laws of nature." Abigail Masham was among those accused of lesbianism. See John Dunton's *King Abigail* (London, 1715).

15. Giovanni Bianchi, Professor of Anatomy at Sienna, *Dissertation on the Case of Catherine Vizzani*, [trans. John Cleland] (London, 1751).

16. See, for example, *Poésies de Sapho Suivies de Différentes Poésies Dans Le Même Genre* (London, 1781); *La Nouvelle Sapho; ou, Historie de la Secte Anandryne* (Paris, 1791); *Anandria; ou, Confessions de Mademoiselle Sapho* ("Lesbos," 1778).

17. See Joan DeJean, *Fictions of Sappho, 1546–1937* (Chicago: University of Chicago Press, 1989). For a brief treatment of the eighteenth-century lesbian, see Martha Vicinus, "'They Wonder to Which Sex I Belong': The Historical Roots of the Modern Lesbian Identity," *Feminist Studies* 18 (Fall 1992): 467–97. For women's same-sex desire in the eighteenth-century context, see especially Lynne Friedli, "'Passing Women': A Study of Gender Boundaries in the Eighteenth Century," in *Sexual Underworlds of the Enlightenment*, ed. G. S. Rousseau and Roy Porter (Chapel Hill: University of North Carolina Press, 1988), 234–60; Elizabeth Mavor, *The Ladies of Llangollen: A Study in Romantic Friendship* (London: Joseph, 1971); and Kristina Straub, *Sexual Suspects: Eighteenth-Century Players and Sexual Ideology* (Princeton: Princeton University Press, 1992). Susan K. Cahn, "Sexual Histories, Sexual Politics," *Feminist Studies* 18 (Fall 1992): 630, reminds us that "lesbian relations remain, as they have through much of history, unnamed and contained within the framework of heterosexual marriage."

18. Elizabeth D. Harvey, *Ventriloquized Voices: Feminist Theory and English Renaissance Texts* (London: Routledge, 1992), writes of the Donne poem, "This neglected text has disturbed and offended critics and editors, and until very recently they have by turns ignored it, questioned its authenticity, and censured its subject matter" (117). Donne speaks in the feminine lesbian voice.

19. In Martial the classical vigorous tribade Philaenis lusted after girls, played handball, and lifted weights, while in Virgil she was a talented prostitute. Don Cameron Allen, "Donne's 'Sapho to Philaenis,'" *ELN* 1 (1964):

190, says that Donne portrays her as both "a tough Lesbian and a skillful heterosexual courtesan" who also wrote erotic poetry. As I have pointed out in the discussion of Cleland, lesbian and prostitute are often closely aligned.

20. Elizabeth Harvey argues that "Sappho comes to master both Philaenis and herself though the objectifying, controlling power of the gaze" (*Ventriloquized Voices*, 130), but the eighteenth-century *Epistle* emphasizes permanent union rather than mastery.

21. *The New Epicurean; or, The Delights of Sex Facetiously and Philosophically Considered* (London, 1740; repr. 1875), 78.

22. In her pathbreaking study over a decade ago, *Surpassing the Love of Men: Romantic Friendship and Love between Women from the Renaissance to the Present* (New York: Morrow, 1981), Lillian Faderman preferred the notion of romantic friendship to lesbian practices in the eighteenth century, hesitating to believe that actual homosexual genital activity occurred. Martha Vicinus, "'They Wonder to Which Sex I Belong,'" dissents from Faderman somewhat to argue that erotic desire between women involved both female friendships and actual sexual activities between women and "female husbands." Janet Todd, *The Sign of Angellica: Women, Writing, and Fiction, 1660–1800* (New York: Columbia University Press, 1989), 115, believes that lesbianism "disappeared from female writing as the century progressed, although it continued to exist intermittently in male pornography and reportage." See also Valerie Traub, "The (In)Significance of 'Lesbian' Desire in Early Modern England," in *Queering the Renaissance*, ed. Jonathan Goldberg (Durham: Duke University Press, 1994), 62–83.

23. Randolph Trumbach states that *A Sapphic Epistle from Jack Cavenish to Mrs. D***** (1782) offers the first instance of the use of "tommy," but *The Adultress* used the term nearly a decade earlier without appearing self-consciously to create a neologism. Trumbach, "London Sapphists: From Three Sexes to Four Genders in the Making of Modern Culture," in *Body Guards: The Cultural Politics of Gender Ambiguity*, ed. Julia Epstein and Kristina Straub (New York: Routledge, 1991): 132.

24. *The Sappho-an. An Heroic Poem, of Three Cantos. In the Ovidian Stile, Describing the Pleasure which the Fair Sex Enjoy with Each Other. According to the Modern and most Polite Taste. Found amongst the Papers of a Lady of Quality, a Great Promoter of Jaconitism [sic]* (London, [1749]).

25. Harvey, *Ventriloquized Voices*, 118; Andreadis, "Sapphic-Platonics," 34–60; Delarivier Manley, *The New Atalantis*, ed. Rosalind Ballaster (New York: Penguin, 1992), 154.

26. *The Travels and Adventures of Mademoiselle de Richelieu*, [trans. Mr. Erskine], 3 vols. (London, 1744), in Caroline Woodward, "'My Heart So Wrapt': Lesbian Disruptions in Eighteenth-Century British Fiction," *Signs* 18 (Summer 1993): 838–65. Interestingly, Woodward suggests that Erskine could be a pseudonym for Lady Mary Wortley Montagu.

27. Terry Castle reviews Anne Lister, *I Know My Own Heart,* ed. Helena Whitbread (London: Virago, 1988), in *Women's Review of Books* 6 (January 1989): 6–7. Castle characterizes Lister as "remarkably self-aware and guilt-free."

28. See Jill Campbell's unpublished paper, "Illicit Enthusiasms: Methodism and Lesbian Desire in Fielding's *Female Husband.*" I am grateful for permission to consult this paper.

29. Trumbach, "London Sapphists," 112–41.

30. Vicinus, "They Wonder to Which Sex I Belong," 467–97.

31. See Julia Epstein, "Either/Or—Neither/Both: Sexual Ambiguity and the Ideology of Gender," *Genders* 7 (Spring 1990): 99–142.

32. *Satan's Harvest Home; or, The Present State Of Whorecraft . . . etc.* (1749) attests to disgust with lesbian practices in French nunneries and sodomy in Italy.

33. Alexander Russell, *The Natural History of Aleppo and Parts Adjacent* ([1756]; repr. London: A. Millar, 1856), 113.

34. *The Present State of the Ottoman Empire . . . ,* translated from the French manuscript of Elias Habesci (London, 1784), 170.

35. Ibid., 171. See also Paul Rycaut, *The Present State of the Ottoman Empire* (London, 1668), a text on which Lady Mary Wortley Montagu relied: "This passion likewise reigns in the Society of Women; they die with amorous affections one to the other; especially the old Women court the young, present them with rich Garmets, Jewels, Mony, even to their own impoverishment and ruine, and these darts of *Cupid* are shot through all the Empire, especially *Constantinople,* the *Seraglio* of the Grand Signior, and the apartments of the *Sultans*" (34).

36. *A New Relation of the Inner-Part of the Grand Seignor's Seraglio. Containing Several Remarkable Particulars . . .* (London, 1677), 88.

37. *The Correspondence of Alexander Pope,* ed. George Sherburn, 5 vols. (Oxford: Clarendon, 1956), 1:368.

38. In the satire *The Sappho-an* (1747) the women take sexual pleasure in using carrots and parsnips as dildoes.

39. See the preface in Walter M. Crittenden, ed., *A Description of Millenium Hall,* by Sarah Scott (New York: Bookman, 1955), 5–22.

40. Sarah Scott lived with Barbara Montagu from 1748 until Montagu's death in 1765, and in spite of the usual historical caveat that brides often travelled with a female companion, their friendship may well have been sexual too.

41. See, for example, Moira Ferguson, *Subject to Others: British Women Writers and Colonial Slavery, 1670–1834* (New York: Routledge, 1992), 101–11. In *The History of Sir George Ellison* (London, 1766), written as Granville Sharp was pursuing his emancipation campaign, Ellison is a merchant and

benevolent slaveowner whose imperialist and racist activities are justified because of his kindness in conducting them. Ferguson harshly critiques the novel for promoting a sentimentalism that substitutes for political action and the eradication of slavery.

42. Mr. D'Avora, the Italian master to Misses Melvyn and Mancel, also possesses colonizing curiosity, "the curiosity of wisdom, not of impertinence" (*Millenium Hall,* 44), on his travels through Asia and Africa. Haggerty, "'Romantic Friendship' and Patriarchal Narrative," posits that D'Avora could be interpreted as a gay man who instructs the women in alternative sexualities, or at least symbolizes them. D'Avora seems to me to occupy instead the place of the mediating eunuch.

43. In fact, Sir George Ellison imitates the plan for a female academy in *The History of Sir George Ellison.*

44. In the introduction to the edition of *Millenium Hall* cited here, Jane Spencer notes that the novel is directed at men and is "primarily concerned with disabusing men of their errors about women" (xv).

45. Ruth Perry suggests that community is made possible in the novel by "the mix of self-sustaining labor and expressive pleasure, the balance between personal freedom and responsibility for others, the proper ratio between production for subsistence and production for art" and "a set of interventions in both the labor market and the marriage market." See Perry, "Bluestockings in Utopia," in *History, Gender, and Eighteenth-Century Literature,* ed. Beth Fowkes Tobin (Athens: University of Georgia Press, 1994), 162–63.

46. This maternal relationship of the women to their charges is reinforced in George Ellison's later comment that "they should have better performed a mother's part" (*The History of Sir George Ellison,* 256).

47. George Haggerty, "'Romantic Friendship' and Patriarchal Narrative," 113, finds that maternal relations in the novel are eroticized "as a way of challenging eighteenth-century assumptions concerning female subjectivity and the place of the mother in domestic relations." Treating primarily the Mancel-Morgan relationship, Haggerty associates lesbian narrative with breaking the bonds that heterosexuality and the cult of domesticity have held on women's alternative figurings of sexuality, but his argument for self-determination ignores important hierarchies that are necessary to the production of this feminotopia.

48. Their relationship is a counterexample to Lillian Faderman's claim in *Surpassing the Love of Men* that even sensual romantic friendship was not regarded with concern because genital contact was unlikely.

49. To Lady Mary, 3 Aug. [1716], in Halsband, *The Complete Letters of Lady Mary Wortley Montagu,* 1:249.

50. Aline Miller, "Sights and Monsters and Gulliver's *Voyage to Brobdingnag,*" *Tulane Studies in English* 7 (1957): 20–82, cites the 1711–12 advertise-

ment for the midget Negro: "A little Black Man lately brought from the West Indies, being the Wonder of his Age, he being but 3 Foot high and 25 Years Old."

51. *A New Relation of the Inner-Part of the Grand Seignor's Seraglio*, 6.

52. Ibid., 79.

53. William Beckford, *Vathek*, ed. Roger Lonsdale (Oxford: Oxford University Press, 1983). The dwarves in the harem sing and address Vathek in a "curious harangue," and objects of pity swarm about the Caliph: "At noon, a superb corps of cripples made its appearance; . . . the completest association of invalids that had ever been embodied till then. The blind went groping with the blind, the lame limped on together, and the maimed made gestures to each other with the only arm that remained. The sides of a considerable water-fall were crowded by the deaf; . . . Nor were there wanting others in abundance with hump-backs; wenny necks; and even horns of an exquisite polish" (61).

54. *The Correspondence of Alexander Pope*, 1:364.

55. *A New Relation of the Inner-Part of the Grand Seignor's Seraglio* also describes the deformed in the seraglio: "The language of the Mutes, by signs, is as intelligible in the Seraglio, as if they had the liberty of speaking, and the Grand Seignor, who understands it as well as any of them, as having been accustom'd thereto from his Infancy, and commonly discoursing with them" (87). Mutes were employed in the Turkish court to amuse the sultan but also to teach pages the sign language used to avoid distracting the monarch with the sound of voices. Habesci's *State of the Ottoman Empire* indicates that "such unfortunate beings, as are thus 'curtailed of fair proportion,' have been, for ages, an appendage of Eastern grandeur. . . . The dwarves are employed in the same manner as the mutes. If a dwarf happens to be a mute, he is much esteemed; and if likewise a eunuch, they esteem him as a great prodigy, and no pains or expence is spared to procure such a rarity" (164).

56. Edmund Burke, *A Philosophical Enquiry into the Origin of Our Ideas of the Sublime and Beautiful*, ed. J. T. Boulton (London: Routledge and Kegan Paul; New York: Columbia University Press, 1958), 103.

57. In another association between the monstrous and the African, "Alexander Carbuncle" writes in the *Spectator*, No. 17, about the Ugly Club, a society of the deformed that mounts speeches in praise of the hunch-backed Aesop. He assumes Mr. Spectator would know nothing about the monstrous "unless it was your Fortune to touch upon some of the woody Parts of the *African* Continent, in your Voyage to or from *Grand Cairo*." Richard Steele, *The Spectator*, ed. Donald F. Bond, 2 vols. (Oxford: Clarendon, 1965), 1:76.

58. *Spectator*, No. 17 (Tuesday, March 20, 1711), 1:75: "It is happy for a Man, that has any of these Oddnesses [*sic*] about him, if he can be as merry upon himself, as others are apt to be upon that Occasion. . . . As it is barbarous in

others to railly him for natural Defects, it is extreamly agreeable when he can Jest upon himself for them."

59. In his *Analysis of Beauty*, Hogarth argues that fitness, variety, uniformity, simplicity, intricacy, and quantity interact to produce beauty. Hay adds that after the initial prejudice against people of deformity, people sometimes "believe [the handicapped] better than they are" and may even take disability to be a sign of good luck. The modern term for this patronizing attitude is "handicappism."

60. Burke, *A Philosophical Enquiry into the Origin of Our Ideas of the Sublime and Beautiful*, lxv.

61. Caroline Gonda, "Sarah Scott and 'The Sweet Excess of Paternal Love,'" *SEL* 32 (1992): 511–35, identifies the dangers of beauty and sexual attraction but focuses on the father-daughter relationship rather than the homosocial nature of ugliness and deformity.

62. Seyla Benhabib, *Critique, Norm, and Utopia: A Study of the Foundations of Critical Theory* (New York: Columbia University Press, 1986), 13.

63. Benhabib (ibid., 41) notes Marx's profound ambivalence about utopia and indicates that he "does not acknowledge the radical otherness that the determinate negation of the existent brings with it."

Chapter 7: "An Affectionate and Voluntary Sacrifice"

1. See Ramkrishna Mukherjee, *The Rise and Fall of the East India Company: A Sociological Appraisal*, 2nd ed. (Berlin: Deutscher Verlag der Wissenschaften, 1958).

2. See the introduction to Peter J. Marshall, ed., *India: Madras and Bengal, 1774–85*, vol. 5 of *The Writings and Speeches of Edmund Burke*, ed. Paul Langford (Oxford: Clarendon, 1981), 23.

3. Sara Suleri, *The Rhetoric of English India* (Chicago: University of Chicago Press, 1992), 49–74, provides a subtly nuanced account of these matters.

4. Percival Spear, *The Nabobs: A Study of the Social Life of the English in Eighteenth-Century India*, 2nd enlarged ed. (London: Curzon, 1963), 129.

5. See Ketaki Kushari Dyson, *A Various Universe: A Study of the Journals and Memoirs of British Men and Women in the Indian Subcontinent, 1765–1856* (Delhi: Oxford University Press, 1978).

6. J. M. S. Tompkins, *The Popular Novel in England, 1770–1800* (Lincoln: University of Nebraska Press, 1961), 181–83, takes note of this phenomenon.

7. See Renu Juneja, "The Native and the Nabob: Representations of the Indian Experience in Eighteenth-Century English Literature," *Journal of Commonwealth Literature* 27 (1992): 183–98.

8. *The Indian Adventurer; or, The History of Mr. Vanneck* (London, 1780). See Alexander Hamilton, *New Account of the East Indies in 1727* (London, 1727). The story of having freed a Hindu woman about to be immolated

on her husband's funeral pyre is a common trope of European men's travel writing.

9. The term *sati* signifies both the rite of widow immolation *and* the woman who has burned herself on her husband's pyre. See Arvind Sharma et al., *Sati: Historical and Phenomenological Essays* (Delhi: Motilal Banarsidass, 1988), 1. The word entered the English language in the eighteenth century (ibid., 39).

10. Records of intermarriage and British wills showing British men's provision for their Indian mistresses and children appear in Suresh Chandra Ghosh, *The Social Condition of the British Community in Bengal, 1757–1800* (Leiden: E. J. Brill, 1970), 180–81.

11. Lata Mani, "Contentious Traditions: The Debate on *Sati* in Colonial India," in *Recasting Women: Essays in Colonial History*, ed. Kumkum Sangari and Sudesh Vaid (New Delhi: Kali for Women, 1989), 88–126.

12. The novel, in two volumes, was published in Dublin in 1797.

13. Gary Kelly, *Women, Writing, and Revolution, 1790–1827* (Oxford: Clarendon, 1993), 126–64, discusses Elizabeth Hamilton's counter-revolutionary feminism in her various works.

14. Eleanor Ty, "Female Philosophy Refunctioned: Elizabeth Hamilton's Parodic Novel," *Ariel* 22 (October 1991): 111–29, believes the novel demonstrates a double attitude of parody of and sympathy toward revolution.

15. Spear, *The Nabobs*, 134.

16. [Sophia Goldsborne], *Hartly House, Calcutta: A Novel of the Days of Warren Hastings*, rpr. from 1789 ed. (Calcutta: Thacker, Spink and Co., 1908; Bibash Gupta, Calcutta, 1984), 13. All subsequent quotations are from this text. Isobel Grundy, "'The Barbarous Character We Give Them': White Women Travellers Report on Other Races," in *Studies in Eighteenth-Century Culture*, vol. 22, ed. Patricia B. Craddock and Carla H. Hay (East Lansing, Mich.: Colleagues Press, 1992), 73–86, discusses the authorship of the novel. Apparently Gibbes did not visit India herself, though her son died in Calcutta. See also *Hartly House Calcutta: A Novel of the Days of Warren Hastings*, introduction and notes by Monica Clough (London: Pluto Press, 1989).

17. A pirated edition appeared in Dublin in 1789, and a German translation was published in 1791 in Leipzig. See A. L. Basham, "Sophia and the 'Bramin,'" in *East India Company Studies*, ed. Kenneth Ballhatchet and John Harrison, Asian Studies Monograph Series (Hong Kong: Asian Research Service, 1986), 13–30.

18. Spear, *The Nabobs*, 127.

19. Ibid., 79.

20. Harriet Guest, "The Great Distinction: Figures of the Exotic in the Work of William Hodges," in *New Feminist Discourses: Critical Essays on Theories and Texts*, ed. Isobel Armstrong (London: Routledge, 1992), 296–41,

comments evocatively on Hodges' femininizing of the Hindu people of Madras and his pose as an impartial European spectator gazing on Asia. Guest also notes significantly that the feminization of the Madras people should be counterbalanced by the representation of the Muslim man as excessively masculine.

21. Hodges is not alone in seeing India in feminized terms. See also Mrs. [Jemima] Kindersley, *Letters from the Island of Teneriffe, Brazil, the Cape of Good Hope, and the East Indies* (London, 1777), 127, who describes the dress of Indian men as effeminate.

22. Robert Sencourt, *India in English Literature* (London: Simpkin, Marshall, Hamilton, Kent, 1923), provides a catalog of these and other references to India in Restoration and eighteenth-century literature.

23. Kindersley, *Letters*, 124.

24. Ibid., 226. Kindersley remarks that she admires the Muslim women's eyes and prefers the complexions of those who are the lightest in color, the least yellow, and the furthest from black.

25. The idea of employing the Other as aesthetic contrast or as the exotic deformed occurs elsewhere, including Janet Schaw, *Journal of a Lady of Quality: Being the Narrative of a Journey from Scotland to the West Indies, North Carolina, and Portugal, in the years 1774 to 1776*, ed. Evangeline Walker Andrews in collaboration with Charles McLean Andrews (New Haven: Yale University Press, 1921). Schaw describes Lady Bell as standing beside a "little Mulatto girl not above five years old, whom she retains as a pet. This brown beauty was dressed out like an infant Sultana, and is a fine contrast to the delicate complexion of her Lady" (123). See also the famous portrait by Jonathan Richardson, Sr., of Lady Mary Wortley Montagu attended by a Negro servant, reproduced as the frontispiece to volume 1 of *The Complete Letters of Lady Mary Wortley Montagu*, ed. Robert Halsband, 3 vols. (Oxford: Clarendon, 1965).

26. On the significance of rape to empire, see Jenny Sharpe, *Allegories of Empire: The Figure of Woman in the Colonial Text* (Minneapolis: University of Minnesota Press, 1993).

27. The character Sabrina in Sarah Scott's *Journey Through Every Stage of Life* (1754) says, "There is no divine Ordinance more frequently disobeyed than that wherein God forbids human Sacrifices for in no other light can I see most Marriages." Quoted in Caroline Gonda, "Sarah Scott and 'The Sweet Excess of Paternal Love,'" *SEL* 32 (1992): 524. Richard Allestree in *The Ladies Calling, in 2 Parts* (Oxford, 1673), 2:58, compares forced marriages to "a more barbarous Immolation then that to *Moloch*; for tho that were very inhumane, yet . . . the pain was short: but a loathed Bed is at once an acute and a lingring Torment."

28. Gayatri Chakravorty Spivak, "Three Women's Texts and a Critique of

Imperialism," *Critical Inquiry* 12 (1985): 243–61, argues that Western female individualism depends upon empire for its formation.

29. Parliamentary Papers on Hindu Widows, 1821, xviii, 316. The passage is cited in Lata Mani, "The Production of an Official Discourse on *Sati* in Early-Nineteenth-Century Bengal," in *Europe and Its Others: Proceedings of the Essex Conference on the Sociology of Literature* (Colchester: University of Essex, 1985), 109.

30. Rajeswari Sunder Rajan, "The Subject of Sati: Pain and Death in the Contemporary Discourse on Sati," *Yale Journal of Criticism* 3, no. 2 (1990): 4.

31. Hodges, *Travels in India*, 80. See also J. Z. Holwell, *Interesting Historical Events, Relative to . . . the Empire of Indostan*, 2 parts (London, 1765–67).

32. *Raja Rammohun Roy and Progressive Movements in India: A Selection from Records (1745–1845)*, ed. Jatindra Kumar Majumdar (Calcutta: Art Press, 1941), 139. Neither do eighteenth-century women emphasize scriptural tradition as authorizing the practice, as nineteenth-century commentators will do. Lata Mani, "Contentious Traditions," argues that "the concept of tradition is reconstituted in the nineteenth century, that women and scripture are the terms of its articulation, and that this development is specifically colonial" (126).

33. Mrs. Eliza Fay, *Original Letters from India, 1779–1815* (New York: Harcourt, Brace and Co., 1925), 213–15.

34. In "The Subject of Sati," Rajan, working with Elaine Scarry's notion of the body in pain, has argued that recovering sati's material reality will help dispel the notion of widows' dying voluntarily.

35. For contemporary feminists who challenge reductive understandings of sati, see Lata Mani, "Cultural Theory, Colonial Texts: Reading Eyewitness Accounts of Widow Burning," in *Cultural Studies*, ed. Lawrence Grossberg, Cary Nelson, and Paula A. Treichler (New York: Routledge, 1992), 392–408. See also Antoinette M. Burton, "The White Woman's Burden, British Feminists, and 'the Indian Woman,' 1865–1915," in *Western Women and Imperialism*, ed. Nupur Chaudhuri and Margaret Strobel (Bloomington: Indiana University Press, 1992), 137–57.

36. Ania Loomba, "Dead Women Tell No Tales: Issues of Female Subjectivity, Subaltern Agency, and Tradition in Colonial and Postcolonial Writings on Widow Immolation in India," *History Workshop Journal* 36 (1993): 210–27. Loomba questions the reliance on the authenticity of experience.

37. Mani, "Cultural Theory, Colonial Texts"; Loomba, "Dead Women Tell No Tales," 219.

38. Loomba, "Dead Women Tell No Tales," 221.

39. Jenny Sharpe, *Allegories of Empire*, 1–24, argues that the fear of interracial rape was not strong until after the 1857 revolt.

40. *The Writings and Speeches of Edmund Burke*, 5:17.

41. Basham, "Sophia and the 'Bramin,'" 15.

42. See especially Gayatri Spivak, "Three Women's Texts," and "Theory in the Margin: Coetzee's *Foe* Reading Defoe's *Crusoe/Roxana*," in *Consequences of Theory: Selected Papers from the English Institute, 1987–88*, ed. Jonathan Arac and Barbara Johnson, n.s. no. 14 (Baltimore: Johns Hopkins University Press, 1991), 154–80.

Epilogue

1. As Moira Gatens puts it, "In the past the concept of the 'universal citizen,' or neutral rational agent, has not been universal or neutral but masculine." Gatens, "'The Oppressed State of My Sex': Wollstonecraft on Reason, Feeling, and Equality," in *Feminist Interpretations and Political Theory*, ed. Mary Lyndon Shanley and Carole Pateman (University Park: Pennsylvania State University Press, 1991), 112–28.

2. Mary Wollstonecraft, *A Vindication of the Rights of Woman*, ed. Miriam Kramnick (Harmondsworth: Penguin, 1975), 80.

3. Carole Pateman has demonstrated that it is not the case that "'individual' is a universal category that applies to anyone or everyone. . . . 'The individual' is a man and a classcoded one as well." Pateman, "Removing Obstacles to Democracy" (paper presented to the International Political Science Association meeting, Ottawa, Canada, October 1986). For a recent reevaluation that remarks on the significance of feminism to new histories, see John Bender, "A New History of the Enlightenment?" *Studies in the Eighteenth Century 8*, in *Eighteenth-Century Life* 16, n.s. 1 (February 1992): 1–20.

4. Fredric Jameson, "Postmodernism and Consumer Society," in *The Anti-Aesthetic: Essays on Postmodern Culture*, ed. Hal Foster (Port Townsend, Wash.: Bay Press, 1983), 118.

5. Ibid., 125.

6. Michel Foucault, "What Is Enlightenment?" in *The Foucault Reader*, ed. Paul Rabinow (New York: Pantheon, 1984), 43.

7. See Nancy Fraser and Linda Nicholson, "Social Criticism without Philosophy: An Encounter between Feminism and Postmodernism," in *Universal Abandon? The Politics of Postmodernism*, ed. Andrew Ross (Minneapolis: University of Minnesota Press, 1988), 83–104, and Jean-François Lyotard, *The Postmodern Condition: A Report on Knowledge*, trans. Geoff Bennington and Brian Massumi (Minneapolis: University of Minnesota Press, 1989).

8. Max Horkheimer and Theodor W. Adorno, *Dialectic of Enlightenment*, trans. John Cumming (New York: Continuum, 1990), xiv.

9. Foucault, "What Is Enlightenment?" 32–50.

10. Nancy Hartsock, "Rethinking Modernism: Minority vs. Majority Theories," *Cultural Critique* 7 (1987): 190.

11. David Harvey's *Condition of Postmodernity: An Enquiry into the Origins*

of Cultural Change (Oxford: Basil Blackwell, 1991) argues on the side of Habermas, who would like to transform the Enlightenment project rather than find it "creatively destructive" (in Nietzsche's terms) or abandon it altogether.

12. I take the term *ludic* from Teresa Ebert, who formulates the concept, as opposed to "resistance" postmodernism, in "Ludic Feminism, the Body, Performance, and Labor: Bringing Materialism Back into Feminist Cultural Studies," *Cultural Critique* 23 (1992): 5–50.

13. Michèle Barrett, *Women's Oppression Today: The Marxist/Feminist Encounter,* rev. ed. (London: Verso, 1988), xxxiv.

14. Immanuel Kant, "What Is Enlightenment?" ("Was ist Aufklärung?"), trans. Peter Gay, in *Introduction to Contemporary Civilization in the West,* 2 vols., 2nd ed. (New York: Columbia University Press, 1954), 1:1071–76.

15. I am indebted here to Onora O'Neill's discussion in *Constructions of Reason: Explorations of Kant's Practical Philosophy* (Cambridge: Cambridge University Press, 1989).

16. Michel Foucault, "Kant on Enlightenment and Revolution" (1984), trans. Colin Gordon, *Economy and Society* 15 (February 1986), 88–96.

17. Hubert L. Dreyfus and Paul Rabinow, "What Is Maturity? Habermas and Foucault on 'What Is Enlightenment,'" in *Foucault: A Critical Reader,* ed. David Couzens Hoy (Oxford: Basil Blackwell, 1986), 117.

18. Foucault, "What Is Enlightenment?" 45.

19. Jürgen Habermas, "Modernity—An Incomplete Project," in Foster, *The Anti-Aesthetic,* 12.

20. Jürgen Habermas, *The Structural Transformation of the Public Sphere: An Inquiry into a Category of Bourgeois Society,* trans. Thomas Burger with the assistance of Frederick Lawrence (Cambridge: MIT Press, 1989).

21. Thomas McCarthy, introduction to *The Philosophical Discourse of Modernity: Twelve Lectures,* by Jürgen Habermas, trans. Frederick Lawrence (Cambridge: MIT Press, 1987), xiv.

22. Terry Eagleton, "Nationalism: Irony and Commitment," in *Nationalism, Colonialism, and Literature,* intro. Seamus Deane (Minneapolis: University of Minnesota Press, 1990), 34.

23. Chantal Mouffe, "Radical Democracy: Modern or Postmodern?" in *Universal Abandon? The Politics of Postmodernism,* ed. Andrew Ross (Minneapolis: University of Minnesota, 1988), 33. Mouffe refers to ideas developed more fully in Ernesto Laclau and Chantal Mouffe, *Hegemony and Socialist Strategy: Towards a Radical Democratic Politics* (London: Verso, 1985).

24. Seyla Benhabib, *Critique, Norm, and Utopia: A Study of the Foundations of Critical Theory* (New York: Columbia University Press, 1986), 352.

25. Nancy Fraser, "What's Critical about Critical Theory? The Case of Habermas and Gender," in Shanley and Pateman, *Feminist Interpretations and Political Theory,* 260. John Barrell notes that "those who are not citizens

are excluded as firmly from participation in the republic of taste as they are from the political republic, and they include two groups in particular: the vulgar and women." Barrell, "'The Dangerous Goddess': Masculinity, Prestige, and the Aesthetic in Early Eighteenth-Century Britain," *Cultural Critique* 12 (Spring 1989): 103.

26. While David Harvey recognizes the problem that the possession of reason is largely limited in Enlightenment terms to a white male elite, he finds its predicament of attempting to translate "Enlightenment principles of rational and scientific understanding into moral and political principles appropriate for action" still timely. Harvey, *The Condition of Postmodernity*, 19. But Harvey's promise to take up the reason that "women, gays, ecologists, regional autonomists, etc." are hostile to postmodernity (ibid., 48) is never fulfilled.

27. Gayatri Chakravorty Spivak with Geoffrey Hawthorn, Ron Aronson, and John Dunn, "The Post-modern Condition: The End of Politics?" in *The Post-Colonial Critic: Interviews, Strategies, Dialogues*, ed. Sarah Harasym (New York: Routledge, 1990), 19–20. In Peter Gay's 1100-page interpretation of the Enlightenment, the status of women receives four pages.

28. Hartsock, "Rethinking Modernism," 191.

29. Jane Flax, *Thinking Fragments: Psychoanalysis, Feminism, and Postmodernism in the Contemporary West* (Berkeley and Los Angeles: University of California Press, 1990). See also Jane Flax, "Postmodernism and Gender Relations in Feminist Theory," in Nicholson, *Feminism/Postmodernism*, 42.

30. Sandra Harding, "Feminism, Science, and the Anti-Enlightenment Critiques," in Nicholson, *Feminism/Postmodernism*, 83–106.

31. Henry Louis Gates, Jr., "Critical Remarks," in *Anatomy of Racism*, ed. David Theo Goldberg (Minneapolis: University of Minnesota Press, 1990), 319–29. Gates's essay parallels Richard Popkin's earlier argument, which states, "It seems to me that all theories of knowledge and theories of human nature, especially in the period from the Renaissance to the Enlightenment are theoretically non-racist." Richard H. Popkin, "Hume's Racism," in *The High Road to Pyrrhonism*, ed. Richard A. Watson and James E. Force (San Diego: Austin Hill Press, 1980), 266.

32. Immanuel Kant, *Observations on the Feeling of the Beautiful and Sublime*, trans. John T. Goldthwait (Berkeley and Los Angeles: University of California Press, 1960), 110.

33. Soame Jenyns, "Disquisitions on Several Subjects; Disquisition I: On the Chain of Universal Being," in *The Works of Soame Jenyns . . .* , 2 vols. (London, 1790), 2:133.

34. Richard H. Popkin, "The Philosophical Bases of Modern Racism," in Watson and Force, *The High Road to Pyrrhonism*, 79–102. The essay is reprinted as "The Philosophical Basis of Eighteenth-Century Racism," in *Studies in Eighteenth-Century Culture: Racism in the Eighteenth Century*, ed.

Harold E. Pagliaro (Cleveland: Case Western Reserve University Press, 1973), 3:245–62.

35. After reviewing these early racial theories, Popkin concludes, "If we are to overcome our racist heritage, I think we have first to realize that the question of human origins implies nothing about the merits of present-day human beings" ("The Philosophical Bases of Modern Racism," 100).

36. Linnaeus [Carl von Linne], *A General System of Nature Through the Three Kingdoms of Animals, Vegetables, and Minerals,* trans. W. Turton, 7 vols. (London, 1802–6), vol. 1. Hume's racist note in the 1753–54 edition states, "Mr. Hume challenges anyone to cite a simple example in which a Negro has shown talents. . . . So fundamental is the difference between these two races of men [black and white] and it appears to be as great in regard to mental capacities as in colour." Immanuel Kant, *Observations on the Feeling of the Beautiful and Sublime,* quoted in Popkin, "Hume's Racism," 259–60.

37. Thomas Hodgkin, *Nationalism in Colonial Africa* (New York: New York University Press, 1957), 174–75, cited in V. Y. Mudimbe, *The Invention of Africa: Gnosis, Philosophy, and the Order of Knowledge* (Bloomington: Indiana University Press, 1988), 1.

38. Kumari Jayawardena, *Feminism and Nationalism in the Third World* (London: Zed Books, 1986), 17. She adds, "Similarly, the indigenous bourgeoises had no intention of applying the concepts of natural rights, liberty, equality and self-determination to the masses of women or to the workers of their own countries."

39. Aihwa Ong, "Colonialism and Modernity: Feminist Re-Presentations of Women in Non-Western Societies," *Inscriptions* 3/4 (1988): 79–80. In associating that history with the Enlightenment, Ong does not note that although feminism found many of its arguments in the Enlightenment's emphasis on reason and the rights of man, it was also a contestatory discourse that acknowledged its tentativeness and its opposition to many of the *philosophes.*

40. Jayawardena, *Feminism and Nationalism in the Third World,* 2.

41. Wahneema Lubiano, "Shuckin' Off the African-American Native Other: What's 'Po-Mo' Got to Do with It?" *Cultural Critique* (Spring 1991): 156. Lubiano critiques postmodernist theorists such as David Harvey for omitting slavery and genocide as examples of the horrors that defied Enlightenment optimism.

42. As Foucault himself notes in "What Is Enlightenment?" Enlightenment is "located at a certain point in the development of *European* societies" (43; italics mine).

43. Chandra Talpade Mohanty, "Cartographies of Struggle: Third World Women and the Politics of Feminism," in *Third World Women and the Politics of Feminism,* ed. Chandra Talpade Mohanty, Ann Russo, and Lourdes Torres (Bloomington: Indiana University Press, 1991), 10.

44. Chela Sandoval, "US Third World Feminism: The Theory and Method of Oppositional Consciousness in the Postmodern World," *Genders* 10 (Spring 1991): 16.

45. Trinh T. Minh-ha, *Woman, Native, Other: Writing Postcoloniality and Feminism* (Bloomington: Indiana University Press, 1989), 76, 40.

INDEX

Page numbers in italics refer to illustrations.

Turkey, 12, 16–18, 20, 31, 33–36, 136–38, 147–49, 157, 214 n.41; in *Adeline Mowbray*, 41; women of, 35, 41, 90–92, 137–42, 148–49, 161, *165*, 178, 210, 237 n.19
Turkish dress: in *Adeline Mowbray*, 41; in *Roxana*, 36–37, 39, 40, 218 n.33
Turkish Embassy *Letters*. See *The Complete Letters of Lady Mary Wortley Montagu*

Ugly Club, 158, 244 n.57
Unsex'd Females, The (Polwhele), 121

Vathek (Beckford), 127, 157
veil, 4, 5, *72*, 94, 118, 120–26, 137–38, 236 n.11; blush and, 19, 20, 117, 133, 209; Turkish women and, 91
Vicinus, Martha, 147
Vindication of the Rights of Woman, A (Wollstonecraft), 11, 92, 192–93
Vizzani, Catherine, 143, 147
"Volunteer Laureat, No. 1, The" (Savage), 60–61

Voyage to Guinea. See *New Voyage to Guinea, A* (Smith)
Voyage to the River Sierra-Leone, A (Matthews), 82
voyeurism, 140, 142, 151, 178

Wallace, Michelle, 65
Walpole, Horace, 74
Wanderer, The (Savage), 47
Warton, Joseph, 24
Weil, Rachel, 33
Weitzman, Arthur, 128
Welch, Saunders, 98
West, Cornel, 21
Wheatley, Phillis, 65
Widow of Malabar, The, 169
Wollstonecraft, Mary, 11, 41, 88–89, 92–93, 121, 171, 192–93
Woodward, Caroline, 146

Yeazell, Ruth, 122

zanannah, *164*, 177–78, 186

Library of Congress Cataloging-in-Publication Data

Nussbaum, Felicity.
   Torrid zones : maternity, sexuality, and empire in eighteenth-
century English narratives / Felicity A. Nussbaum.
        p.   cm.—(Parallax : re-visions of culture and society)
   Includes index.
   ISBN 0-8018-5074-6 (cl).—ISBN 0-8018-5075-4 (pbk.)
   1. English prose literature—18th century—History and criticism.   2. Women and literature—Great Britain—Colonies—
History—18th century.   3. Women and literature—England—
History—18th century.   4. Imperialism in literature.   5. Motherhood in literature.   6. Narration (Rhetoric)   7. Sex in literature.   I. Title.   II. Series: Parallax (Baltimore, Md.)
PR756.W65N87   1995
820.9'352042'09033—dc20   95-11801